NAGA PATH

URSULA GRAHAM BOWER

NAGA PATH

LONDON 1952

READERS UNION : JOHN MURRAY

TO

PAM AND PHILIP MILLS

This Readers Union edition was produced in 1952 for sale to its members only, by Readers Union Ltd at 38, William IV St, in the City of Westminster and at Letchworth Garden City, Hertfordshire, from either of which address full particulars may be obtained. This book has been newly set in 11 point Fournier, and printed at the Selwood Printing Works, Frome, Somerset, by Butler and Tanner Ltd. The first edition was published by John Murray.

CONTENTS

ILLUSTRATIONS

All the plates appear between pages 84 and 85

CHAPTER I

IN THE BEGINNING

IN the extreme north-east corner of India the long inlet of the Brahmaputra Valley cuts back deeply into the ranges running down from Tibet and the Roof of the World. The warm, green, thickly-populated valley floor forms one part of the Indian province of Assam, and the surrounding hill-tracts and their variety of tribes make up the rest. On the north side of the valley are Monbas, Akas, Daflas, Miris, Apa Tanis and Abors and other groups yet unclassified or never seen by a foreign eye, for the hinterland along the foot of the Great Himalayan Range is still unexplored for a good part of its length. On the southern bank a stretch of mountain country —a long skein of parallel ranges—runs down between India and Burma, and in the upper half of this live the more or less Mongolian tribes known as the Nagas and Kukis. I say 'more or less Mongolian', for nobody yet knows all the strains and races which have contributed to their make-up or what eddies of migration brought them there. The Kukis lie to the south with the Lushais and Chins below them, the Nagas are to the north, and there is a belt in the middle where the two overlap.

The Nagas are divided into a number of different tribes and sub-tribes, Angamis, Rengmas, Tangkhuls, Lhotas, Semas, Aos, and many more too numerous to cite here. They live in hilltop villages which were, and often still are, defended by stone walls, dykes, thorn fences and spiked palisades, and before the Pax Britannica stopped them they were head-hunters to a man, celebrating the deed in elaborate rituals and recognizing its worth by the right to special insignia. Beyond the frontier, in the considerable tract which still remains unadministered, head-hunting and its ancient rites persist unabated—aggravated, indeed, by the modern weapons the war left behind when it receded.

Under British administration the Naga country and the

other Assam hill-tracts formed 'excluded areas'—excluded, that is, from the control of the Provincial Legislature and left in the hands of the Governor. The object of this was neither repression nor the artificial preservation of primitive cultures; it was designed to protect the hillman from exploitation, to reduce to a minimum the bureaucracy with which he had to contend, and to cushion him against the impact of civilization until he was educated to withstand it alone. Should anyone doubt the propriety of withholding the benefits of civilization for even a short time, may I point out that prostitution and venereal disease are unknown to the untouched tribes but are the first blessings imported by the higher races.

The administration of hill districts was a very personal matter, depending almost entirely upon the individual officer and his influence. It called for men with integrity, tact, infinite patience and real devotion to their often obstreperous charges. Speaking as one who has seen the process of government from a worm's eye view and not from a coign of vantage in official circles, I should like to pay tribute to the remarkably high standard attained. The district of Naga Hills in particular was fortunate in its officers, and under such men as Hutton, Mills and Pawsey it enjoyed a long period of just and sympathetic control to which Naga loyalty and co-operation in two wars are a tribute.

In the administered areas Mission and Plains influence have altered the tribes much. Caps, boots and trousers replace the former simplicities, and a desire for sinecures and soft jobs seduces men from the old, hard way of the soil. There are, though, blessed oases in the drab desert where beads and feathers, red-dyed goats'-hair and rich-hued plaids still gladden the eye; where the ancient candours and ancient moralities survive uncorrupted, where chipped enamel and cheap glass have not ousted the hand-carved product; where men go armed with spear and dao instead of notebook and fountainpen; where the dog-eat-dog existence of modern economics has not swamped the primitive decencies, and where life is simple and pagan and brief and happy.

Of such an oasis is this book written.

It all began in 1937 when, as a girl of twenty-three, I was on a visit to India.

A broad belt of jungle ran along the hill-foot. Its long, thin trees strained upwards, their trunks wound round, choked and netted with a welter of creepers. The road ran straight through in a cleft like a railway-cutting, and beyond was a rampart of hills, blue-black with rain-forest.

The small car bumped and hustled along the road, dipping in and out of the hollows where the morning mist still lingered. It pulled up at a sentry-post. We showed our papers, the car moved on, and we had entered Naga Hills and the excluded area.

Hillsides rose suddenly on either side and a gorge enveloped us. We climbed steadily beside a wild, green stream which slid through sunlit pools and between grey boulders, and above us cliffs thick with cane, fern, palm and matted tree mounted to an invisible skyline. The road looped round elbow after elbow, the little car rolling at each, and as suddenly again we shot out over the gorge's lip and were rushing past stony flood-courses full of plumed reeds. Again the road lifted and climbed. The car hummed on, round steeper bends, between bamboos, through lighter, drier forest—the hazy plain falling lower and lower behind—and up the feet and knees of the great Barail Range itself.

A group of hillmen scattered before us and stood on the roadside, staring. They were not the slim-built Assamese of the low ground. The sight of them was a shock. Here were the Philippines and Indonesia. Bead necklaces drooped on their bare, brown chests, black kilts with three lines of cowries wrapped their hips, plaids edged with vivid colours hung on their coppery shoulders. Tall, solid, muscular, Mongolian, they stood, a little startled, as we shot by.

I turned on Alexa beside me.

'Lexie! Who on earth are they——?'

'Why, Nagas,' she said, surprised.

It's twelve years now since that moment, and I still don't know what happened. There was a sudden surge of recognition. I must have sat there like a fool, gaping. Nagas!—of course!—illumination so plain, so known and obvious, that I was speechless at my own stupidity in not remembering sooner.

And suddenly, in the split second before it reached full consciousness, the knowledge was gone. It vanished as cleanly and completely as writing wiped off a slate. The car swept on up the twisty road; and I sat there dumb in the back seat, trying to snatch from the edge of my mind the vital, the intensely important, thing which a few seconds earlier had been so clear.

I never did.

We breakfasted at Kohima, whose tidy bungalows and red-roofed lines spread out along the spurs in the shadow of Japvo. I don't remember much of it. My ordinary winter visit to India was taking unexpected twists. Beyond the town there lay a progression of ranges which faded out into the haze of the east and the unmapped country. Bridle-roads led there, winding down bare spurs and curving round contours till they were lost in the intricate folds. On every ridge there was a shaggy village, its thatched roofs smoke-stained and weathered. One behind the other the hills stretched away as far as the eye could see, in an ocean of peaks, a wilderness of steep fields and untouched forest, of clefts and gulfs and razor-backs which merged at last into a grey infinity. That landscape drew me as I had never known anything do before, with a power transcending the body, a force not of this world at all.

Dazed, tired, bewildered, and not sure what had happened, I was decanted from the car that evening in the middle of Manipur.

I woke next morning to as pleasant a backwater as anyone could wish. Manipur State lay deep in the hills between Assam and Burma. Part of its territory was mountain country, but the heart of it was a level plain, an old lake-bed now drained and cultivated and covered in little square rice-fields yellow with stubble. Raided with hideous cruelty by the Burmese early in the nineteenth century, notorious for its rising of 1891, it slept now in a warm quiet. The one long road to the railhead cut it off effectively from the rest of the province. A mule-track linked it to Burma through Tamu, and that was all.

A European community of less than a dozen lived in the neat Imphal cantonments. Bougainvillea sprawled over their tiled bungalows and beds of snapdragon and lupin edged the lawns. At the lip of the Manipur River, which ran shallow and brown in a deep cutting through its own past sediment, stood the brick walls of the old fort, with the ruined Palace and Coronation Hall beside them—relics of '91. The new Palace, white and crisp as icing-sugar, stood on a grassy level outside the town. Beyond cantonments sprawled a dusty bazaar, all rickety balconies and peeling paint; and from that spread out the native Imphal, a vast conglomeration of bamboo-cloaked villages, hut upon hidden hut, pond after pond, a green, dank, feathery labyrinth which overflowed far on to the surrounding plain.

Life turned over pleasantly, with leisure. There were shaded lawns to sit on. There was golf at the Club and tennis at the Residency; there was duck-shooting on the lakes at the south of the valley. We womenfolk idled comfortably. We shopped at the Canteen, we dined; we visited the Arts and Crafts showroom; and twice a week we went to watch the polo. But above everything there was one daily spectacle which took the eye. Every evening in the Imphal bazaar was held the Sena Kaitel, the Golden Market.

When the heat was out of the day and the light fell long and warm, files of villagers came padding in with their produce through the soft, thick dust of the roadsides. Along the edge of the polo-ground passed one endless procession of purple and scarlet, russet and green, and the ever-recurring yellow of the women's shawls. Girls passed, their stiff, striped *faneks* wrapped round them and belted in. Women, their hair sleeked back and knotted, pressed by in groups of black-and-purple and black-and-gold. Men, turbaned and swathed in white, pulled jade or amethyst wraps about them against the growing chill. Here were hillmen, tousled and nude, here were dogs, here were children, here were beggars—one jostling tide of colour on white and white on colour, streaming into the market-place in a cloud of golden dust.

By dusk the great square space was crammed. Hundreds of small lamps, wicks burning in saucers of oil, glimmered down the long aisles where the women sellers sat behind goods whose colours glowed again in the half-light—quilts in mauve and pink, stacks of white muslins, red-and-yellow loin-cloths, and the broad-banded scarlet-and-white cloths which the Tangkhul Nagas wore. There were brass wares and brass jewellery, bowls and dishes, armlets and bracelets and crowns in imitation of Manipuri goldwork; a dried fish section, smelling to high heaven; the potters' place, stacked with red earthenware jars; and betel, coco-nut and food-sellers of every kind, who overflowed from the stalls and cluttered the packed roads with titbits displayed on trays or on strips of plantain leaf. There was a tingling smell of smoke, spices, dust and marigolds in the air, there were lorries nosing and honking through the press, there were half-naked hillmen stopping to stare, and away and beyond it all was a bronze-green twilight and hills of black velvet against a shot-silk sky.

In the ordinary way I might never have gone further than the valley. Life centred on Imphal. Though the forested mountains ran right round the level like a rim to a tray, officers visited them occasionally and in the course of duty, and outsiders never. But ten days after I arrived, the Civil Surgeon and his wife, who were going on tour to Ukhrul in the Tangkhul Naga country, offered to take me with them. Almost before I had unpacked, certainly before I knew what I was in for, I was bundling a scratch camp outfit into jappas, the tall carrying-baskets used for hill-transport. The car at the door, a flurry of forgotten oddments, and we were bouncing eastwards along the Yaingangpokpi road.

We spent the night in a mud-walled rest-house at the foot of the hills, and next morning entered them. The outer slopes were barren and dry, seamed with red gullies and covered in dense grass which held the heat. Then, as we climbed, we came to woods and cool air, and crossed to the inner slopes and a greener landscape.

It was a glorious, open world, with a sense of infinite distance. Sometimes we marched through oak-scrub and dry leaves, like a winter wood at home, with blue sky and white clouds behind the bare branches; sometimes we dropped to tropical forest as dank as a cellar, all broad leaves and coarse, crowding growths and wild banana-trees rearing out of the tangle. The track itself was a shelf on the side of the hill, and at intervals along it there were patients waiting for Colonel Taylor, his medicine-chest and the compounder. Naked, grimy, smelling of sweat and wood-smoke, they stood and squatted with their small offerings of eggs and fruit on the ground before them, their round-faced, slit-eyed children peering at us from behind them. With them were their head-men, tall and statuesque in black and crimson togas. Great rings of silver distended their ears. Collars of beads and bone hung down on their chests, and they wore the Tangkhul hair-cut, the sides of the head shaved clean while a stiff cockscomb of hair ran over the top like the crest of a classical helmet.

Each night we slept in an earth-floored bungalow with crumbling mud walls and nothing between us and the spar-rows in the thatch, so that debris and blessings rained on the dinner-table. Every morning we left a cactus-hedged com-pound, marched for four hours, and camped again in another just like it. The bungalows varied only in situation and decrepitude. Daily the road dropped into a chasm of a valley and crawled laboriously out of it by a ladder of zigzags; it wound in and out of ravines, crossing bouldered streams by roofed timber bridges, and once in a while it wandered along a crest, through woods and grassland, and let us see ridge lifting beyond ridge in the distance. Mist boiled in the hollows, rising raggedly as the sun struck it. Villages were perched here and there, scattered Kuki hamlets, compact Naga settlements, and sometimes a tin-roofed converts' chapel. Bamboos arched below us, graceful and feathery; dark, aboriginal forest covered the hilltops; and everywhere the wet-rice terraces swept down row on row in fan-shaped staircases two thousand feet deep to the rich, irregular curves of the valley fields, whose banks made a black tracery on the bright water.

When, ten days later, we returned to Imphal, life had changed. There is no describing the fascination of the hills. Neither heat, sweat, dirt nor discomfort could break their hold. It was as though I had re-discovered a world to which

I had belonged the whole time; from which, by some accident, I had been estranged. Seen again, Imphal and the life of its small community had indefinably altered. I saw them, rather, at a new angle; the perspective was subtly different. They had become a little hostile, a little foreign. Not yet of the hills, but already divorced a fraction from my own race, I wanted nothing now but the lovely, wild reality of mountain and jungle. I had to go back.

There wasn't long to wait. Alexa, unable to join the Ukhrul trip, had already arranged for the pair of us to go to Tamenglong and the Barak River with Mr Jeffery, the State Engineer, on his next tour of bridge inspection. She broke the news to me almost as soon as I reached the house.

At that time the hill districts of Manipur fell into two subdivisions. Ukhrul was the headquarters of the eastern, and Tamenglong that of the west. Both areas ran from the Naga Hills border to the Chin and Lushai Hills on the south, and in both the tribes were of two groups, Naga and Kuki.

The former were an early migration, the latter recent arrivals akin to the Lushais and Chins. The southern half of both districts was wholly Kuki; to the north, where the full tide of their invasion had not reached, they were peppered here and there among the Nagas in scattered clans. To a certain extent they were still moving. Though their larger communities were static, the smaller tended to shift and break up, drifting from place to place in search of fresh land as though their migratory urge were not yet spent. The Nagas, on the other hand, were well-settled. Their last migration was several centuries behind them and they lived in clearly-defined tribal areas. To the east, round Ukhrul, were the Tangkhuls; on their fringes were a small pocket of Marrings and some Khoiraos; and there were border villages which shaded off into the Angamis of Naga Hills. On the west, at Tamenglong, there were three allied tribes, the Kabui, Zemi and Lyeng, which together formed the group known as the Kacha Nagas.

The Ukhrul trip had been short and over bridle-roads. This was to last three weeks, we should be lodged in jungle-camps, and much of the route was over native paths. It wasn't usual then for women to tour in the hills. There were protests; our plan was criticized.

'You'll never stand the marching,' said a captain, with gloom. 'You'll go sick on the Barak and be carried in, and then you'll know all about it.'

But Mr Jeffery ignored all pessimists. We left on the scheduled day, in the worst weather possible, and the station sat back to await our bodies. We climbed into the car, broad-sided our way to the starting-point through a foot of mud, and met our porters in a damp bazaar. The peepul-tree above the cigarette-stalls dripped heavily on the men and baggage; and then we were gone, tramping away up the slope in thick mist, wind-blown drizzle and deepening twilight, on as unpromising a start as ever a trip had.

The weather cleared in a day or two, and, razor-back after razor-back, the ranges came out of their cloud. Where the Ukhrul side had been dry, with grassy stretches and oaks and pines, the country here was covered throughout in dense rain-forest. Blue and dark green, black, almost, where cloud-shadows crossed it, it coated everything. By Haochong and Lukhambi and the giant bamboo of the Irang valley, we came, on the fourth day out from Imphal, to Tamenglong. Struggling up the wicked ascent of Khebuching—stretch after stretch straight up without a bend to ease it—we met beer-bearing interpreters a little below the summit, and, refreshed, tramped on the last half-mile. The road turned downward. The trees ended suddenly; and we overlooked Tamenglong.

The long ridge on which we stood here fell away in eroded knolls and hummocks. On these stood the station, its tin roofs patches of red below us. The S.D.O.'s bungalow was perched on one pinnacle; the rest-house lay below it on another; and a primitive stone fort stood detached a little on a third. The town, if you can call the straggle of clerks' and interpreters' houses that, ran winding along a spur lower still, and right out at the end of the tongue and jutting above the deep Barak valley was a Kabui village. But beyond the station was such a view as is seen in dreams—one vast sweep of rolling green hills ran right round the horizon, here rising in a peak, there dropping in seas of bamboo to a river and the faint streak of a waterfall.

We halted a day in Tamenglong, visiting the fort with its spike-studded glacis; and then we marched again, down the long, level spur to the Kabui village, and through its dung-littered street to the lip of the hill. The path fell suddenly into space. Down through the fields it went, through grass and woods; down by zigzags, by steps, by twists, by long slants —down, down, down, turning and dropping, out of the cultivation and into the jungle beyond. A vaulted tunnel of bamboo received us. Its endless vista stretched on, grey-green, winding a little, always sloping down. Knees ached, toes bruised; down, still down. Milestone after lichened milestone we passed. The river murmured a very little louder—we saw it for a second, bright with rapids in the sun, with a thread-like suspension-bridge stretched across it. The wind of the hills was gone. A warm, wet, muggy quiet enveloped us, the heat of the deep valleys. Tiger-mosquitoes swarmed on us when we sat. Giant bamboos replaced the lighter types. The road was thick with decaying leaves, perpetually damp. And then, at last, the slope ended. The river roared now on our left. A few yards more, through jungle and river-grass; over old courses and sandbanks, through scrub and reeds—and there was the bridge, high, light and web-like, and under it our small bamboo-built camp.

Next morning the sandbank beside us clattered with bamboos and the whop-whop of cutting. Twenty or thirty Nagas were building rafts for our downstream journey, and on the day following we launched forth. The rafts were long, triangular structures, mere bundles of bamboos secured at the bows and braced amidships. Low platforms kept us out of the wet, as the bottom boards were awash. Of terrifying instability—the least tilt shot you off sideways—yet of sur-prising endurance, they could not, so far as I know, be capsized. One boatman forward and another aft poled, pushed or paddled, as the case required, and so, bumping over shallows, wading, portaging and sometimes sliding serenely down long, deep pools, we proceeded south.

We were well into the wilderness now, in a world of green

water and green jungle, of bamboos and elephant-grass and trees, of glaring, sunlit shingle and bright rapids. Our camps were in tiny clearings cut out of the woods and tiger-tracks appeared overnight on the paths and sandbanks round them. Barking-deer took nightly exception to the glare of the pressure-lamp; otters slipped into the water as the rafts approached.

It was a new world, too, in another way. Jeffery had a friendly, tolerant liking for the hillmen. At any rate, he saw them as human beings. If their world differed from his, he was prepared to recognize theirs as a distinct entity, complete in itself, and respect it as such. There was a great difference here between his view and Imphal's, which, at least on the non-administrative side, inclined to be strongly European, and poked fun at anyone, of whatever race, whose standards were not exactly its own. It is an understandable reaction, perhaps, in a small group of people isolated, surrounded and pressed in upon all sides by the strong tides of native life, by cultures and standards quite other than those to which they must conform on their eventual return home. There are those so detached from the world, saints so supported by an inner strength, that they can move untroubled through half the conflicting cultures of the globe; but the ordinary mortal has only his small props and stays of precept and custom to sustain him, and when they crack under outside pressure, he can but close the ranks and defend the shell bravely.

Every evening brought a new camp-site and new people crowding it, brown, slim, curious, unhurried, with a strangely unsavage courtesy. Even now I get a catch at the heart from the sharp, clean smell of new huts—the fresh-cut bamboo and thatch, and the scraped wet earth of the floor. Night after night the mists shut down on the valley, the moon shone thinly through, and the porters, like young bronze statues, came up to sit by the fire. We passed the three great falls of the Barak, each sliding in a giant step between ever-rising walls of grey sandstone, and started below them with new rafts, paddling down long, still reaches on a widening stream. And then, at last, we came to the suspension-bridge carrying the Silchar track, and the end of our river journey.

It was the end of a dream. Already the outer world was near us, Silchar, and Imphal, where Nagas were an obscene joke, and the incredible beauty of the jungle meant nothing. There was this last camp, with the Kabuis of Kambiron, who, old friends of Jeffery's, had moved down in a body seven miles and taken us to their hearts in a family picnic, but every moment was sharpened by its impermanence. And then the end came. The logs smoked out in the sunlight in the abandoned fire, the porters took their loads, the long file started, and the camp was left deserted under the trees.

We returned by train up the Hill Section, which everyone in Silchar had been at pains to praise; but it was dust and ashes after the cool Barak. The carriage was a grim and dusty coop. The few Nagas along the line were thin and dingy. For all I know, my future bodyguards sold me oranges at Mahur; I cared for nothing, and slept, tired and liverish, all the way. By Christmas we were back in Imphal. Things would never be the same for me wherever I went. What Ukhrul had begun, the Barak had clinched.

In April I was at sea and bound for London, with no idea that I should ever see India again.

CHAPTER II

SOLO FLIGHT

Back in England that following summer three things happened which influenced events profoundly. Firstly, the photographs I had taken were far better than I had expected. I thought of them as snapshots, but when I brought them home they proved to be pictures of professional standard. Secondly, Mrs Southcott, a family friend, took an interest in them and me and introduced me to the Royal Geographical and Royal Central Asian Societies as well as to individual friends of hers, some of them anthropologists. Many of the people I met asked me if I were going back. I had made a start, so why not follow it up? That set me thinking seriously. It might be worth doing, there might even be a career in it, but at present I had neither money nor backing nor even a prospect of returning to Manipur. I needed an opportunity.

Then the third thing happened. Our old friend Jeffery wrote to say he planned a last trip to the Barak before retiring. If I liked to find myself a chaperon and come along, I could join his party. Here was my chance, and it was up to me to use it. I should be going through country where very few people went and there was no point in travelling aimlessly and wasting time and films on casual pictures. I must concentrate on something, and as I was interested in the tribes the obvious field was anthropology. I knew nothing at all about it and I had no training, but I felt that there might be some worthwhile work simple enough for a layman to tackle. So I wrote to Professor J. H. Hutton at Cambridge, to Professor Hodson, to the Pitt-Rivers Museum at Oxford, and elsewhere, and I found that there was. Very little photography had been done in the Manipur hills, and there were many technical processes, brass-casting, weaving, pottery-making and the like, described by trained observers but not yet pictured. Good sets of still photographs illustrating these, or better, ciné-films, would be welcomed.

Autumn brought the Munich crisis but Chamberlain flew. At the end of October I was once more eastbound. I had my list of subjects, I had spent my savings on films. I had found I could lecture, I thought I could write, I could sometimes take good pictures; I knew I wanted adventure. There wasn't a scrap of certainty that I should ever make anything of it, but I saw—which matters more at twenty-four—unlimited possibilities.

The Barak trip over, I applied to the Political Agent for permission to go into the hills alone to do my anthropological photography. Leave was, after a delay, granted—a revolutionary step.

Now that it had come the adventure was rather alarming. No institution was backing me; I had no money except my allowance from home. My camp equipment was minimal and was borrowed, camp-bed, chair, table and bath, some forks, spoons and knives, a set of cooking-pots and a plastic picnic-set. I had some cheap cotton shirts and drill shorts, a warm sweater and a golf-jacket, and that was my camp wardrobe. For marching, and you had to walk every mile in the hills, I had Pathan-type sandals called *chapplis* and Army socks. I hardly spoke the language. I owned, and these were my only really good items, an almost new Leica and additional lenses, and a Bell and Howell ciné-camera, a Model E. It was all I wanted and I felt it was adequate. If I had not the skill to get results with that, then no patent tents or expensive extras would help me. The human element was what was going to count.

Feeling very cold and small one January morning, I climbed into a truck. My baggage was piled on behind and my servants were piled on top of it. We rolled off towards the foot of the hills and I was alone with my abilities.

A month later, with the first few films and notes secured and the preliminary canters safely over, I left on my first real expedition—to Ukhrul, to Nungbi and the Tangkhul country.

My companions were two. The first was my servant, Abung. He was a Kabui Naga; small, faithful, furry, and no cook, but he smoothed over more difficulties for me than ever I realized at the time. The other was a Manipuri compounder.

A gentle, kindly soul, he was being sent with me by the new Civil Surgeon.

In the drought of February, in a pillar of dust, we set out across the dry plain towards Yaingangpoki and three days later reached Ukhrul. It lay on a long ridge at a height of six thousand feet, the square stone fort to the south, then the straggling Christian settlement, then the S.D.O.'s bungalow, which stood on a shelf on the eastern slope and commanded a superb view of the great peak of Sirohi; and lastly, some way along the ridge to the north, the three-hundred-house Naga village, its street descending in a series of stone-faced platforms, and its tall, bare genna-posts—barked tree-trunks set up to commemorate feasts—standing in clusters against the pale sky. The houses were timber-fronted with massive planks; their shaggy, smoke-blackened porches overhung, and some, the houses of rich men, were partly roofed with wooden shingles and boasted house-horns on the gables. .

We halted a day in Ukhrul to refit and re-organize, and then, on the 13th, primed with advice from Mr Duncan, the S.D.O., I set out at last for the two Nungbi villages, Khulen and Khunao, marching through scattered pinewoods and over a carpet of red needles towards hills which showed green, brown and Madonna-blue in the rain-clear air. We camped that night at Nungbi Khunao, in grass and matting huts through which a bitter wind swept, and next day I went to the village to take the pictures of pottery-making I had come to secure.

Their situation near a bed of clay gave these two villages a local monopoly. Day after day in the cold weather one could see columns of smoke rising above the houses as the pots were fired, thin brown pillars climbing into the sky.

The Tangkhul potter uses no wheel, nor does he, like the Manipuri, shape his pot on a board turned on his knee. Instead, he gives the clay its first circular shape round a bamboo and then moulds the pot by hand. The workshop was the village street, with the villagers for audience. The potters stripped down their wine-red cloths to work, girding them round their waists like petticoats. First of all stones were brought in a basket, and one or two of them hammered to a fine powder.

They crumbled easily, and in a few minutes were dust. Then the dust was mixed with half as much powdered clay, and enough water to make a firm, damp mass. This was pounded in a wooden trough till smooth and then divided into two parts.

One was made into a flat, round cake for the base of the pot. The other was laid on a board and shaped into a long strip, three inches wide and perhaps an inch thick, which was beaten out to twice the length and half the thickness. The edges were trimmed and squared off with a bamboo knife, and it was ready.

The potter fetched a section of giant bamboo. He rolled the strip of clay up round this, stood the whole upright on the clay base, shook the strip loose from the bamboo, which he removed, and coaxed the strip round to form a cylinder. Joining the ends, he worked it to the base; and there it stood, a pot in embryo. The rest was but thinning and shaping. Round and round the pot he backed, patting, moulding, curving. The sides swelled, the neck contracted. He rolled two strips of clay in his hands, spitting to moisten them, and set them on as handles. A last smoothing; he cut the pot from its base; and there it was, rimmed and twin-handled, ready for the fire. The potters posed for a final picture, solemnly, their work before them, and all was done.

Unexpectedly that night, in the dusk by the camp-fire, we found a new retainer. His name was Luikai. A small, grimy, snub-nosed Tangkhul, he had run himself into debt over his wife's funeral. Either in ignorance or perversity, he had given the prescribed parts of the sacrifice to the wrong people, and had had to right the matter by doing the whole ceremony again. He wanted to come along with us to earn the money. Anxious, shivering in his tattered cloth, with the compounder as advocate, he waited the verdict. I took him on. He had the itch, unfortunately; but then most Tangkhuls had.

Then down from Nungbi we went, and away to the north, to the hills I had looked at so longingly the year before. It was like a dream now to be walking their rise and fall: the air of morning in one's face, the mist clearing, the file of porters in front, the pad-pad of barefooted followers behind. Never had

I known such exhilaration, such passionate happiness; your loads up, your porters off, the mountains round you and the world ahead—can anyone twenty-four and adventurous ask for better?

The day's routine was simple. With the first gleam of day-light through the hut walls, in came Abung with a cup of tea. Next we packed the kit and sent off the porters, the compounder and I staying back to hold a final dispensary. Our route lay well off the beaten track, and there was urgent need for it. With luck we were off by eight, but when we got in depended on the roadside villages, for we stopped to hold a dispensary session in each and seldom got off again in less than an hour. After medical aid, when confidence had been established, came photographs—sometimes posed, grave headmen against their house-fronts, to show the sweep of the Tangkhul haircut, the fine features; sometimes unstudied, snatched at the right moment, a quick portrait of a laughing boy. When we reached the night's camp there was a short lull while we settled in, ate and rested; and then there would be one long dispensary till dark or after.

Photography was no strain. The actual dispensary work was not hard; but the rough conditions and the numbers who flocked to us made it so. The crowd of patients was generally marshalled by a headman, but it always pressed in as close to us as it could, a tight ring of bare, brown, unwashed bodies, all wriggling and jostling to be the next for attention. Scabies, worms and malaria were the chief troubles, but coughs and bronchitis ran them pretty close. Then there were septic wounds and ulcers, often of horrible size. There were minor operations—lancing abscesses and extracting teeth—and sometimes a lady who had to take me aside and tell me all about it in Tangkhul before she could be coaxed along to the compounder. In wayside villages it was much the same, except that the medicines had to be set out on a bench, a woodstack, or the ground, and it was one long battle to keep the flies and dust off them.

It was not that Manipur was unprovided with facilities. The Civil Hospital in Imphal was well-equipped for its size, improvements were added as funds allowed, and there were smaller hospitals at Ukhrul, Tamenglong and Mao. But there were no travelling dispensaries, and the rural areas went untouched. In addition, the hillman's conservatism, his fear of a hospital, his tendency, like a child's, to cling to the familiar when things went wrong, all combined to keep him from the help available. But if it could be brought to him, then he was glad of it; and, used in this way, a few plain drugs could relieve a disproportionate amount of suffering.

From village to village, the stock of photographs growing, we crept on east and north. One camp I have cause to remember.

We had passed the salt-wells at Mariem, where Tangkhuls were boiling brine in iron pans to make the flat cakes of earthy salt which the hillmen love, and we came at the end of a hot march to a group of rest-huts in a wood near Luchai. The men's shelters were dotted about in the shade under the trees. Mine, a big, plank-walled building, stood in the middle of them. When night fell and it was time to lock up, I found the crude wooden door had no latch or bar. It wouldn't wedge, and when pushed to, merely swung open again.

I leaned out and looked at the camp. The fire was down to ashes. The night was still and calm; not a thing stirring, not a breath of wind, we were even out of earshot of Luchai, the village. It was so quiet, so peaceful, that I could hear the breathing of the men asleep in the nearest huts. I left the door open and slept like a top.

Next morning the camp was in a flutter. The porters had heard a tiger among the huts in the night. Round and round it had gone, and they had lain listening. They were frantic to leave; Abung was pop-eyed, and even the compounder uneasy. I alone was sceptical. Tigers aren't common at that altitude in the cold weather; and still less often—unless they are man-eaters, and we should have heard if there was one about—do they venture in among buildings and close to fires. But I asked Mr Duncan about it on the way down, a fortnight later, and learned that Luchai harboured a were-tiger, the son of a were-tiger, and of the most evil reputation possible. I remembered, vividly, that open door.

Climbing round and over the shoulder of a great hill, we came, through fields and woodland, to Chingjaroi.

It was an odd village. The site had once been occupied by a Tangkhul settlement, but this had been wiped out by raiding Kukis. Gradually, to the empty place, came emigrants from the surrounding tribes; a handful of Tangkhuls here, some quasi-Angamis there; and their descendants, marrying, had fused the two into a unique community. They had their own village dialect, and the women spoke nothing else. The men, more travelled, were bi-lingual, speaking Tangkhul or Angami as well, and sometimes a little Manipuri, the lingua franca.

There were three settlements in the group. The main one, Chingjaroi Khulen, had a hundred and fifty houses and ran in steps and terraces down a southward slope. Behind it, at the back of the hill, the ground fell sheer; and from the fringing wood one looked far down on rice-fields and little black blots of cattle nibbling among the stubble. High on the top of the ridge, the village dropping below it in a dark fan, stood the headman's house. Great wooden barge-boards, prolonged into horns, edged the front gable; one saw them sharp and black and curved against the turbulent spring sky. But dominant as the house was, it did not stand on the old traditional site of his ancestors, the place reserved for the founder's line. Had he occupied that, and taken on himself the full burden of ritual headmanship, he would have been bound by taboos of every kind, on washing, food, work, on every least part of his daily life; and he was young and liked his creature comforts. He ruled, therefore, as a secular headman, an unconsecrated king, and, perched on another house-site with his gentle wife and fat, golden baby, ate, did and lived as he liked. An offshoot village, Chingjaroi Khunao, was two miles away down a pine-covered ridge; and below that again was a small Christian settlement.

It was a good centre, and we halted. The March winds had begun. We came in a gale, and throughout our stay the trees roared, the air was full of dust and flying leaves, and the draughts whistled ferociously through the cracks in the basha. Constant nagging had by now got Luikai fairly clean; but here some criticism of mine drove him down to bathe at the water-point in spite of the bitter wind. Next morning even the tea tasted of soap, but Luikai was three shades lighter. Treatment had reduced his scabies, and he had learned all kinds of odd jobs. When not on the march, he was washing, scrubbing, chopping wood, or running about on a dozen other chores. He was hard-working and willing and Abung swore by him.

Most of the time was spent in photography and dispensary work, clambering up and down the stepped village, through dust and corn-cobs, with camera, lenses and medicine-jappa. But I went one day to climb Chingjui hill. This, seven thousand feet high, rose just behind us. The path up was almost vertical. Long out of use, it had to be re-cut for the expedition; a second cutting-party, a dozen bucks armed with long, fishtailed Eastern Angami daos, accompanied us in case more cutting was needed.

For a long time, in steamy heat and an aura of jungle mosquitoes, I toiled up this green cliff with the others crawling respectfully after. Then, as we topped the ridge and met the view, I stopped short. Beyond the first, forested hills below us lay range on range and ridge on ridge, in endless shades of grey, as though the steep winter waves of the Channel had frozen suddenly on a vast scale. Featureless, cold and uncanny, they rolled on till they melted into the lowering sky, and where the two met was one snow-capped peak, standing out against the ominous unknown country in a blaze of white. It was Saramati. There was just the one glimpse of it, bright, unearthly; and then the sun went, and the greyness swallowed it up.

From Chingjaroi we bore back to the south. The elders said good-bye to us under the bare bauhinias at the ford. Their red blankets showed for a minute on the far slope, against the earth banks, the dry leaves and the wintry trees, as they turned back again up the hill; and we, crossing the river, set our faces to the Paowi climb. Within the first few hundred yards I was aching with 'flu.

It'll be a long time before I forget that march, the endless road, the hill extending, apparently, like a telescope, with every foot I trod. I made it, but even in camp there was nothing much to be done. The drugs which might have been of use were all expended; and I had to get better as best I could.

There were lepers here. The compounder found one at the first dispensary. He was a young man, a buck in his twenties. Already the disease showed a little in his face, a thickening here, a coarse lumpiness at the lips. We were still talking to him when the crowd drew back, and through the gap came hobbling a woman with a child of eight or so at her skirts.

She too was a leper. Crude soles were tied to her feet with string; the sores had developed there, and she could not walk barefoot. Even shod, she shuffled painfully. The little boy turned round, hugging his mother and laughing up at her, and we saw, in the sharp sunlight, the first patches of leprosy on his back. We sent them away. She would not go to the leper asylum at Kangpoki; and there was nothing that we could do.

Then we reached Ukhrul again. I still had 'flu, but money and stores were short, and we could not halt a day. We turned to the west, and, arrived at Tuinem, stopped there a day to photograph Tangkhul weaving.

Tuinem was a weaving centre. With the other Naga tribes, weaving is a universal industry. Each woman supplies her own household, and only specially-talented workers make cloths for sale. But with the Tangkhuls the trade is confined to half a dozen villages, and these supply the whole tribal area. Nowhere have I seen such a concentration of textiles as there was at Tuinem—racks of blue and crimson cloths were airing outside every house; skeins of dyed thread, red, white, black, orange, green and gold, were stretched to dry or lay beside the women as they worked. In every porch was a loom, with a cloth on it at one stage or another; and all up the street of dark, smoky houses and sudden gleams of colour there were plum-trees in flower, the pink sprays arching over against a clear blue sky.

It was almost over now. From Shongphel we marched down to the plain, the waiting lorry and Imphal; and every step away from the hills was a separate pain. For the first time I had known responsibility, loneliness, worry and exhaustion. I'd been revolted by wounds and filth, hampered by lack of the language, but nevertheless I was going back to it if it killed me. And I couldn't have given one sane reason why.

CHAPTER III

SECOND ATTACK

A WEEK later, fortified by experience and stocked up with medicines, we left again. But, on this trip, anthropology took second place. I had covered all the items on my list, and I went now partly for sheer adventure and partly because I knew the need for medical help in the remoter hills.

Our start was unpropitious and proved prophetic. It had been raining, and it was doubtful at first if the lorry could reach the end of the road. When, after many skids and alarums, it did, Abung the cook slipped and hurt himself on the bungalow path and my new compounder had a violent row with the caretaker over the state of his quarters. They really were very foul, and I had to lodge him in half the tiny house, to the loss of all my comfort. I had been warned, too, to keep an eye on the man. He was a tall and sullen Kuki, and not, the Civil Surgeon said, to be trusted; I was to keep the medicines by me and issue them myself. I did not know, though, that he had twice been transferred for dishonesty, and was going out with me as a last chance to reform. Far from reforming, he set out to give all the trouble he could, and succeeded admirably.

The next day we marched right through to Lambui, a matter of seventeen miles and very steep. At the top of Lambui hill, another of my servants, Luikai—who, a few days before, had asked to stay on, so that I had not engaged an alternative man in Imphal—suddenly said he wanted to quit and go home. He could have chosen no more inconvenient time or place to say it (I have since wondered whether the compounder put him up to it) and I reached Lambui, in the blue, shadowy dusk, so furious that it startled even myself. But Abung, always a peacemaker, talked him round, and we reached Ukhrul much the same party as left it. A short halt; and we pushed on to our old camp at Nungbi Khunao, where it was blowing as cold as ever in the huts.

The last morning there broke warm and sunny. The light slanted in through the flimsy walls, spotting the floor and silhouetting the humped jappas. I reached for my tea while Abung, a pint-sized figure, poured water into the washing basin. The door closed behind him. I slipped out of bed. It was warm and windless; I stripped my pyjamas and began to dress.

The door flew suddenly open. There was a dazzle of light and a man came in. I cried out sharply—I was half-naked. I fell back, snatching at the nearest thing, a towel, and then saw that the man was the compounder.

'I'm not dressed yet—please go away!'

He took no notice. He didn't even reply. His head averted —he conceded that—he slouched across the hut to the other corner. He reached the medicine-jappa; removed the lid; and, squatting down, began to unpack at leisure the fifty pounds of drugs. The door flopped open, and in came a flood of patients, pushing, unaware of the scene.

I still didn't grasp it. I thought he hadn't heard.

'What is it, please? Is it urgent? I want to dress. I'd rather you came back later.'

The Tangkhuls saw me. Shocked and embarrassed, they stopped. But there sat the compounder, sullen and slow. His hands played with the medicines; he lifted them up; he looked at them; put them down. A cigarette hung on his lip. He didn't trouble to remove it when he spoke, nor turn, nor apologize; he jerked the words out backwards over his shoulder.

'I want medicine.'

Sitting there on my bed, half-covered, the Tangkhuls shuffling uncomfortably and looking the other way, I understood. It was deliberate; and quite deliberately he had brought in the Tangkhuls, to shame me just that much more. I found myself shaking. I jumped up and ran over to him. I told him, over and over again, to go. He rose, and walked out slowly. The Tangkhuls had gone. I slammed the door. Trembling, nearly crying, I crammed my clothes on. The camp was quiet outside.

I sat on the bed till I felt better. Then I went out.

The open space in front of the door was sunlit. In the

middle of it was a heap of baggage, packed; and squatting by it, the compounder. This was his moment of triumph. Shortly, and not looking at me, he complained to me that I had been rude, and proposed to return at once to Imphal.

I contemplated his plan in silence. How thoroughly, how brutally, had the incident been engineered; and what a mind had planned it! There was no other compounder. Here was an end of the trip to the north, an end to my photographs; to the medical help we had promised the villages there, help they so much needed. At one stroke he had freed himself and ruined my enterprise, and that with as much humiliation and indecency as he could contrive in so short a space of time. And then I saw why he turned his face away. He couldn't suppress, in his moment of victory, a triumphant grin.

It was that which did it. This grin was the last straw. All my personal considerations went like smoke. Come hell and high water, that compounder was going on and the hillmen would get their medicine. If it was the last thing I did, I was going to win this battle. There was one stroke on which I knew he was not counting. He had complained of my rudeness, therefore he required an apology—I let him have it, an exquisitely polite apology.

It took the ground out from under him like a trap. He tried to recover; but it was no use, I had him. My daimon had taken charge. My other self, small at a distance, heard my own voice talking rings round him with alien fluency. When, half an hour later, we left for Chingngai, the next camp, I felt as though I had been wrung out like a dishcloth, but a black-sulky and disgruntled compounder was with us.

Instead of following our previous route north we were moving parallel to it and one range to the east, and along the top of the ridge beyond us ran the Burma border. Among the people who came into camp was a Tangkhul girl from the Somra Tract. She wore huge crystal-disc earrings, so heavy that they had to be held by a band of thread across the head or they would have torn the lobe. I tried to photograph her; but the people here were wild and shy and ran from the camera. Here, too, Luikai and the porters picked up a rumour that the Tangkhuls of Somra village, just across the border, had killed two Manipuri traders recently and taken their heads, but we never found out whether this was true.

The next stop was at the Kuki village of Paotong, where an old lady who came to get liniment was excessively friendly and tried to give me a chaw of tobacco as well as a string of revolting dried fish, and on the following day—the fifth out from Ukhrul—we reached Kharasom. This was the most northerly Tangkhul village. There were traces of Somra influence, and the genna-posts were tall, straight shafts with one side nicked in deep points, instead of the branched, barren trees which the Ukhrul Tangkhuls used. The porters were to go back from here, and I sat up till ten o'clock labouring over mail to go down with them. As I pored, who should appear but Abung, with a strange yellow object the general shape of a chef's cap—a home-made loaf he had baked for me, because, he said, he thought I was looking depressed.

At Nungbi we had collected another new follower. He was a tall Tangkhul called Chinaorang, and he was without exception the best porter I have ever known. As the now-clean Luikai had been polished by a brief training and was acting as house-servant, Chinaorang took over the medicine-jappa; and, once past the last village and given his head, he would steam away over steep and level under a sixty-pound load, leave me panting behind him, and reach the camp three-quarters of an hour in front of everybody. His lean, angular body gave him an Ancient Egyptian look; he had the broad shoulders and slim hips of a tomb-painting; and he was the shining light of the spear-throwing contests we held on slack days in camp. He had, too, an unexpectedly romantic history. A poor villager, he had fallen in love with the daughter of a rich family. But they disapproved, and married her off at once to a well-to-do youth in another village. The match was not a success. The lady sent over for help to Chinaorang, who did not fail her, and the resulting charge of wife-stealing cost him, when it came to court, a fine of Rs 100/–, which he was doing his utmost not to pay. But the wronged husband had been rather outspoken lately, and talked of complaining to the S.D.O., so Chinaorang, too, had joined us to make money. Whether the husband would ever see it was another story.

We were to have halted at Kharasom; but at noon on our first rest-day, when the camp was festooned with washing and all the porters dispersed up the village, in came the Chingjaroi headmen to say that there was an urgent case there and they needed help at once. Then ensued fearful confusion, but we were packed and off in an hour, and, half-running, half-walking the eight miles, reached the familiar camp in the early dusk. We now discovered what no one had thought to say before, that the patient lived in the Christian village, two miles further on; so leaving the rest of the party to settle in, the compounder and I and Chinaorang with the jappa pushed on down the spur.

It was almost dark when we got there. The house stood tall and shut against a green twilight sky—green with a line of coppery-red over the hazy Manipur plain. The headman spoke at the door. It opened, and we stepped in.

A fire burned in the middle of the oblong room inside; by it sat a man, nursing a bundle of rags. The rags whimpered; it was a baby. A woman, her hair loose, left us to shut the door and went back to the hearth to stir a rice-pot. Clothes, hoes, baskets, gourds, all the soot-blackened odds and ends of a Naga household, were dumped and littered about in the untidy darkness. The heat was incredible—the air felt solid. Food, smoke, stale clothes, the dungy, dusty smell of the village, they were there; and added to them a reek of sweat and a sweetish, horrible odour.

We asked for the patient. They pointed across to the far wall.

She lay on a bed of rags. Her face and body were swollen, her skin a yellowish-grey. She levered herself off the bed when the headman spoke, and part-crawled, part-dragged herself to the fire for us to see her. The trouble was all too clear. She had had a difficult labour, and the villagers, mid-wives, with their gnarled and filthy paws and twisted nails caked with the dirt of years, had delivered the child by hand. The results were shocking; and our resources were few.

We did what we could. We worked for an hour. The firelight flickered and often died; the others, watching us, forgot to make it up. We used a flashlight, and held it by turns. The sharp smell of disinfectant thickened the mixed reeks in the air. Suddenly I found myself faint and sweating. I made a dash for the door.

It was cold outside. The headmen and Chinaorang were squatting by the wall. Over them the night was clear, a pattern of stars; and down below was a procession of pine-tipped ridges, a landscape like a dim transparency.

'Will she be all right?' asked the headman. She was his cousin.

'She'll be all right,' said I, and thought—What a lie. I went back in.

The compounder was sitting waiting. It needed two pairs of hands. We were nearly finished; we applied a dressing and drew the bandages firm. The syringe was lying sterilized in its little pan; the compounder gave an injection; the other woman and I helped her back to bed. She was quite exhausted and pitiably ill. But she tried hard to give us no trouble; she turned her head, her face so swollen it was hardly human, and said something in thanks. Her thick black hair splayed out on the rag pillow. I had felt it over my arm—it was wet with sweat and harsh as a horse's tail, and as full of tangles. I watched the other woman pull up the covers. We turned to go. The husband, nursing the baby, stared after us. His thin, Mongol face was sharp with misery.

It is so difficult on these occasions to find words. One tends to speak with a crisp, professional assurance:

'That's all for now—we'll come in the morning. Just a day or two now, and she'll be better.'

The dark of the porch, with a pig snorting disturbed in its bed of chaff. The open street—cool, marvellous after the fetor inside. The compounder, stalking off in the dark to spend the night with his friend the pastor. Chinaorang, sitting to the jappa, pulling the strap over his head, hauled up by a friend, humping, adjusting his load, and looking round for the others. And then the torches—brought out from a house, the glare lighting the headman carrying them; distributed, two, three, four, perhaps up to a dozen; the whole street bright, alive, flickering between the closed houses; the dogs slinking on the edge of the glow, the rocks seen, the dust pitted and visible, the distance solidifying into a backcloth to our lit stage. We turned, the headmen leading, and set off in single file along the steep path to camp.

There is no magic, no beauty, like that of pine-torches at night. The spirit-fed fakes at military tattoos are a mockery. We moved in a red cave of light, black darkness receding ahead and closing behind. The pine-trunks stood like palisades on either side of the road; the wind moved through the night over us and touched cold on our faces, and the Nagas' long, crested shadows rippled along the needle-strewn ground. The torches burned with a rich, deep, smoky glare. The scent of burning resin came from them, pungent and nostril-tingling. They dropped fat sparks and gobbets of fire on the road; the needles caught and smouldered till the men following stamped them out. Now lit, now silhouetted, the file moved; the pattern, the ripe, red-orange luxuriance of colour, changing, deepening, shifting always—with every change a new picture, an æsthetic experience so deep as to make one catch the breath; so, in an hour's journey, we reached the camp—and the transcendent gave place to the mundane, to chairs and lamps and an anxious Abung.

At noon next day the compounder returned, looking haggard. The woman, he said, was better. He had given a second injection, and thought she might now pull through. But the Christian village was full of infant diarrhœa; anxious parents had been pulling him out of bed all night to attend cases, and he had had no sleep at all. So saying, he went to bed in his hut.

We stayed on a day or two, till our patient was out of danger, and then prepared to resume our tour as planned. But the compounder pointed out that we had exhausted most of our drugs, Chingjaroi having, as usual, a wealth of cases, and suggested he should go back to Imphal to fetch more. As we still had more than half the tour in front of us, this was the sensible course, and I agreed, though privately doubting whether I should ever see the slippery brute again; so he turned south next day, while I marched back to Kharasom and the north.

CHAPTER IV

BLACK MAGIC

OUR next stage on from Kharasom was to a village called Jessami, on the long tongue of Manipur which juts into Naga Hills. The moment the name was mentioned, the men showed an odd unease. One after another they came to me with undefined reasons why we shouldn't go. But from no one —neither Abung, nor Luikai, nor Chinaorang, nor the Kharasom headman, who was reluctant to produce porters—could I get a clear statement of what was wrong. At last I said that if they could give me no reason against it, why, go we would; and we went.

It proved an elusive place. The road wandered on and on and up and down through dusty, scrubby jungle. At one point a pinewood burned, and we ran the gauntlet through smoke and sparks, jumping smouldering logs. We came to a Kuki village, which held us up for an hour and a half while we ministered to all the ailments in Asia; and not until afternoon did we drop suddenly from the wooded ridge into fields, from fields to a firewood reserve, and through that, by a broad, worn path, to a camp at the Jessami village gate and a settlement which, seen through the gap in the palisade, seemed Eastern Angami.

The old headman was ill, but his subordinates met us. The camp was excellent. There were ample supplies; the elders were the soul of courtesy. Only the Tangkhul porters and my servants struck a discordant note. They shied from the rice-beer as though it were brewed from arsenic. They huddled in camp in a wild-eyed bunch, glancing over their shoulders each time a villager passed; they could hardly have looked on the headmen with more terror had the old gentlemen worn horns, hoofs and tail. Had it not been so inexplicable their fear would have been comic.

Next morning I held a lone-hand dispensary which was well-attended. At eleven o'clock I was reading in peace, when the door burst open. There was a surge of men, and the hut was suddenly full with Abung, Luikai, Chinaorang, and the whole body of porters.

Never have I seen men in such a state of fright. Their eyes bulged. Nor was it easy—they were shaken to gibbering-point—to find out what was the matter. I got it at last from Abung.

There was something in the gateway—something put there to harm us. He kept insisting it was *jadu*—black magic, that is, of the most unpleasant kind. I pushed past them and went out to the village gate.

The others halted in the hut veranda. Abung, as my lieutenant, paddled after me. A few yards from the gate he stopped and pointed; and there on the bank ahead, at the foot of the thin, tall hedge which formed the palisade, was a little bamboo basket.

It sat there, small and harmless. I walked up to it to have a closer look.

It wasn't even a basket, really—a fragile, handled container of the simplest kind. In it was a white egg; and laid on it, and tied to it with a scrap of thread, was a lint square which must have come from the morning's dispensary, for it was smeared with ointment. I straightened up, and found I was alone with the thing. Abung had fallen back. Inside the gate, but at a very respectful distance, was a crowd of Jessami men, who watched me in silence.

It was a nice dilemma. I knew nothing about Jessami's sickness ceremonies. For all I knew it was a piece of innocent magic. On the other hand, the silent crowd suggested—there was a stillness, a waiting tension—that it was nothing so simple. I went back to Abung and asked, but he was positive —this was *jadu*. I returned to the gate, then, and picked it up, and as I carried it back to the hut the porters retired before it as though it were an unexploded bomb.

As I stood there with it, not at all sure what to do next, I saw, suddenly, one of the headmen. Unaware that things were wrong, he was peering into the empty cookhouse and searching, in a bewildered way, for the servants who should have been sitting there. I called him over. He came, astonished. I showed him the basket, and said: 'What's this?'

His eyes opened, his lips fell apart; he turned a dull yellow. He threw out his hands and took a step backward. If ever I saw consternation, it was then. He stood there, his mouth was trembling; he didn't speak.

'*Jadu*,' said Abung. The matter was clinched.

The porters all began talking at once. They squashed in a mob round the headman. The bolder spirits of the Jessami crowd came up; they stuck their heads over the porters' shoulders, the headman's, any gap that came handy, talked in whispers, and peered at the basket and egg. I was still holding it out to him; and he was staring at it as I should have looked at a severed head. I was tired of the thing. I forced it into his hand, keeping only the scrap of lint. Someone had been down to the dispensary to get that, with witchcraft in mind. It was the necessary physical connection, the link through which the curse could be directed. I burned it with ceremony, later.

For a second the headman held the basket. The crowd was still. Then, as if suddenly discovering it to be red-hot, he thrust it into the hands of a small boy next to him. The small boy bore it away at arm's length into the village; and more in sorrow than in anger I told the headman, through Abung, what I thought of it all, and withdrew with dignity into my hut. Through the cracks in its wall I presently saw the headman turn from the door with the others after him, and they followed him into the cookhouse in a gabbling flock. I heard afterwards that he wept for shame. They had tried so hard to welcome us, to have everything right; and now this unknown witch!

For the rest of the day the Tangkhuls continued in a state of alarm and I in a huffed seclusion. The headmen, I think, were holding emergency meetings in the village. The very large cat was, of course, now out of the bag—Jessami was a nest of wizards; it was this that the Tangkhuls had been afraid to tell me. I thought perhaps they might bolt in the night, but morning broke, and they were all still there. Abung regained his customary poise; and presently in came the headmen, laden

with peace-offerings—fowls, eggs, beer, rice and pumpkins—
and made it clear that the basket was in no way whatever
an insult from Jessami as a whole. They were, in fact, so
genuinely distressed about it that by general consent we
dropped the matter. The headmen and I behaved as though
the painful incident had never happened; dispensaries and
entertainments went on as usual; and in a day or two not only
did the Tangkhuls go into the village without me, where
before they had moved as though gummed to my shadow, but
drifted up at all hours, daylight or dark, to drink as much as
they could of the Jessami rice-beer. Jessami themselves, however, did not let the matter drop. I heard later that, unable to
find the culprit, they held a public cursing to cause his death
—which, Nagas being what they are, it almost certainly did.

We were still at Jessami when the compounder returned,
which he did after an unexpectedly quick journey—expedited,
perhaps, by a Civil Surgeon who knew him. After a day or
two longer, to give Jessami the benefit of the new supplies,
we turned back to the south and trailed laboriously once more
along the ridge to Kharasom. When, tired and hungry, we
came out of the woods to it, we found the village shut and
barred against us. When a headman was at last produced to
parley, we heard that smallpox had broken out at Lai-yi, our
next halt, and that every village for miles had closed its gates.
Day after day Lai-yi had sent messengers to know if we were
back; and, when Kharasom drove them away, they left a
scrawled letter begging us to come and save them.

The compounder and I held a hurried conference in the still
half-unpacked camp. We checked up on the party's vaccinations. Only he and I were safe; of the others, not one could
enter the danger-zone. But even if he and I were to go alone,
we still had no lymph or lancets. The only thing we could do
for Lai-yi was to send for help.

The shortest road to Imphal lay through the infected area.
That meant sending round through Ukhrul, a matter of eighty
miles. But it couldn't be helped; it was the only chance. We
picked the youngest and best of the Tangkhuls. A note was
scribbled, and he left that night.

The Duncans at Ukhrul forwarded it by a fresh runner.

It reached Imphal the evening of the second day. The Civil Surgeon immediately despatched a relief-party, which got to Lai-yi on the fourth day after my letter was written. But, quick as they were, short as the time was, there had still been thirty deaths. Yet there are people opposed to vaccination. How many of them, I wonder, have seen a smallpox outbreak?

Our message despatched, it remained to consider our own plans. It was inadvisable to stay where we were. There was risk of infection to Kharasom, should Lai-yi send over to call us again; they were on tenterhooks to be rid of us. Did we delay, we should get no porters ahead. There's nothing shuts up an area like an epidemic. We therefore decided to move slowly south, through the villages west of Paowi, where there was need for medical work but where we should be within call if the Lai-yi rescue squad needed us. So south we went; and the next evening we were with our old friends at Chingjaroi.

We asked for our woman patient. Oh, yes, they said, she was better. We went to call.

The house looked smaller by daylight, and shabbier, too. It had lost its sinister tinge; the weather-worn planks and bleached grey thatch were homely and humble. We rapped at the closed door.

It was opened by a pink-cheeked young woman, who stood in confusion at the sight of us all. Her hair was down, she was holding the baby—the mother's help, surprised at her morning chores. We asked for the convalescent and made to go in.

The girl protested.

'But isn't she here?' we said.

Then everyone talked at once. There was a chaos of tongues, misunderstanding in four languages. The headman came up. He thrust himself into the group, and when the compounder had finished—

'But this is the one,' he said.

There was a deathly silence. We stared so hard that she blushed.

The ten days' change was staggering—from a shapeless, swollen, half-conscious figure, to this robust young mother;

shapely, comely, plump, as though she'd never been ill a day. Embarrassed she nursed the child, and laughed.

'I think,' said the compounder, 'it is with the help of God.' I thought he was just about right.

From our old camp at Paowi we turned westward and scrambled up and down Naga paths in wild spring weather which grew steadily worse, and from that moment things began to go wrong. We arrived at Huimi soaked to the skin, Luikai paddling along at my heels with his cloth over his head, and we were not even settled in when Chinaorang reported sick with fever and an infected cut on his leg. We decided to turn back, then, instead of going on to the south and west, and, cutting up over the hills to the Ukhrul-Chingjaroi road, strike it at a camp known to exist at Phungam.

Next day we climbed up through the misty forests and over the range. Chinaorang was still lame, the men had coughs and chills, and Luikai, glooming along behind me, was prophesying pneumonia for everybody. When at last we descended shivering on the promised haven, we found, not the sound huts for which we longed, but a half-derelict camp looming up through wet mist, a wild, gusty wind driving the clouds past, and thatched roofs which leaked on the pitted earth floors. The villagers were not expecting us, so it was not their fault; but when at last we secured some firewood, it was soaking wet, and the fires smoked as only Naga fires can, with acrid persistence; there was hardly a dry space large enough to hold the camp-bed and we went round and round the hut with it, defeated by drips at every place where we tried to put it down, and to top all off, a violent thunderstorm blew up and removed with one roaring blast the mats we had laboriously spread over the leaks in the roof. With one accord we all gave up the struggle and went dumbly to bed.

We halted next day in only slightly improved conditions and then pushed forward to Huining, the weather, thank goodness, clearing as we went, and the men's spirits picking up with it. It was now mid-April, and between storms the country steamed with a threat of the heat to come. I had meant to go on to Ukhrul, but the bungalow there was booked; so I made a day's excursion in to say goodbye to the kindly Duncans, and then turned homewards direct from Huining.

There was no through road from there to Tuinem, but a complex of field-paths could be made to bring us there. At first it was fairly plain sailing along paths leading to the cultivation, but presently these began to subdivide—China-orang breaking down a green frond at each fork to guide the stragglers—and grew less trodden, and before long we had lost the path altogether and were scrambling down a great sweep of hillside by the banks of the water-channels and wet-rice terraces. At last our zigzag and precarious course brought us out in the valley bottom, and we teetered along the narrow field-banks to the edge of the central river.

I brought up short. There was no bridge. In the middle of the deep, brown water was a row of stepping-stones, round, wet, water-polished, and a yard apart. With a jump I reached the first one, and stuck there, wobbling.

On the bank behind me, Abung shouted directions. Luikai clucked. The porters spread out, jabbering. And at that moment, a Tangkhul in a field-gang on the far side downed his hoe and ran to my assistance. He darted down the steep bank and into the water. He waded the stream, the water swirling round his lean thighs. Straight from his work, he was mud-stained and stark naked. He caught my hand. Slowly, from rock to rock, he took me over, and I clung to him thankfully.

Behind me I could hear the loud guffaws of Abung, while the school-trained Luikai blushed.

We all reached Tuinem late, tired and hot. The compounder lost his way entirely and turned up hours later from some village quite off the route. He celebrated his arrival by a row with his porter, but I was too tired to care. What with the marching, and the long dispensaries, and the un-ending struggle with him—he never left an unpleasant remark unsaid—I was worn out. The only course was to go home now and refit, use the material I had, and return again in the autumn to try for more.

As a final touch, the Kuki watchman at Shongphel rest-house was drunk and fought the men. The next night we were in Imphal. My three months of paradise were over.

From a lorry bouncing along the road to the railway I watched the landmarks passing one by one—Maram village on its high hill, the windy pass at Mao, near Kohima. Then the road swept downwards and on, to the heat, to the plains, to the docks, and to England.

CHAPTER V

CHANGE OF COURSE

ARRIVED home in 1939 I at once laid plans to return in order to continue work amongst the Nagas. At first everything went swimmingly. My photographs were the best I had ever taken, and as a programme for the winter took shape it looked as though I might really be able to achieve something even if it did mean a big outlay in film stock, fares and camp equipment. But the moment my passage was booked and it all seemed settled, luck turned. From then on, the more the kit and the films piled up, the less and less chance there was that I should ever use them. On one hand, things at home had gone as wrong as they could; and on the other, if there wasn't war in the autumn, it would be a miracle. Between the two it was a grim summer. By the end of August they were cancelling sailings. My booking was twice switched. At last, at dawn on the day I was due to sail, we were called to ambulance-stations, and I cancelled my berth and sat down to wait for the blitz, quite certain that I had seen the last of Assam and the Naga hills.

On a grey day three months later I sailed after all. All the way out and across India, I still couldn't believe my luck; but there at last was the Manipur Road platform, the backcloth of forest, the familiar rest-house. I walked on air up the path. It was unbelievable, it was true—I was there.

Half-way to the bungalow the watchman met me with a letter. Still in a daze, I opened it, and pulled out a pass for the road and a letter from the Political Agent, whose last line brought me up all standing. He regretted that this time it would be impossible for me to tour the hills.

It was the final blow. Fate couldn't have found a better place nor a more cruel time to deliver it.

I hadn't realized before that a shock of this kind could stun one physically. I remember almost nothing of the next twenty-four hours. I made my way up to Imphal, though, and saw the Political Agent. He was not unkind; but he would not change his decision.

It was evening when I left the Residency. I had never been in such a state before. I daren't go back to my quarters. I walked and walked. It turned dusk, and then dark. I still went on, round and round cantonments. I passed the bungalows, the homes of lucky people with careers laid down. I walked till I was exhausted, till I was too tired to think, too tired to do anything but sleep. Tomorrow was another day. I'd worry about it when it came.

The breakdown lasted about a fortnight. Following as it did on the long strain of the summer, it was a bad patch, much worse than I dared tell anyone. But I had just enough sense left to keep control. I put away or locked up anything which could be of danger in a fit of depression. I rented the small Forest Bungalow, I shopped, I furnished it; collected a staff, learned Manipuri, clung to anything, everything, all the small, fussy chores of daily life. It was a giddy path. The holds were so small; one clung by a hand, a finger. I kept away from the rest of the station. They didn't know, and, at the worst time, the least rough touch would have meant disaster.

And then, in the very middle of it all, came the dog Khamba.

Luikai, one of my servants, was back, and hard on his heels had come a pockmarked Tangkhul friend selling dogs in the Naga market. He called on me to know if I needed one. I told him No; but he came back an hour later, and behind him, at the end of a chewed string, rolled a fat, soft, fubsy, solemn toy, black-and-white like a giant panda. It fell over its own feet and sat down; and it was mine for a rupee.

With that, not a dog but a personality entered the household. He was, it is true, a hound of the old, true Naga breed; big, massive beasts resembling Chows. But nobody could have confused Khamba with a mere canine. His independence, his dignity, alone marked him as apart. By the time he was full-grown he knew exactly where he came in the household; directly after me, but above the men, whom he treated always with an affectionate courtesy. He never fawned. Caresses he asked for when he wanted them, took, and departed. His life was lived in parallel with mine, together, but apart, as bachelor friends might share the same house. Yet he had, all the same, a sentimental and tender nature. He and I were deeply attached. Despite our one or two disagreements (such as over the question of the village goats), each went to the other for comfort in adversity, and his arrival did much to cheer me at this particular time.

In January I went to Shillong to see Mr J. P. Mills, then Governor's Secretary and Director of Ethnography in Assam. He was extremely helpful, proposing a whole list of alternative fields. Hope sprang again, but my heart was still with the Nagas, and the name on his list which caught my eye was that of North Cachar, the district immediately west of Manipur.

I had already read Soppitt's monograph on the Zemi Nagas. They were, one supposed, the same sad, shabby lot we had seen in 1938 along the railway. But they were akin to the Kabui, a tribe I had hoped to study and had seen; such notes as I had on the latter would be of use. Besides, the district was large and of great interest. There were other tribes, and archæological remains which were well worth seeing. So North Cachar it was; and a month later I was on my way there up the Hill Section, with a Tangkhul staff and a wildly-excited Khamba.

The S.D.O. met me at Haflong Hill, the railway halt, and we climbed to the town above.

It was a pretty, park-like semi-hill station, on a ridge round which the railway ran in a great loop. It was the administrative centre of the subdivision. It held, too, a small railway colony, and had at one time been a resort for the Cachar planters. But the new road to Shillong had killed it, and the Club and the bungalows were decaying away. The lay-out was lovely. Slopes dotted with pines and oaks surrounded a winding lake. The only roads were footpaths, lined with flowering trees; and in the small bazaar, two old, grey Kachari statues, small-waisted, staring-eyed, looked out from under a vast rubber-tree.

The subdivision whose centre it was linked mountains to plateaux, the Naga Hills and Manipur to Jowai and Shillong.

Haflong itself stood just where the two types joined. To the east of it towered the high Barail; to the west were grassy hills, the so-called Western Plateau, which merged into the tablelands of Jowai next door.

The Kacharis were the district's major tribe. Once the rulers of the Assam Valley, the Ahoms had driven them from their capital at Dimapur in the sixteenth century. Re-established at Maibong, they had, two centuries later, been driven from that too and down into the surrounding plains. There their ancient kingdom had become extinct, but here, in the lowlands, the northern foothills and the main valleys, a considerable section of them survived, and with it much, in language, tradition and costume, which had been lost elsewhere. Then there were the Zemi Nagas, who lived chiefly in the Barail, but had a few villages round Haflong and on the plateau beyond. There were Mikirs in the northern forests; and almost throughout the area, except for the lowest ground, there were scattered Kukis—Rangkhols, Bietes and Khelmas on the plateau, and Thadous and Chongsens among the Zemi on the Barail.

Its history was stormy and brief. The first inhabitants were an aboriginal jungle race, whom the invading Kacharis wiped out. Then came the Zemi, migrating down the Barail Range from the north-east. They found the Kacharis ensconced at Maibong, and, settling in the mountains south of it, lived for many years under Kachari suzerainty.

At last the Kachari kingdom fell. The warlike Angami Nagas, who had come to power since the Naga migration, raided the Zemi constantly and exacted tribute. Before their pressure the weaker Zemi villages of the north and east moved westward, passing through the crowded Barail and colonizing the rolling hills beyond the Diyung valley. They still spoke the Zemi dialect of Naga Hills, and not that of the earlier Barail settlers. Then from the south came Kuki immigrants, the first fringe of a great wave, and, filtering through the Zemi, squatted wherever they could on the closely-populated land. Kachari and Manipuri chieftains disputed the overlordship, but the hillmen acknowledged neither; and during the nineteenth century they were gradually brought under British rule. Since then there had been but two major disturbances. Both, however, coloured local politics yet. One was the Kuki rising of 1918; the other the Naga troubles of '31.

The key to both lay in shortage of land. Though the area involved was large, it was immensely steep, and only a very little of it could be cultivated. Within a few years of the Kukis' coming the pinch was felt by both tribes. Intense rivalry arose between them for the means of subsistence, and under administration the matter could not be resolved by war.

In 1918 the Kukis rebelled. Though their revolt was primarily against the British Government, they took the chance, while the hills were out of control, of paying off old scores against the neighbouring Nagas. When, therefore, some ten years later the Kacha Nagas—the Kabui, Zemi and Lyeng —grew restive in their turn, their grudges against the Kukis were many and deep. They planned, and were only just prevented from carrying out, a general massacre of Kukis; and when the Government intervened, their hostility was extended to it as being on the side of the enemy. There had thus been a reversal of roles. In 1918 the Nagas assisted the troops against the rebel Kukis. They had taken heads, too, on their own account. There were at least five Zemi who wore headhunter's ornaments, the victim's tresses in the ears and the shield tufted with human hair, on a Kuki score. In 1931 the Kukis, now apparently loyal, were, not without zest, aiding the British power against the Kacha Nagas. But, in 1940, while the Kuki movement appeared to be quite dead (in actual fact it was not), that of the Kacha Nagas still smouldered. The Kabui were quiescent, as were the Lyeng, but the Zemi were, with reason, regarded as disaffected. Only a few years earlier officers had toured their territory with armed escorts, and search there still continued for wanted men.

The Kacha Naga movement was odd and interesting. It began at Kambiron.

For generations there had been a prophecy that one day a Naga king would arise, drive out the British, and rule over 'all who eat from the wooden platter'—that is, all Naga tribes. In 1929 a seer of Kambiron, a man named Jadonang, proclaimed himself the promised Messiah. He conceived and founded a new religion—a blend of Hinduism and Christianity, grafted on to a Naga Animist stock—but, though the authorities heard early of his activities, he was not breaking the law. They let him be.

About that date or soon after four Manipuri traders disappeared on a trip to Silchar. Inquiry found no trace of them. A year passed; and some bucks from Kambiron went to a feast in neighbouring Kekru.

In the course of the feast there was a drunken quarrel. A Kambiron buck, in a frenzy of rage, shook his full-dress cloth at a Kekru rival, and shouted out: 'Be quiet, you!—or I'll do to you as I did to the Manipuris!'

The onlookers saw that his cloth was tufted with human hair.

When the Political Agent and the S.D.O. arrived at Kambiron, the buck, sobered and frightened, had burned his cloth. But they dug up from the village outskirts other evidence, which, if not by that time directly identifiable with the Manipuris, was eloquent of foul play; and they recovered from the village cloths, pots and other relics which were more certainly theirs. They found enough, in fact, to hang Jadonang for murder by human sacrifice, and to jail for several years the bucks who had done the butchery for him. But, when all was done, when they had wrecked his temples and shot his sacred python, there still remained his disciple and priestess—a sixteen-year-old Kabui girl called Gaidiliu.

Now what the two officials did not know fully then was that Jadonang and Gaidiliu had been worshipped as Gods for the last two years. They had amassed an enormous amount of tribute; and they had secured the allegiance of all the Kacha Nagas by proclaiming the Naga Kingdom and threatening to cast out all who refused to pay and conform. Their programme was an attractive one, the very blue-print of a Naga heaven—the millennium was at hand, the faithful were to spend everything in one stupendous feast, massacre the Kukis and live in plenty ever after on their Gods' miraculous bounty; and cash and converts came rolling in. So, too, did every crook and gangster in the three tribes, and the girl who faced the

Political Agent that day was not only the figurehead of as pretty a mob as ever graced Chicago, but was herself the hub of a money-spinning God-racket. The Agent sent her home, as too young to jail. She made an immediate dash for the north, her gang and the faithful, and a few days later the whole Kacha Naga country was alight.

There then ensued something almost comparable to the hunt for Prince Charlie.

Troops were sent out to all the three districts in which the Kacha Naga country fell—Manipur, Naga Hills and North Cachar. Outposts were set at strategic points; searches were instituted; patrols went out; and local movement between villages was sternly restricted. But Gaidiliu, piloted by her North Cachar agent, Masang of Kepelo, remained at large. The bulk of the Zemi were on her side, and those who were not were afraid to speak. The country was a warren of game-trails, field-tracks, paths, caves, forests and ravines. Every settlement had its own private ways, its back entrances revealed to none, its secret hide-outs. Abetting villages signalled, by beacon, the movements of patrols. She came and went like a ghost. To make things worse, she was often present only in spirit, and panting sepoys, sent out on the best information, found Nagas dancing solemnly before an empty throne. To crown it all, she was—on the principle of 'darkest below the lamp'—concealed for three months within sight of the outpost at Hangrum. The village sent out to worship her every day; and when she left she told Hangrum that they could attack the outpost without getting hurt. She had, she said, bewitched the sepoys' rifles. Their bullets were water; they would not kill.

It would be interesting to know now whether she really believed in her own powers. At any rate, Hangrum (who could, had they been attacking rationally, have crept up by night through the dead ground and rushed the outpost easily) made a massed charge, in daylight, down the only slope on which the sepoys commanded a field of fire. It will always be a mystery to those who know the place why three times the number were not killed. When the first volley, fired over their heads, brought them howling on, encouraged, the next was sent into them at thirty yards' range; with the obvious consequences.

Meantime the Gaidiliu movement went merrily on. Where-ever she went there were agents to support the racket. They sold 'Gaidiliu water' at Rs 10/- the bottle—one draught, and you'd never be ill again—though the contents were drawn straight from the Thingje village pond! They did her patent infallible magic ceremonies for the sick faithful, for a large fee and their dinner; they collected tribute on her behalf and took commission; and above all, they took great care that she stayed at large. When the ordinary villager grew tired of it—and it was he who was being harried and worried and fined by an angry and pursuing Government—they took care of him, too; and when a few dissenters had been found dead it was harder than ever for officers to gather information. But it had to stop one day; and it did.

She had just reached the edge of the Angami country, and there was a risk that the powerful villages round Khonoma might become involved. At that point, the Kuki caretaker of Lakema rest-house heard of her whereabouts and passed the news on to the Deputy Commissioner at Kohima—at that time Mr Mills. To defeat the spies she was known to have in Kohima bazaar, a false expedition went off by day, in a blaze of glory, and in the wrong direction; and the real one left at dusk, unnoticed, on a thirty-mile night march.

They found her sentries drunk, for, primed with wrong information, everyone had been celebrating their supposed security. The sepoys swarmed over the palisade and sur-rounded her house, but when she began to shriek spells and call on her bodyguard to resist, the men who composed it perhaps remembered Hangrum; for they laid down their spears and surrendered, and it was left for the sepoys to go in and pull her out, screaming, scratching and kicking and inflicting the only casualty on the expedition by biting a Naik severely in the thumb. A few hours later she was telling Mills that it was very hard work being a goddess—people wanted to worship her night and day, and she never had time for a bath. So she had her bath, in the rest-house, with sentries at every exit; and the goddess, queen and terror of the Kacha

Nagas, the elusive sorceress, the evasive divinity, went off to Manipur and trial—and a sentence of fourteen years for abetment of murder.

But it wasn't quite over yet. Her intimates had escaped the raid—Masang, Ghumeo and Dikheo, to name but three—and one night Dikheo, with thirteen others of whom Masang was one, went to take revenge on the Lakema caretaker. They didn't find him, as he had gone to Kohima to collect his pay; but they found his wife and children in the rest-house lines. They strangled them all and then set fire to the house.

When I reached Haflong eight years later only Dikheo was still at large. Ghumeo had been captured; Masang had done six months and had been released. But before Gaidiliu was arrested she had told Masang and the rest that even if she were caught it would not matter; the Government would imprison only her simulacrum and her real and divine self would be safe elsewhere, to return in the course of time in such a shape that her enemies would never know her and only the faithful could recognize her. Masang had not forgotten. After all those years he was still looking for her reincarnation.

I didn't know it at the time, but he found it in me.

CHAPTER VI

INTRODUCTION TO THE ZEMI

THE few Zemi who hung round the bazaar were shabbier, even, than anything on the line—dirty, draggled, huddled up in whole ragbags of cast-off European clothing, and opium-eaters for the most part. The real Zemi were those in the Barail, and it was decided that I should go out there with the S.D.O. as soon as it could be arranged. The start was delayed for a day or two by rain, and in the interval two Zemi from the Barail came in and gave me a new idea of what I was to meet. One was Gumtuing of Nenglo; the other Masang of Kepelo.

Gumtuing walked round the corner of the bungalow one morning with a bottle of rice-beer in one hand and a fowl in the other, his headman's scarlet blanket slung round him and a red hibiscus in his ear. From head to heel, from kilt to haircut, he was of the very Barak. If these were the Nagas I was to work among, I was in clover!

Masang appeared a day or two later. He too was swathed in a scarlet blanket. He had been made a wet-rice demonstrator in the hope of winning him to the Government side. Where Gumtuing was tall, Masang was short and deep-chested. His thick black hair was cut in a page-boy bob. His little sharp eyes were never still. They flickered ceaselessly, alert and wary; he missed nothing. In front of strangers he wore a silly grin and clowned continually. It was a clever disguise. He was a cunning devil, was Masang, as clever a ruffian as they come—and yet I never quite made him out, right to the very end. There was something in him that was not wholly the villain.

We left Haflong at last on March 4th, tramped down a half-made road to the station, and took train up the line to Mahur. Here the Haflong-Kohima bridle-path came out on the railway and there was a wayside halt, with the high, black, forested Barail towering wall-like over it. Beyond the tracks was a little muddy bazaar, a stream, and a midget rest-house, with the lowest doorways I have ever met. Next morning we struck off along the north face of the range by an easy contour-road; and, after a detour or two to visit villages, we came to our first halt at Asalu.

It was a pleasant camp in park-land, with the site of an old headquarters station on the spur beyond. A wood like a Hampshire beech-hanger hid the village; and in it, thirty or so houses, whose steep-pitched roofs jutted in front as porches and sloped away behind, faced on to an irregular street of bare earth dotted with large, flat gravestones. There were two morungs, or 'bachelors' halls', each three times the size of a private house, and their huge front rooms served as clubs and dormitories for the men and youths. Small granaries on stilts and patches of fenced garden were scattered about on the village outskirts. Stray fruit-trees, plum and pomegranate, grew at the wood's edge. Beyond the houses, whose thatch was weathered to silver-grey, one saw the dim blue distances of the low ground.

The temporary interpreter the S.D.O. had found for me in Haflong was of little use. The chance came here to replace him by an ex-Government servant, a Zemi named Namkiabu-ing, who had lately resigned and lived now in a village a mile away. A man in his thirties, muscular, well-made, tall for a Zemi, he looked intelligent and capable. He didn't seem particularly keen on the job; but the S.D.O.'s orders were orders; he took over the red cloth of office and went to collect his things, and next morning we picked him up at his home at Impoi, a little way up the hill.

The road was now a rocky shelf along the face of the Barail. It climbed and climbed through tall-trunked mountain forest, till the trees thinned and gave way to scrub and old fields and we crossed a pass at some 4000 feet. Then close on our right rose Thumjang Klang, the highest peak in the district; and from it, and from the main range running on to the left, ridges stretched southward like teeth from a comb and cut the country into parallel valleys—first the steep cleft of the Jenam before us, then the still steeper one of the Jiri, then the Makru, then the Barak, and so on all the way to the Imphal plain, and from the pass we could see the intervening ridges, dark and whale-backed, shouldering one behind the other along the skyline.

Normally we should have stayed at the Laisong rest-house, where the foot-track crossed the Jenam river. But, for my benefit, we were to camp at Laisong village itself.

We were still in the grassy foothills and half a mile from the stream when a path came up from below, met the track at right angles, and vanished up a steep hill on the left. We followed it. For three or four hundred yards we climbed precipitously, at first towards the foot of a line of crags, and next along below them; and then we saw the jutting roofs of the village morungs above the surrounding copse. The path widened; we passed a stone sitting-platform, and entered the wood; and then we debouched into the head of the village street by a side-alley littered with chaff, dung, refuse and all the storm-washings of the ground above it.

Laisong was a village of perhaps eighty houses. It stood on a spur which sloped from the main range. In the middle of the rocky street there was a widening into an open space—not a square, it was too irregular for that, but a space where stood two huge wooden water-troughs, like dugout canoes, each fed by a bamboo pipeline from springs on the hill behind, the sacred jumping-stone, the *hazoa*, beside which heads taken in war were buried, and the long mound of earth where the jumpers landed. The two morungs stood one at each entrance to this space, as though guarding it, and from the head of it one looked away to the east past cliffs and over vast, airy gulfs to a valley flanked by tremendous fells. At the head of the valley was a pass, a deep U scooped in the mountains, and framed in the gap was a far-distant rock-ribbed giant of a peak, a monstrous wall blued and made soft by atmosphere.

Beyond the lower morungs the street dropped steeply, the houses ended, and the path forked. One branch fell away through a stone-walled gateway and disappeared down the cliff; the other climbed up the round hummock which ended the spur. Here, frail and contemptible among all those immense summits and sweeping, blue-shadowed chasms, was the little thatched camp which had been built for us. The place was an eyrie, a castle rock. On the south and east its sides fell sheer in grassy cliffs; on the north was a wooded ravine; and the Jenam itself, a streak of water among rocks, wound round the foot of the hill eight hundred feet below the barren top. Enormous hills, cragged, tree-sprinkled, yellow with sunbleached grass and capped with black forest, loomed over it on three sides and from across the valley; but to the south it overlooked an open green basin, through which the Jenam wound, a shimmer of light between bamboos and reed-beds, before it disappeared again into a maze of spurs.

There was to be a mass gathering of the Zemi here, with a feast and dance at which they and I might meet one another. By the second day the headmen and their dance-teams were coming in, and I, for my part, was negotiating for a big bull mithan—the Naga domestic bison—for the feast. The Zemi have a genius for celebration, and dancing is a tribal art. Each village has its special numbers and its stars, and their merits are discussed as technically, and with much more practical knowledge than are those of ballerinas and companies by Western balletomanes. Touring companies of bucks and girls go round performing for fees which vary with the strength of the company and the distance travelled. The dancers get the cash and a free dinner, the villagers get a free show; but the rich man who pays for the performance has to be content with the accruing honour. The Zemi have more methods of getting cash in exchange for 'honour' than anyone else I know.

Never in the whole history of the Zemi, though, had there been such a gathering as this. The camp and the village swarmed with interpreters' red-fronted waistcoats, and the Jacob's-ladder street to the lower morung was speckled with the scarlet blankets of ascending and descending headmen. Men and boys in all stages of full dress, from the first sketch to the complete achievement, sat about outside the houses or wandered, like dogs at a fair, among our huts. The whole male population of Laisong itself had gone down to catch the mithan. An old bull and a mighty beast, he was resisting capture. A whole day had already been wasted on him; and still we could see him from the camp, an elephantine blob, moving a mile off in the open valley. About mid-morning Masang came up again, gasping and sweating, his hair full of burrs and his grin gone, and called down every man available. An hour later they all returned, triumphant, and the mithan was led at last to the sacrificial post before the lower morung. All was now ready. The bull and a buffalo were killed that afternoon with proper ceremony, and in an amazingly short time converted into hot, rich, chilli-filled stew; the feast began; and presently silence warmed into a roar of voices as rice-beer drinking began.

By dusk the village hummed. After dark the drums began to thud, first singly, then more and more, as the leaders gathered their teams together. Lights danced up and down the street; and team after team came into camp, their torches trailing in orange streamers against the blue night sky. The wide top of the spur had been levelled to form a floor some forty yards long. Round this were ranged the spectators, and the singers with cymbals and drums. Great bamboo torches ten or twelve feet long were brought down from the morungs and set at intervals round the field; some held high, and flaring in the wind, and some flung down on the ground, where their glow lit bare, brown legs and the big eyes of squatting children.

Then more than a hundred dancers, bucks and girls, slipped out through the crowd and formed into line. The men massed on either side started a lilting, leisurely song in strophe and antistrophe. The drums and cymbals joined in; and the dancers began to sway, rocking from one foot to the other as they picked up the time. Then they were away, slowly at first, with a dipping, easy step. Hornbills' feathers were in their hair and in their hands, beating time, or shimmering in the red torchlight, which shone on the bucks' smooth-muscled backs, on the girls' bare shoulders, and on horned bracelets of polished brass on arms held out and up. Round and round they went, coiling, meeting, parting and winding, till the whole spur moved with a maze of human figures.

Now the time changed. Slowly, but inevitably, it quickened. Forward went the leaders in high, springy leaps, far off the ground and perfectly controlled. Behind them followed the long lines, uncoiling, and choir and drums were swaying and rocking to the tune. Faster, faster, lighter, higher, leaping feet and glinting armlets, a forest of hornbills' feathers glimmering in and out of the dark, rising and falling, rising and falling; it was one wild intoxication of sound, colour and movement. The deep thudding of the drums shook the ground underfoot and jarred the body. On and on, in and out, went skein within skein of dancers, springing, curving, turning in endless recombination under the sheen of the black-barred feathers and the glare of the torches. Dance followed dance; torches burned to stubs and were renewed and the bamboo-ash blew about the bare ground like tufts of grey hair. Stars rose over the far hills, climbed over us and dipped away, and still the wild music shook the spur, still the torches flickered in the night wind, and still the kaleidoscope of dancers melted, changed, and swung leaping on, on, on.

CHAPTER VII

RECONNAISSANCE

THE next day I parted from the S.D.O. at the village gate and set off on my own for the first time in a year.

The tour was one of exploration, of search for the best places for field-work, but as a tour it was notable only for the number of things which went wrong. It made it clear, though, that the Zemi were an exceptionally interesting people; so much so that I determined to stay a year and make a full study of them. Not merely that; they were the most extraordinary Nagas I had ever met; and fully half of them were mad. That, at least, was the only explanation which occurred to me at the time. By no possible conception was their conduct rational.

The tribe seemed to be arbitrarily divided into two halves. One, which included Namkia, regarded me with dislike and suspicion. The other fell on me with a hospitality which was frightening.

Take, for example, Hangrum and Guilong—Hangrum in its fantastically dramatic setting on a knife-edged ridge; range after range of the Manipur hills looming blue and green out of the cloud on one side of it, razor-backed spurs sweeping down to the Jenam on the other, the forbidding mass of Hemeolowa blocking the outlook to the south; its smoke-stained houses a study in shades of brown and tan and darker brown, like a sepia drawing. It was nine years since the ill-fated charge against the Sepoys' rifles, but most of the men in the village had suffered in it, or as a result. They had seen their fellows killed and wounded and their village burned, and they themselves had been punished. The most powerful village in the area, it was still unreconciled. The first time we passed through it, there was not a woman to be seen, and the men were ranged in silent rows, two deep, on the house-platforms. In absolute stillness, not a word spoken, between these human palings, we walked its quarter-mile length.

Then take Guilong. There, too, there had been shooting in the troubles. I expected just the same resentment there as at Hangrum.

But not a bit of it. The villagers, men and women, swarmed on me like bees. Cup on cup of rice-beer was forced into my hands. They caught hold of me, pulled me by the wrist, tugged at my clothes, and even prised my hand open to make me accept, in person, the gifts they offered. In fact they behaved as I had never known a Naga village do before, with raving insanity. I hadn't a second's privacy the whole time I was there. No matter what I was doing, sleeping, eating, resting, or even bathing, the hut was invaded regardless by somebody crying parrot-phrases: 'O my Mother! O Queen, O Goddess! You are our mother, you are a goddess, there is none greater, there is none better than you!'

There was no stating of a request, no calm discussion. Down the intruder plumped and claimed my whole attention. If it strayed back to my book (and Guilong's conversation was not exciting) an impatient hand tweaked at my clothes and recalled me, not to a sane discourse, but to an awful, unreasoning babble of set words.

'Mother, mother, mother! Mother, you are our mother! O my mother—*asui i kasang da*—I am very happy! O my mother, bless me, say good words for me. O my mother, you are our mother, you are a goddess, you are greater than all, there is none greater than you—*Apui, anuipui-da, nang soa ka-i-va ga-le, nang soa ka-di-va ga-le!*'

A barred door made no difference. Jam it, barricade it as I would, a brown arm was sooner or later forced through and the bar flung sharply down. They were really hurt if I shut them out—hurt and angry. I gave it up. There was no dealing with it. I simply suffered.

At Guilong, too, we ran into a party from Bopungwemi, Dikheo's village, the stronghold of the Gaidiliu movement. They were on their way to Maibong to buy salt, and they had scarcely seen me when they vanished behind the houses and appeared again with a present of three worn cloths, all neatly folded, but still warm from the wearer, and clearly stripped that minute from the youngest member of their party. Guilong then wound up the whole lunacy with a dance; and never have I seen such a three-ring circus—the drums and choir each doing something different and the dancers wildly at variance with each other, even to having two dances going at once in opposition—a performance of stark, staring, undiluted anarchy.

Next morning, thank goodness, we left.

The S.D.O. agreed to let me stay a year to make a detailed study of the Zemi. Laisong was chosen as the best centre, and arrangements for a camp there were set in train. Luikai and his fellow-Tangkhul had gone on leave, and I had to find some Zemi servants. Where at Ukhrul I had had more applicants than I could find jobs for, here intensive search produced two; which gave me a staff of (besides Namkia) Ramgakpa the scullion, a stocky youth from Gobin; Degalang the dog-boy, slim, young, and from Impoi; and the new Manipuri cook, a Mussulman.

At Laisong the camp on the eyrie was under construction. Workmen swarmed on the skeleton of the big house. From there we passed on southward, to Hangrum again, and Shongkai beyond it; and ten days later, as we came down from Haijaichak in the U-shaped pass, we saw the new-thatched roofs of our camp catch the morning sun. It perched on the hilltop like a Rhine castle, the house-tops just showing above the low scrub-jungle.

The day was sultry. On the steep climb up from the river the baked ground radiated heat like hot metal. It glared on our faces, it beat off the high bank beside the road. It was with infinite relief that we climbed the last rock-steps and reached the gateway. The breeze across the col met us, blowing sweet and cold. Turning, we tramped up the long rise of the knoll, and came thankfully, for the first time, into the tall, cool, airy bungalow.

There were two verandas and five rooms. It was all of matting on a timber frame, and the roof was thick grass thatch. Behind the big house were the cookhouse and the men's quarters, two long, low huts facing north. Filled with immense content at a home at last, I looked up at the tall posts and their intricate cane lashings and at the solid roof-beam eighteen feet overhead. I watched the jappas brought in and their contents unpacked, ate my first meal by the new hearth, and then, tired out by the grilling march, I went to sleep for the afternoon in the shadowed bedroom.

I woke. The shuttered room was so dark I looked at my watch. It was half-past one—I'd slept for less than an hour. I realized then what had woken me. A wind had risen, the doors were banging, and the bungalow had begun to creak. I got up and looked out.

It had clouded over blackly and the wind was rushing down through the valley behind us. I caught hold of the heavy veranda door—slung from an overhead beam, and flapping madly—and started to pull it shut. It wouldn't close. It shook and lifted in the increasing wind like canvas in a gale; and as I fought it, swearing, there was a tap and a rattle on the back wall.

Then the hail hit us.

The whole bungalow leaned over, groaning. The groan was lost in the noise of the hail on the walls. It was not now a rattle, but a roar, a continuous, shaking roar, like an express train in a tunnel. Though I was in the lee of the house, it took my full strength to force the door to, for the wind was flinging it about like a piece of paper. Inside the bungalow, small hailstones, twigs and shredded leaves were blowing in through the back eaves and up over the inner partitions, and showering down over everything in the place. The half-grown dog Khamba, terrified, was dashing about. As I grappled the second door he broke out past me. I ran after him into the veranda. The whipping hail at the corner stung him; he doubled back. I caught him and dragged him in and shut the door on us both, and out of the open window I saw the hail outside.

The stones were the size of golf-balls. The wind was carrying them horizontally across the spur and off again into space. Only those which hit something fell; and then they rolled and lay about the turf.

For perhaps ten minutes the storm blew at this strength. It was useless to worry whether the house would stand; there was nowhere to run to, and nothing could live in the hail. I slipped a lead on Khamba and stood by the front wall, where we had most chance if the house collapsed. At last I heard the roar lessen; slowly the wind-pressure decreased. The whole house above us creaked its way back to the upright, and a watery sun came out. I waited a minute or two for the last stones to fall and then ran over to the cookhouse to see what had happened there.

It was at least, as I saw when I got outside, still standing. A crowing and hysterical cook met me just short of the door. He stood there, flapping like a goose; I had to push past him to get in. Ramgakpa was sitting on the bamboo bench, looking strained but calm. The floor was streaming with melting ice, and the hut had been blown fifteen degrees from the upright; but there was no serious damage. I went out again and looked round. The ground at the back of the house was thick with a mat of white hailstones which had bounced from the back wall, the rear entrance had a two-foot drift in it, and a small grass hut left over from the old camp had been blown to ribbons. Then I turned and looked back the way the storm had come.

There had been little damage in the lee of the Barail, but the exposed north side of our spur had been devastated. I had never seen anything like it. There was nothing left of the scrub-jungle but a stripped, ripped, barren expanse of naked twigs—every leaf had been torn off in a belt a mile wide. Banana-trees were battered as though machine-gunned, their stems pitted and pulped; the bark was scarred and splintered even on the big timber. As I stood, Masang and my newly-hired caretaker came running up, shouting to know if we were safe. It then seemed that, blasted though we had been, we had still escaped more lightly than the village. Hail beat so violently into the morungs that the bucks had to shelter under the benches, and even there were hurt; and every pig, dog, goat and fowl caught in the open had been killed outright.

However, hailstorms or no, the films I had planned to use from November onwards were sitting untouched in Haflong. It was time to get on with the job. I set off at once to bring out the rest of my gear. But I hadn't reached the top of the pass on the way to Asalu when down I came with fever, and after a hideous march I fell into bed in the camp there with my first real illness.

To my impotent fury, the men were broken reeds. The cook had more hysterics. He stamped and raved in the hut when I wouldn't be carried in. Namkia, on whom I was dependent for nursing, went out and got drunk. When I painfully whispered that I was really bad, and wished he'd stay within call, he said: 'Oh, take some medicine and get better!' and walked off home. I was so blazing angry I spent my lucid intervals that night in rehearsing what I'd say to him if I lived till morning; and when morning came, and with it Namkia, I rose on my pillows, launched what must have sounded like a dying curse, and then fell back in a semi-coma. It scared the daylight out of him. He nursed me loyally all the rest of the time.

A fortnight later we moved in at Laisong on permanent occupation. But the Jessami *jadu*, or whatever jinx was in operation, had not quite finished yet. No sooner were we in there than the newly-returned Luikai went sick in the lines and was no more use. I went down again with malaria; and I was still in bed when an interpreter arrived from Haflong. There was trouble reported among the Zemi, another rising was possible, and I was to come back at once.

When, exhausted and nearly heartbroken, I reached Haflong, Luikai was found to have an attack of venereal disease he must have concealed for weeks. He had to be put in hospital and Chinaorang quarantined; and, with the precious film-stock rotting and all my fine hopes in ruins, I fled at the beginning of June to the western plateau.

CHAPTER VIII

EXILE

Quite the most interesting things on the plateau—which was rolling, shadeless and unbelievably hot—were the urns.

The Zemi villages were small and disappointing. The people had lost some of their Naga character. They were dull and poor, dependent largely on work in Haflong bazaar; the settlements were often split into Pagan and Christian, a house divided against itself; their morungs were decaying, always a bad sign. It was depressing to come to this from the Barail, where Zemi culture still survived in so complete a form, even in villages, such as Asalu, a bare three miles from the railway. Much that would have been of great interest had here been neglected and forgotten. The beauty and vitality of Zemi life were gone. The heart was out of it; and though, for comparison's sake, there were notes to be taken, it was not here that the main work must be done.

The urns, however, were worth the heat.

At the main urn-field, outside the Naga hamlet of Bolosan, several hundred of them stood on a low knoll. The site was preserved, and, looking down on it from the steps across the fence, the monoliths cropped out of the thick jungle-grass like enormous mushrooms. Roughly pear-shaped, each cut from a single block of stone, and of all sizes from eighteen inches to six feet high, they stood on the narrower end, and in the broader top was cut a deep, cylindrical hole. Bolosans is not the only urn-field; there are other smaller sites, and not improbably others await discovery. There are none, so far as is known, in the eastern hills, where the pre-Naga remains are of a different kind. They were funerary in purpose. A fragment of charred bone recovered from the hollow of one by Mr Mills and Dr Hutton was identified as human. But their age, the reasons for their limited distribution, their makers (though the Khasis, now living round Shillong, are possible candidates) are mysteries still.

Touring the plateau was much better than sitting in Haflong, but it was still no picnic. The heat was killing, for the plateau inclined to be low and dry; there were no trees, the camps were miserable, and the move had so unsettled Namkia that he gave notice regularly every day. I could no more make him out than I could the rest of these inexplicable Zemi. But, under the pressure of common adversity, the ice was beginning to crack. One day in the middle of a long, hot march, as we sat down for a rest under the only shade-tree between Muchudui and Chenam, he unbent suddenly, and for the first time talked like a human being. I was so taken aback that I froze up myself, and he gave notice that evening as usual; but after that I was the richer by a good friend and a sterling interpreter.

His was an unusual character. A pagan humorist, a Zemi to the backbone, with all the faults and virtues of his tribe and race, he still had an inner core, a moral citadel, which made of him a Hampden. He had an intense, a vivid, sense of right and wrong. They were to him a personal responsibility. He could no more compromise with wrong than he could stop breathing; nor see a wrong done, nor an injustice, and not right it, at whatever cost to himself. It was not a quality to endear him to all masters, and neither was Namkia (whose intelligence, though it worked on different lines, equalled any European's) the man to be a mere obedient instrument; and as a mere obedient instrument was, in most cases, all that the harassed district officer required, Namkia had recognized that he was not wholly suited to Government service and resigned. But not without repeated applications. 'Sea-lawyer', infuriated officers might sometimes call him; but he was an honest man, an accurate interpreter, an organizer, an expert in tribal law, and a notable man among the Barail Zemi.

His family were of Kabui origin. Migrating northward to Hangrum heaven knows how many generations ago, they had passed on to the Asalu-Impoi group at an early stage in that community's history. Even then, it appears, the family had character. They founded, and were hereditary headmen of, the village of Gareolowa, third of the group's settlements;

and while there they worked as liaison officers to the
Kachari Kings, who granted them Gareolowa's land in
perpetuity.

But they, and the Asalu group as a whole, had fallen on
hard times. No longer able—since the administration, not
understanding the system, had reallocated the land—to follow
their custom of cycle-migration round three or four village
sites over a period of many years, they were left stranded on
Asalu's worn-out and eroded soil, which should long ago
have been left to lie fallow while the community moved
elsewhere. All Gareolowa's land and the village site itself was
in the hands of the Kukis. The grave-monument of Namkia's
grandfather, dead only a few years back, had been pulled
down by the Christian Kukis, who found it a convenient
stone-quarry, as they did Gareolowa's complex and unique
stone fortifications. But Namkia was not to be done. He
asked permission to colonize Impoi, another site belonging
to the group, where a little rested land remained. He was at
first refused, but persistence won him sanction; and he had,
in 1940, been settled there some three years. Already, the
colonists said, they found the site healthier than Asalu, lower
down. Namkia was the second headman. Although the
obvious candidate, he had refused the senior post. It was not
according to custom. He did not 'belong' to Impoi; he was
not of a founding family. To give him a foothold in the place
at all in Zemi law his brother-in-law, who was 'of' Impoi,
made over to him a couple of house-sites. But, though the
senior headman was of the proper descent, there was no
question who was the leading man; it was Namkia.

At the end of July we returned to Haflong and found out
what had been happening in the Zemi country. The storm-
centre had been in Naga Hills, a day or so beyond the North
Cachar border. A woman lunatic had established herself
there, and by all accounts used to utter prophecies while lying
in the village water-trough. One would have thought this a
peculiarly damp and unconvincing pulpit; but the Zemi
faithful apparently found it valid, and there had been quite
a stir. She had been arrested and removed by the Deputy
Commissioner from Kohima; the village headmen of Ngau-

long, where she had been, were in trouble for allowing it all; and peace had been restored.

The S.D.O., however, thought Laisong too far away in case of sudden trouble, so for the time being we settled down in the leaky Asalu bashas and started to make them habitable. Chinaorang, out of quarantine, had rejoined us, and so had Luikai; but in the latter his disease had produced a mental change, and though he had previously been a most obedient little man and the perfect servant, he was now so unmanageable that he had to be sent home. Poor little maggot! There were tears and protestations. He had been with me some time and had served me well, and I was heartily sorry to lose him; but there was no choice.

Chinaorang stayed on some weeks. He mixed well with the Zemi, and never minded being ragged, as Luikai had done. It was a casual jape on him—Namkia faked tiger-tracks round the water-hole one morning, so that Chinaorang, arriving, gave one yell, dropped his buckets, and ran like a deer—which inspired the great Tiger Rag.

Every hot weather a tiger or two moved up from the low ground and roamed the hills killing cattle until someone shot it or the winter cold drove it down again; and one such, a big beast, was then operating a beat from Laisong to Mahur. He hated pushing through the thick, wet jungle, so walked down the bridle-road each night as boldly as a taxpayer. He took a short cut over the Asalu spur from a point about thirty yards from the camp, and had trodden a regular runway for himself in the grass there. The cook was extremely worried at a tiger's passing so close, and one night, when Namkia came back from a call in the village, he told him the beast had been into camp and snuffing round. Namkia was somewhat sceptical; and coming across to me, asked me to stand on guard with one lamp while he took the other and looked about for tracks. Finding none in the camp, he went right out along the road to the runway itself; and when he came back, full of scathing comment, the cook, stung, said instantly he'd never have dared search at all if he hadn't been drunk at the time. Now Namkia, admittedly, had been enjoying Asalu's hospitality; but he was nothing like tipsy. He resented the insult and determined to have his own back. After an interval in which the tiger abetted him (it roared in the forest and scared some Asalu woodcutters) he took me into his confidence and laid on the attack.

On the chosen evening he complained of fever and retired early to the spare hut. As soon as the cook and the others had settled down for the night, he slipped down into the high grass by the cookhouse, thrashed about and roared for all he was worth, and then bolted back to his quarter—I covering his retreat by shouting questions out of the hut window.

There was no answer till my second or third yell; and then three hapless voices—Ramgakpa's, Chinaorang's and the cook's—cried 'Tiger, tiger!' in a concerted wail.

I went out into the veranda. After a minute or two they came across, Chinaorang armed with a piece of firewood, Ramgakpa glancing nervously behind, and the cook, long, thin and anxious, but manfully leading with the kitchen lamp. They trooped up into the porch and all began to tell me about the tiger at once. Its performance improved with every repetition.

Then the cook broke off to reprove me for having come out. He quoted horrible cases of Sahibs torn from their office desks and Memsahibs snatched screaming from bathrooms by tigers (I should have thought that the most difficult place from which to snatch anyone) and I hastily diverted him by asking for Namkia. That set us all to calling; and after a minute there was a muffled reply. Next he came slowly over, wrapped to the eyes in a blanket, carrying a stout staff, and looking like nothing so much as one of the Pilgrims' Chorus.

They all, of course, then had to tell him about the tiger. In the very middle of the story, when tension was at its height, he grabbed the cook by the arm, pointed up the road, and said: '*Look!*'

It made me jump, but Ramgakpa's reactions were far quicker, and he made one flea-hop straight past us into the hut. We others stood. Chinaorang gripped his firewood and prepared to defend me to the last; the cook peered tensely into the night; and after ten seconds' suspense he cried excitedly: 'Yes, yes, I see it! There are its eyes—it's going downhill!'

By that time I was staring over their shoulders, and the dark curve of the hill was as bare of tigers as the palm of my hand. Not a leaf rustled, not a green eye blinked, except in the cook's imagination. It was altogether too much for Namkia. He spun round, and had a veranda-post not intervened I think he would have fallen weeping on my neck. As it was, he clung to the post, and, with choking noises inside his blanket, regained his self-control. But we saw no more eyes, and I packed the men off to the cookhouse. They sat there half the night telling the story to a most appreciative Namkia. It was days before he let out the truth; and by then the tiger was such an established legend that they refused to believe him. The cook said indignantly that never, *never* could the Miss-sahib have been a party to such a conspiracy.

Soon after this incident (though not because of it) China-orang too went home, and except for the cook the staff was now wholly Zemi. The tiger, however, remained; and punctually every morning at six it walked down the road from Impoi and disappeared into the long grass. Equally punctually, and just about the same time, Namkia walked down from Impoi to bring in my morning tea; and his comings and goings synchronized so exactly with those of the tiger that I began to have an uneasy feeling. Was it possible—was it just possible—that my interpreter was a lycanthropist?

One evening after dinner I was taking notes on tribal law and kept him late. Just as he rose to go there was an appalling bellow from the village, followed, after a second's interval, by shouts, shots, screeches, and the frantic barking of the village pack. The half-dozen Asalu cattle had been sheltering in the copse. The tiger had that moment taken one.

I shot an anxious glance at Namkia. As a were-tiger, he should have gone into paroxysms in sympathy with his beast. But no—there was not a sign of a link with a tiger affinity; he was behaving merely as a startled, but normal, interpreter. I decided, with a sigh of relief, that he was, after all, human.

Ramgakpa, as it happened, was in the village when the kill occurred. The late evening is the usual time for bucks to call on the objects of their admiration; and he and three others were seated unobtrusively in the porch of the girls' dormitory, waiting their turn. At that moment came the agonized bellow. Then, hard upon it, the whole mithan-herd and the rest of the cattle stampeded panic-stricken down the village street. With one cry of 'The tiger!' the four boys rose. They leapt as one for the doorway, reached it together, and jammed. The girls inside woke up and began to scream. The male visitor in occupation sat up and began to swear. And then the heaviest boy fell through; the dam collapsed; and the four fell flat in a heap as the inner door flew open and out rushed the beldame in charge, breathing fire and slaughter and waving a purposeful ember. In a flash all five bucks had clapped their cloths over their heads and bolted, incognito; and, tiger or no tiger, they never stopped running till they tumbled into the safety of the lower morung.

About this time, just before we went back to Laisong, there was an addition to the staff in the shape of Haichangnang the mail-runner. He was Namkia's brother-in-law, a simple, lovable, child-like little man. He hadn't been with us long when his small daughter caught the common summer diarrhœa. Almost the first we knew of it was the death-cry in the village.

A little later, as I sat reading, I heard grunts, as of a laden porter coming. I was just rising to see if it were a messenger from Haflong, when a shadow flitted along the thin matting wall of the hut and Haichangnang appeared suddenly in the doorway. His face was all disfigured by weeping; the grunts had been his sobs as he ran up the path. He fell at my feet, clutched my knees, and began to cry out in Zemi.

I got him up again and called Namkia. When he arrived, Haichangnang asked quite rationally whether I had any medicine to poison him. He couldn't bear his daughter to go the long, dark road of the dead alone.

I don't remember how we calmed him down, except that sal volatile entered into it. But I do know that his remaining baby was our chief argument.

Zemi infant mortality is very high indeed. He returned with the next mail to hear that, an hour before, the baby too had died.

CHAPTER IX

FIRST-FRUITS FESTIVAL

By the end of August everything was still quiet, and we were allowed back to Laisong at last.

We found that the gardener and caretaker had kept the place up, and that a water-supply had been laid on, at the S.D.O.'s orders, by running an extension down from the lower morung's pipeline. Now only the garden remained to be made, but Samrangba the gardener's initial efforts with it were not encouraging. Where there should have been rows of carrot and cabbage there was an aching desert of stony soil, raked into humps and innocent of manure. We cherished several small green things for a week before finding them all to be weeds, and then dug the whole thing up and started again; but patience and manure triumphed, and by mid-September the peas and beans were up and flourishing and the garden never looked back.

It was soon clear that life at Laisong would be no bed of roses. Funds calculated for conditions in Manipur went just half as far here. To make it all the more difficult, Laisong was notoriously the most miserly and unhelpful village in the area —as Namkia took care to point out as soon as we were irrevocably committed to it. It had had weak headmen for years, and was now a thoroughly anarchic community run largely by the three chief bullies of the lower morung. This trio came down on us at the start with large schemes for business partnerships—we, of course, to provide the capital—and were sent packing with such home-truths from Namkia whistling after them that they never forgave us. There was a better element, though, to which the caretaker and his sons and the two permanent porters belonged. The old man, Zhekungba, looked like a minor prophet. His elder boy, Ramzimba, was a pleasant youth with a slight moustache which would have been very fashionable in the West; the younger, Sonning, was a merry young Mongol just sprouting into a buck. The porters were both respectable householders; which left Samrangba the gardener, who was not respectable, but a scapegrace whom his uncle the headman—an inane old goat—had pushed into the job.

And now that I was established and in constant touch with the Zemi, the pieces in the puzzle fell into place. Here were no treacherous savages, but honest, stubborn, conservative cultivators, excitable and credulous, it is true, and living by simpler and sometimes more brutal standards than ours; but the vast majority of them decent folk and good citizens. Between them and the Government had been built up a wall of misunderstanding, fear, suspicion and mistrust. A conspiracy of silence cut the tribe off from all strangers, and behind the invisible barrier their tribal life went on, warm, human, and rich with tradition. When I first reached Laisong, I was outside it. As their reserve melted, the wall dissolved, and I found myself on the far side and looking back at a familiar world seen topsy-turvy, as Alice passed through the looking-glass and saw her own room reversed when she looked back. So seen, the world I had left did seem odd; there was foundation for the Zemi attitude. Civilization had certain features which were only apparent to an outside view. Nevertheless, it was all wrong that so profound a misunderstanding should exist. I made up my mind to do what I could to right it.

It was autumn now, and the first of the great harvest festivals had begun. The early rice was coming in, the lean weeks of the summer were over, and village after village was celebrating the feast called Pokpatngi. This included the traditional mithan-chase. As we had already missed Asalu's and Impoi's, and I still had an uneasy fear that I might be whisked out again without warning, we packed up and went over straight away when Hegokuloa sent to ask us across to theirs.

The Rains were going out in storms and steamy drizzle, and damp grey clouds hung low on the peaks as we scrambled up to the village through fields of ripening rice. There were roars of disapproval from Namkia at the sight of the camp. The old materials had been stretched and re-made to fit a different plan. The hut was now so narrow it was like a passage, and one went round the table by a detour over the bed. Instead of overlooking the village and the pleasant blue and green valley as before, it now faced straight out on to a heap of refuse and a monstrous tree which cut off every breath of air ; but after the huts we'd had on the western plateau I didn't mind anything, so long as it had a roof on.

The mithan-hunt was to be held first thing next morning. At dusk the young men gathered to pad the horns.

The animals—there were two—were in fact buffaloes, which came cheaper than mithan. One was not much more than a calf, with no horns to matter, but the other was a big bull with a magnificent sweep and a most uncertain temper. He was thrown with a struggle. Ring after ring of heavy creeper was applied to his horns and lashed on; and then the whole was bound with bark till it looked like nothing so much as a large and badly-packed bus-tyre. The chase was, by tradition, a stern test of nerve and stamina. The padding was, if used at all (Asalu frequently chased unpadded bulls), a precaution to prevent fatalities. But Hegokuloa were taking no risks. They piled it on and on to a fantastic extent, to handicap the beast; and Namkia's comments were caustic.

It was still dark when Namkia called me next day, but there was a faint tinge of grey in the cloudy sky. I tumbled into my clothes anyhow, gulped a cup of tea, and hurried off down the street to where the runners, almost stripped, were grouped about the bull. Cloaks and necklaces were all discarded; they wore nothing but their small kilts. All the staff except for Haichangnang and the cook were competing. Haichangnang had a poisoned hand, and the cook was no athlete. The local runners were fortified by ceremonies and rice-beer. Our team, so far as I know, had had to dispense with both.

Haichangnang and I backed into the shelter of a convenient porch. The street had emptied magically. The children were shut indoors, and every house-front was tightly closed except where one or two women, bolder spirits, peered out round the door-jambs. The village priest took out a stout stick. His assistant cut the bull's tether with one sweep of his dao, and as he did so, the old priest raised his stick and caught the buffalo a hard blow on the rump.

The big beast threw up his weighted head in pain and astonishment. Then he found himself free, and launched off down the street at a thundering canter with a tumbling, jostling, shoving flood of men full-tilt after him. They swept between the morungs in a mob of bare, brown backs, blue kilts and shaggy black heads. Down in ruins went a woodstack and the village pipeline, men fell headlong and were trampled on and scrambled up and ran on again; the bull jerked suddenly to the right, crashed out through a garden, leaped a stile with unexpected agility, and vanished into the jungle with his pursuers after him. The street was left suddenly void, with somebody's kindling stack littered the length and breadth of it and water spilling from the still shaking pipe.

The headman now came up and asked us to go along for a drink. We perched on three-inch stools in his firelit inner room and were served with rice-beer in pint-capacity bananaleaf cups. But as we sat we heard, suddenly, a distant shouting which could only mean that the bull was being thrown. As soon as some stalwart has a tight hold on the tail, he yells his patronymics at the top of his voice; and the moment he is identified, all the bucks of his morung race to the spot, the first up catching the horns while the rest beat off the rival morung and help to bring the bull to a standstill. Then they band together, to throw it, with much ho-ho-ing; for no throw, no win. We didn't want to miss seeing that. We looked at each other with a wild surmise. Then we rose as one, thrust our drinks back at our hostess—to be poured back into the family beer-vat, for economy's sake—and dashed outside and down the street towards the noise, accompanied at a hand-gallop by several small boys with the same idea.

At the foot of the street a corkscrew path wound down into saplings and thickets. We raced on till we came abreast of the shouting, and then, certain that we should be too late for the fun, plunged headlong into the woods on the right. A gully intervened. We hurled ourselves into it and up the far bank. And there we found, not a captive buffalo in the hands of the young men, but a loose and very angry bull just in front of us and all the young men treed and ho-ho-ing to stampede the brute. Haichangnang's red blanket was too much for him, and he charged us. I had one brief glimpse of the great head bearing down, and another of a frantically-beckoning Naga up the slope. Never had I run as I ran then —my feet were air, I flew. Haichangnang reached the place a second before me and waited, thrust me into a natural cage of saplings into which the other Naga had preceded us, and ducked in after me, and there we stood gasping while the bull stamped and snorted where we had been five seconds before.

He had trampled out an arena for himself in the under-growth and was making short rushes up and down it, smelling enemies everywhere and unable to find them. There was not a sign of our team, but every tree was black with the men of Hegokuloa. One of them was right over my head, clinging to a sapling not six inches thick and rocking in an apelike frenzy as he shouted. Each time he rocked his foot came down on my head, so that with every whoop he lunged and I ducked, like a pair of mechanical toys, till the bull swung suddenly round with a snort and charged away in the under-brush. Instantly brown figures swarmed like monkeys from the trees or dropped like plummets from above and went racing off after him; and for the second time that morning Haichangnang and I were left abruptly alone in a scene still quivering from violent activity. We waited several minutes to make sure the coast was clear, and then squeezed out of cover and made off back to the village as hard as we could pelt.

When we arrived perspiring at the headman's house the first person we saw was Namkia, sitting delicately poised on a stack of folded cloths. He was thickly covered in dust, burrs, sweat and scratches, and, between gulps at a large cup of rice-beer, he told us how the team had fared.

He had been right in the van when the bull crashed through the garden and jumped the stile, and beyond that had been a narrow footpath on which he found himself in the lead. But as he raced down this with the tail and triumph almost in his grasp, both bull and path jinked suddenly to the right, and Namkia, overshooting, went straight ahead into a small ravine. His feet went out from under; he sat with a bump; and for twenty feet or more he skidded down the rocky bank on his bare stern.

Arrived with a crash in the stream below, he found himself once more up with the hunt, which had taken the more conventional route round. Leaping up and joining again in the battle, he was presently in the forefront with the new scullion, Paodekumba, a fuzzy-headed little man compact of muscle and tough as they come. First one and then the other of them took hold of the tail and was shaken off, and at last, in the confused chase which was going on all round in the thick scrub-jungle, Paodekumba grabbed the tail once more, and Namkia, by a supreme effort, secured a grip on the horns. The bull then set off at a rousing gallop with the pair of them flying from him like tails on a kite.

At some point in this passage the bull tried to wipe Namkia off on a tree. He displayed a skinned arm in token. Then it came to a sudden stop with the idea of turning on Paodekumba; but Namkia whipped a providential loose end of the padding round a sapling and made it fast; and there they were with the bull caught and Paodekumba most indubitably on the tail—a clear win for the Bower stable. Then up came Ramgakpa, who had been thereabouts, but dancing round at a safe distance in spite of Namkia's yells at him to help; and, a split second after, the whole of the Hegokuloa pack, who declared as one that never would they allow a visiting team to win on the home ground. They were almost at blows with Namkia over it when the bull broke loose; and as soon as the staff reached safety and stopped running, they put their noses in the air and stalked off home in a huff, while the Hegokuloa contingent shot straight up the nearest trees and were still there when Haichangnang and I burst in on them ten minutes later. And Heaven, as Namkia unctuously pointed out, was revenged on Hegokuloa for their lack of the sporting spirit; for the padding worked off the bull's horns and by midmorning it was as much as a man's life was worth to come within twenty yards of him. They had to send back to the village in the end for the headman's gun, and shoot him with that. However, by then most of the runners had come home disgruntled to start the chase of the second beast; and that turned out an even bigger fiasco.

The animal was tied up, as the bull had been, on the flat space in front of the upper morung. Haichangnang and I stationed ourselves with the cameras in the porch of the lower, where we were almost opposite and had a refuge in case of need. The bucks lined up, the rod came down on the hairy flank, the runners surged forward, and the buffalo gave a convulsive bound; but in the confusion someone had forgotten to untie the hobbles. In a trice half a dozen men had hold of the tail at once, and kicking, yelling, plunging and bellowing, the tangle rolled straight down the short slope on top of us. The next thing I knew I was on top of the morung woodstack, fifteen feet above ground. I had not then, and have not now, any clear idea of how I came to be there. I was, however, filming away quite automatically at a howling maelstrom below, where arms, legs and hoofs waved, black heads bobbed, bodies writhed, the bellows of the buffalo rose above a growing quarrel, red-blanketed headmen bored cursing and cuffing into the riot, and members of rival morungs shrieked abuse, slapped, punched, scuffled, kicked, wrestled and pulled hair.

Then the film ran out.

We spent the afternoon in a sleep of exhaustion. There was a dispensary in the evening to patch up the day's casualties; the two morungs had fought it out for some time. Hegokuloa then earnestly pressed us to stay for the serious drinking, but we had had enough, and in any case it would be some days before Namkia could sit down. We therefore said goodbye, and marched back again to recuperate at Laisong.

CHAPTER X

THE ZEMI

DESPITE their closeness to the railway and the fact that they had been long administered, the Zemis' tribal polity still survived in surprisingly complete form.

Much of it dated back to the time of their first arrival. When their early colonies came drifting into the country, and, casting about, picked on sites for their settlements, each had had a leader. With this leader had been a lieutenant. In nine cases out of ten he was a man of the other exogamous group (the Zemi had only two) and probably the leader's brother-in-law or a similar connection by marriage. These two naturally claimed the soil on which they settled with their clansmen; and from their descendants were chosen the village headmen for ever after, for ownership of the site, and with it virtual control of the village, passed down in the family. These hereditary landowners were called *kadepeo*, 'man of the soil', and only rarely, when there was no candidate of suitable age, did an outsider rise to leadership. No one else could wield the same authority as a true *kadepeo*. The only difference under administration was that the headmen were officially recognized and wore the red Government blanket. The method of choice by the village remained the same.

Each community was ruled by a village council, with the *kadepeo* at its head. He was, in effect, its president. He convened it; and, with the help of the village priest, the other permanent member, chose elders to sit on it at any given meeting. But he was no dictator. The council could on occasion overrule him, if public opinion were overwhelmingly behind it.

Besides deciding all matters affecting the village—what areas were due for cultivation the coming year, whether or no they required a third morung, and if so, who should take charge of it—the council also served as a court of justice. As the area was administered, they were supposed to deal only with minor cases; but in practice they settled everything, as they always had. Only disputes between villages, which ordinarily would have ended in war, were taken up to the magistrate's court.

There was no appeal from a decision of the village court. Judgement once given, it was irrevocable; the parties must accept it or leave the place. In civil cases, therefore (they were mostly suits involving property), the court was less concerned with an outright award than in settling the case by compromise, before it could split the village; a very reasonable system, and one which worked well. Criminal cases were few. They were simply judged in accordance with tribal law; banishment was the usual sentence for serious crimes.

All cases were heard in public. To the unaccustomed ear they sounded like a minor riot. Here were no marshalled facts, no measured oratory; plaintiff, respondent, friends, witnesses, onlookers, anyone with something to say, said it at the tops of their voices and all together. The hearing was, in fact, a violent public argument between the parties, in which allegations, denials, and the testimony of witnesses were hurled to and fro and all the relevant points of the case sooner or later brought out. By the time both sides had shouted themselves hoarse, the old men, who had been quietly listening, had heard what they needed to know and reached a decision; and this was forthwith announced and the court dismissed before anyone had time to argue. The judgements were, on the whole, extremely just. I came to have a great respect for their methods.

There were in all eight village officials, all of whom were chosen by the community. Four were secular and four religious. There were the senior and junior headmen (representatives, as a rule, of the two *founder* families—Namkia, as has been seen, was an exception); and after them two lesser assistants. Immediately, the assistants' task was to deal with official and other travellers, finding them food and drink and arranging quarters, but eventually they would succeed the senior headman; and they were there to learn the job from him.

Then there were the first and second priests, two aged men,

who were responsible for the public sacrifices and the religious life of the village. They decided the dates of *gennas* (to use the convenient lingua-franca term), which were holidays in the old sense, days of abstention from work for religious reasons; they kept the calendar, which was lunar, fixed the dates of festivals and presided over the accompanying rites. Since both were old and frail (none but the very old could call the Gods with impunity) they had an able-bodied assistant to do the heavy work, and a town crier, who took up a proclamation as the old priest whispered it, and shouted it the length of the village. The crier's voice at night, proclaiming the morrow's arrangements, was as familiar a sound as cock-crow.

But of all the features of Zemi life, perhaps the most notable was the morung system.

Each village had at least two morungs, some three or four. The men's club-houses were called *hangseoki* (from the Zemi *rahangmi*, a youth) and the girls' dormitories allied to them *leoseoki* (*heleomi*, a girl). The club members collectively were the *kienga*. An admirable institution, the morung disciplined and educated the young; united the householders, the *hangtingmi*, who were the backbone of the village; and was an instrument by which the elders could control the body public. At once a privileged brotherhood and a public utility, it was the most useful item in the social structure.

You joined your *kienga*, willy-nilly, the day you were born. A detachment from one morung or the other came to the house to claim you as soon as you drew breath. (I have belonged to the upper girls' dormitory of Laisong since 1940, with full member's rights and special permission to pay my dues in tea.) This choosing was an unusual feature. Normally, morungs (which are found, in various forms or stages of development, right through the Naga tribes) belong each to a different clan. By the Zemi system, fathers, brothers and sons may be of different *kienga*, whose loyalties, therefore, cut right across all other divisions; but these other loyalties are, in the last resort, by far the stronger.

At the age of eight or so boys and girls went out to sleep at night in their proper dormitories. It was contrary to all Zemi notions of decency that they should remain any longer at night in the same house as their parents, and from then on the morung became the major influence in their lives.

Girls worked at home during the day, and used their dormitory only at night. There, in the evenings, they held spinning bees, or entertained with music—always for a consideration—distinguished strangers. Strictly proper and public parties, these, to which the headmen and leading elders might, in a fatherly way, drop in. But it was from the young men who came calling stealthily at night—easing the door open, tip-toeing in, feeling along the bench for their particular sweetheart—that they chose their husbands.

On boys the hold of the morung was far deeper. Unlike the girls, they spent the whole of their time there; they came home only for meals, and when seriously ill. Each morung was the enlarged front porch of a private house. Its owner, always a leading villager, was host and headmaster to the boys, as his wife was matron. He taught them by precept and example in peacetime; he led them in war.

But, more important still, the give and take of communal life, the opinions of contemporaries, replaced the disciplinary influence of the father. The people who checked the boy and ordered him round, who told him to wash and twisted his ears if he didn't, were lads of his own age or a little older. He was responsible to a body to which he belonged, of which he was an active member. The system taught early the meaning of co-operation and responsibility. I have known and employed men trained by both methods, the morung and the home; and, where choice existed, I would choose the morung graduates every time. They are of tougher fibre and the rough corners have been rubbed off. They are more self-reliant, with commonsense and better discipline, and above all their loyalty and sense of service to a corporate body is well-developed. They have not lost their individualism; but they have a view of the world in relation to themselves, a grasp of mutual duties as well as rights, a way of giving a fair deal for a fair deal, which is most refreshing.

Within the *kienga*, the small boys fagged for the bucks, keeping the morung clean, washing clothes, carrying wood and running errands, and received in return some measure of protection from their patron, his cast-off finery, and a little instruction when he went out to trap or fish.

Then came the next stage, adolescence.

From the day he assumed the kilt and entered manhood till the day he set up house on his own account were the best years of a male Zemi's life. Excused all field-work, except what he cared to do; indulged by his parents in every frippery and luxury of dress; left all day with nothing to do but drink beer, gossip, make baskets, play music, and finally so to bathe and array himself as to be an object of admiration to all the girls as they came in from the fields; permitted, tacitly encouraged, even, to spend his nights in courtship—what more could a youth want? Life was short; marriage and the cares of a family came all too soon. The Zemi, with their innate love of pleasure and beauty, of dance, music, colour and the good things of life, gave all they could to their young people in the short space stern economics allowed.

Admittedly, in return, the bucks were supposed to form the village guard. This, in spite of administration, could not be left to decay. The Zemi were, like all Nagas, head-hunters; war was the natural state of the hill-tribes, a state in which, to them, the Pax Britannica was but an interlude. The Zemi, never warlike themselves, valued the peace greatly. But the threat remained. There were people living in 1940 who could remember the last Angami raid; and it was two decades since the Kuki rebellion had restored, temporarily, the old conditions. We were, as it happened, to see something like them again.

The elders maintained strict discipline, and loyalty to the *kienga* was strong. *Rahangmi* were supposed, too, under the tuition of the married men, to perfect themselves in hunting, fishing, fighting, and the other manly arts. But still the buck's was a life of gilded leisure, to which the harried householder looked back regretfully ever after.

On marriage, a man ceased to sleep in his morung (except in time of war, when all the men collected there to be ready in case of a raid); but he used it as a convenient club-house. Indeed, the great halls with their long wall-benches, their wide floor-space, their seats round the fire, and their master's house at the back, whence came beer and a welcome for strangers, were indispensable public institutions. Dances, feasts, and informal meetings of the village court were held there; the elders discussed affairs; there the blacksmith worked, there drums, spears, torches and shields were kept, there the bucks lived and there travellers stayed; and all with a warm and friendly informality.

At any time the *kienga* could act as a corporate body. As such, they organized dances, made and maintained the village pipelines, carved new water-troughs, and cleared the village paths; or, hired by an individual, carried the harvest or built a house. (Our wood came regularly from the lower morung; the charge was Rs 15/– for eighty logs, a morning's work for the *kienga*.) On such occasions, members of all ages took part, from the elders to small boys, and the fees received went into the morung's fund for feasts. At the great festivals and on similar public occasions the girls of the allied dormitory appeared. They served as waitresses, carrying beer to the men as they worked. Sometimes they went on formal outings, or picnics, with the bucks and boys; and it was they, of course, who were the main attraction of every dance. Since they married early and so gave up the art, they were seldom such skilled performers as the men; but the Zemi held that even if they couldn't dance, pretty girls were always worth looking at.

In all public activities, it may be noted, it was the men who figured. Girls made only their brief and formal appearances with their appropriate *kienga*; married women had no part in public life at all. They never appeared in court in person, but were represented by a male relative. They could not enter the main hall of a morung; to do so was not taboo, but most immodest. No man could eat game killed by a woman. It was unclean, unnatural. Hunting was a man's job. (This taboo, with us, lasted just one week after I bought a shotgun. Meat was scarce; I was declared an exception on the seventh day.) The legal rights of women were almost none, and to all appearances men were paramount in Zemi society. And yet the women were the most powerful influence in it.

That this was so was partly, but not wholly, for economic

reasons. To men fell the heavier and more arduous work, but not that which was the most productive. Aside from hunting, fishing and war, which were not, in current conditions, of economic importance, their contribution was housebuilding, basketry, and the felling of jungle, all of which took a long time and showed no immediate profit. It was the women's work which was of economic value. They cooked, brewed and pounded rice, and made the little there was go the longest way; they carried wood and water, they sowed, weeded and reaped (though the men took their share here); they spun and dyed, they wove and sewed, they kept the home and raised the family. A man alone was condemned to poverty; and a lad who wished to marry must pay heavy compensation to the girl's father for the loss of a valuable asset. So, too, the death of a wife and mother was the worst disaster which could befall a house. I once saw a village where a smallpox outbreak, by a freak incidence of vaccinations, had spared the men and the children under ten and removed, almost without exception, the women from sixteen upwards. The economic life of the village was at a standstill. The young men worked the fields, a task for which they, as a fraction of the normal labour available, were far too few, and the married men were penned in their houses, coping, with a pathos I cannot describe, with whole families suddenly motherless. It was a most forcible illustration of the Naga women's place.

Women, then, were a very strong folk. The influence they wielded, aside from that which affection and sentiment would in any case have allowed—for family life is everything to a Zemi—was remarkable. Nor did the women take their responsibilities lightly. They were, behind the scenes, the real rulers of the community. They could on occasion take action as such; I have known, in a village riot, the women arm themselves with clubs and go in a body to break it up, each mother collecting her sons and each wife her husband and running them out by force to cool off at home. How many times, too, have I heard a Zemi snort to his cronies about his wife's opinions; plan to do this, go here, buy that, engage upon bold adventures; and come back sadly in the morning to say: 'My wife won't let me'?

CHAPTER XI

THE AFFAIR OF DEGALANG

At half-past ten on a bright October morning Degalang the dog-boy eloped with Dinekamba's sister.

Namkia and I were in the family's rice-field at the time, making a colour-film of Dinekamba and his uncle threshing. Dinekamba was a slim, pleasant-faced boy of seventeen, and he and his sister, who were orphans, lived with their uncle Rangalang in a house at the top of the village street, near the big pomelo-tree. I didn't much care for the girl. She was pretty, in an elfin way, but she looked sly.

Here in the field the cut rice was piled in a red-gold ring. The aunt, a drab figure in mud-coloured clothes, exactly like all the other wives of Laisong, gleaned and gathered the sheaves. Rangalang, his curly, rusty hair full of dust, swept the small sheaves into big armfuls and threw them out to Dinekamba. He, his long ear-tassels bobbing, drew them against his feet on the mat and beat them with a ribbed wooden fan—beat them and shook them up, beat them and shook them up; and the grain fell showering out on the smoky cane matting, a golden rain before the colour-camera.

We came back home in the twilight to find no dog-boy. He had strolled off in the morning, the cook said, and had not come back. The cook himself, always tender towards animals, had fed the vocal and hungry Khamba. We debated the matter in the front room, the lamp lit, the door still open on the veranda and the warm night. I was indignant; Namkia, I remember, non-committal. At that moment, in the doorway, in the spread of light from the hurricane lamp, appeared a breathless, angry, sweating Rangalang. He was panting, having run full tilt from the village. He was still stripped to his kilt and covered in dust and husks, just as he had come up with us from the fields.

'Where's Degalang?' he said. 'Where's Degalang? My girl's missing.'

Namkia turned to him with, I thought, a trace of triumph. '*Ga-le*,' he said. 'Not here.'

There is, in that simple Zemi negative, a finality and an expression of utter absence irreproducible in English. It was not merely that Degalang was not there; he could not possibly have been less present. And in the same word, by some subtle inflection, Namkia conveyed that he knew exactly what had happened and that it was Rangalang's own fault. Rangalang made a noise like a cat spitting; and disappeared, running again, into the dark. Namkia, when he turned round again, was smiling a feline smile.

He was right, as it happened; it was to a large extent Rangalang's own fault.

The young couple had been in love for some time—almost since we first came. But, though Zemi tradition favoured lovers, holding that they should have their way and that interference was wrong, both parents and village had put as many obstacles as possible in Degalang's way. The Laisong bucks resented his intrusion, and even more than that, probably, his success. One night, when he was known to be with her in the girl's dormitory, a band of youths raided it. They pulled him down from the bench and her arms, dragged him to the door, and pitched him out into a rainy night and a cold, wet street with the intimation that he need not come back. There was so much feeling about this in Impoi that, for a time, Laisong bucks were there in danger of assault. From Rangalang and the family he had even less encouragement. Degalang was poor and so undesirable. She had other, more eligible admirers in Laisong itself. As soon as it was clear his intentions were serious, she was forbidden to see him. They were young, they were very much in love; Rangalang might have foreseen the result. That morning, she had told her aunt she was going to fetch firewood. She had taken her axe and basket, which concealed her trousseau, and she had slipped out and off to the woods, the picture of maidenly virtue. Degalang had left his baggage in camp, and carelessly, casually, wandered off and away. Where they met we never discovered; nor does it matter. But at noon they were seen, travelling together, on the road to Impoi; and that night they settled as man and wife in the back room in the house of Degalang's elder brother.

At any other season of the year they would have won; their *fait accompli* would have been acknowledged. But it was the middle of harvest. There was a strict taboo on marriage, as there was, indeed, on everything which magically or actually might interfere with the all-important work. Their sudden act, their violent breach of custom, jeopardized the whole of Laisong's crops. In the utmost agitation a party of headmen and elders went off next day to insist that she return, at least till the harvest was over.

There was an all-day meeting at Impoi at which priests, headmen and relatives argued themselves husky over the merits and implications of the case. But the vital harvest won. She was, at the end of the meeting, persuaded to come back, on the clear and definite promise that she should marry Degalang in the spring, when the New Year feast of Hgangi was over and the wedding season began. As soon as she reached the house again, Rangalang announced that never, so long as he lived, should Degalang have her; but nobody took much notice. The promise was given, if not by Rangalang, at least by the village elders, and considering his loss of face, some such salving statement was only to be expected. The harvest took up our attention, and everyone forgot about Degalang until the following spring.

He had left us by then. I had myself completely forgotten the matter, till one day, on leaving the house, I found the camp full of the elders of Impoi, and in their midst, as they sat on the level space outside the kitchen, a Namkia even gloomier than they. I asked the reason. It appeared that the marriage season had begun. In response to Degalang's anxious requests, they had come over to see Rangalang and make formal application for the girl. They had been met at the door by a stream of abuse, a flat refusal, and a denial that any understanding existed. So there was Degalang in floods of tears in the lines, his cloth flung over his head and the cook weeping in sympathy beside him; and the girl crying herself sick in the village—she was pregnant now, anyway; and the deputation down here to see what Namkia could do.

Namkia himself was not at all sure he could do anything. He came into the house to think it over, and sat there, biting his lip. At last he took leave of absence for the afternoon and went off up the village, prepared, apparently, for a stern struggle, with the deputation trailing raggedly behind him; and that was the last we saw of them till five o'clock.

It was just on the edge of evening and not yet dusk when Namkia came home. He walked wearily. The dust of verbal battle, so to speak, still clung to him. He was very hoarse. In his hand he carried the white cloth of betrothal, the formal, clinching present from bride's father to groom; and he vanished into the lines with it to Degalang.

By all accounts it was a notable combat. The opening rounds found Rangalang strongly entrenched and Namkia probing for an opening. He discovered it. The Rangalang family were hard up; a wealthy Laisong suitor was nosing the hook. Then battle began, barrage upon barrage of accusation, thundering denunciations of their mercenary instincts, reminders of the Zemi tradition of leniency towards lovers, bitter reproaches for their breach of faith, prophecies of shame and disaster, and all in one overwhelming flood of eloquence in which I don't believe Rangalang managed to inject a defensive sentence. I felt considerable sympathy for Rangalang there. Namkia in the full tide of oratory is cataclysmic. Bewildered, outflanked, shaken, Rangalang abandoned his main defences and conceded the principle of the match.

He was lost. Never relaxing pressure, Namkia fought him back point by point and pig by pig through every stage of the marriage-price. Almost single-handed, the Impoi headmen only a murmuring background to him, like distant small-arms heard through the crash of artillery, he beat Rangalang down from Rs 60/- and goods of the same value to Rs 20/-, a necklace, one pig, and a cooking-pot. Now and then, true, Rangalang made a stand; but never for long. By five o'clock it was over and he and his had collapsed, stunned, deafened, and beaten to the ground. The girl was Degalang's at Degalang's own price. It was only a question then of sparing the conquered's feelings. Namkia left the Impoi headmen with a pot of beer to do that, and came on home with the news.

A year later, he and I came into the head of the village street. It was almost dark. We had been out for a turn round the jungle with the new shotgun, and had, as usual, seen nothing larger than a dove. Before us the twilight street was full of evening activity. Field-parties were returning, trudging heavily under full baskets; spear-armed youths, returned travellers, turned in at their morungs, from whose high gables blue smoke curled out into the still air. Indeed, a thin haze of it hung over the whole village, drifting out through thatch, coiling from porches; the friendly and familiar sight which ended every day, infinitely comforting in its repetition and calm security. Below us, the shadow of the hill had swallowed the camp. The rounded spur was blue; blue against the warm Nenglo slope, up whose grass the shadow was now marching.

There, in the porch at Rangalang's, the girl was sitting with her baby.

'Hallo!' said I. 'Why have you come home?—Visiting the family? Ask her, Namkia.'

He did so. She shrugged her shoulders and said that Dega-lang's brother had sent her. There was something wrong. It was in her tone of voice and in Namkia's manner. I asked no other questions. We turned and left.

The following morning the Impoi headmen arrived. All day they conferred with Rangalang and the Laisong elders. Dinekamba, who was now our scullion, was at the meeting. That evening, as I went out for a stroll, I ran into him on the village path. He was hurrying, almost running. He was crying openly; the tears were streaming down his face.

Poor Dinekamba! and poor Degalang, too! The truth was out; the Rangalangs were disgraced. The girl was a klepto-maniac. During the year, she had stolen constantly and re-peatedly from every house in Impoi. Degalang, still in love, had done his best to cure her. He had paid up, worked off the debts, begged for her at the village council; now, when the whole of Impoi demanded her expulsion, his brother had sent her away for the sake of the family name. And Degalang wept, alone, in the back room.

CHAPTER XII

SYMPHONY ON TWO FLOORS

At the end of the same October which saw the elopement I went to Calcutta for a ten days' holiday and shopping-spree. I had been a year up-country; the cobwebs needed shaking off. I took Namkia along.

He had never been farther in his life than Silchar on one side and Kohima on the other, and was not in the least keen to risk more. When I happened to pass his compartment while the train was halted at Maibong he was sitting bolt upright and staring in front of him like a man heading for death. He bade farewell to the few stray Naga fruit-vendors on the platform almost with tears; he dared not look, I think, at his receding hills, lest they unman him. But at Lumding, where we caught the Down Mail, he discovered a stall which sold palatable curry and cheered up.

As to myself, there was a party of Europeans dining in the Lumding refreshment room. They were the first white people I had seen for four months. I stared and stared—how odd, how knobbed and craggy they were, after the smooth Mongol faces; how pallid the woman was, like a plant left in the dark! How strange the usual seemed after the separation; I couldn't stop looking. They must have thought I was mad. Oddly enough, one only notices these things after the first spell away from one's kind; after that the gap seems to close, and one makes the transition between the two worlds, without the same shock of surprise.

At Amingaon Namkia made a friend. As we waited for the train to start, I saw him standing in the doorway of the servants' compartment in all his glory of scarlet blanket, golden-yellow necklaces, black kilt and well-oiled cane knee-rings. In front of him was a growing crowd whose front rank was composed of assorted vendors; gaping spectators formed the rest. In the space which remained in front of the carriage paraded a little brown terrier of a sepoy, belonging,

I ON THE ROAD TO MANIPUR

II KAMBIRON : A KABUI NAGA VILLAGE

III MORNING MIST IN THE TANGKHUL NAGA COUNTRY

IV LAISONG VILLAGE FROM THE CAMP

V ZEMI NAGA MORUNG, HANGRUM

VI MASANG CUTTING NAMKIA'S HAIR

VII KABUI NAGA GIRL WEAVING

VIII MOTHER AND CHILD, CHINGJAROI

IX NAGA GIRL, CHINGJAROI

X ZEMI NAGA LONG JUMP AT THE 'HAZOA'

XI NAGA DANCE

XII THE DOG KHAMBA WITH LUIKAI

XIII BLACK MAGIC VILLAGE : CROWD AT JESSAMI

XIV BLACK MAGIC VILLAGE : THE JESSAMI HEADMAN

XV (*opposite*) ANGAMI NAGA IN FULL DRESS

XVI OLD KUKI, SOUTH-WEST MANIPUR

XVII (*opposite*) TANGKHUL NAGA HEADMAN, TUINEM VILLAGE

XVIII MASANG OF KEPELO

XIX (*opposite*) ZEMI NAGA DRUMMER, LAISONG

XX NAMKIABUING OF IMPOI

XXI (*opposite*) ZEMI NAGA BUCK IN FULL DRESS

XXII PAODEKUMBA, 'V' FORCE SCOUT

apparently, to some military police detachment posted at the station. Curious, I strolled past, and heard the sepoy answering the crowd's questions. Pride and delight were in his very strut, in the tilt of his hat; in his excitement he raised his voice, so that one heard his answers but not what the on-lookers asked.

'Yes, he is an important person. He is of my own caste. He, too, is a Naga. We may eat from the same dish. Seller! Bring some soda-water for my Naga brother! Oh, there!—bring some cigarettes!'

Both vendors jumped to it, and passed their wares up, with blandishments, to Namkia.

'Nothing is too good. I will pay all!' The little man swung suddenly round on Namkia. 'O my brother! Take, please, some cigarettes as a present from me! It is so very long since I saw another Naga; and it has made me so happy!'

Namkia, the old sinner—what he must have been as a buck!—posed there, so statuesque and conscious of himself, in the narrow doorway; the heavy scarlet drapery falling from his bare shoulders; under the bare lights and the black, barren, girdered roof, he was a magnificently barbaric figure. Europeans were stopping to look now, at the back of the crowd. And how Namkia enjoyed it; and how, without catching my eye openly, knew that I knew he did, and enjoyed that, with his own particular humour, a puckish savouring of his own misdeeds. With polite reluctance he took a packet of cigarettes from the vendor, chose and lit one, and said, the crowd hanging on his words:

'Yes, my brother, we are both Nagas. I thank you for your presents. Though you are an Ao and I am a Zemi, yet we are both of the same caste.'

The train gave a shrill shriek and jerked forward and I fled for my carriage.

This encounter not merely raised his morale, but boosted it to well above normal level. I had to wait till Calcutta, though, to hear his subsequent adventures. These began after the change of trains at Parbatipur. There was then no ser-vants' compartment, and he found himself lodged, as one of sixty or so, in a crowded third-class carriage. Such an exceptional figure could only arouse curiosity. Courteous, like all Zemi, he answered fully at first and most politely. But with a few the thirst for information overbore good manners. Newcomers bombarded him with the same old questions. Earlier inquirers, emboldened by his mild manner, pushed matters to prodding point—to fingering, to demands, even, for scraps of his dress as souvenirs; and his patience began to shrink. At last some innocent crowned it all by asking, in a hushed voice, whether Nagas were really, as the plainsmen all believed them to be, cannibals. Namkia took a deep breath.

'Oh, yes!' he said, and resettled himself in the slight space which appeared, by magic, it seemed, on the crowded bench. 'I couldn't tell you the number of times I've tasted human flesh.'

There was a sharp backward movement from his vicinity.

He shifted a little to give himself elbow-room, and went on with an air of simple veracity:

'In the last famine, my wife and I decided we should have to eat one of the children.

'We couldn't make up our minds (we had four, you know) whether to eat the eldest, who was about ten, because there would be more meat on him and we could smoke it down, or whether to take the youngest, which was quite a baby, because we shouldn't miss it so much, and we could easily have another. We argued for hours.

'I decided at last against killing the eldest. He'd been such a trouble to rear. Unfortunately, my wife was fond of the baby. You never heard such a scene—eventually, though, I insisted on killing it; and it really was extremely good, most tender—boiled, with chillies. But my wife, poor woman, was most upset. She cried the whole time and couldn't touch a mouthful.'

By this time, not only was the bench on which Namkia sat empty, but most of the passengers had congregated, with starting eyes, on the far side and at the opposite ends of the carriage. With a final look round him and a benign smile, Namkia spread out his bedding and slept in comfort, at full length, all the way to Calcutta; and every time a fresh entrant approached him with a hint to move over, the rest of the

carriage said, as one: 'Look out! Man-eater!' and Namkia
turned slowly over and murmured: 'Now the last time I tasted
human flesh——'

He told me the story with immense delight as soon as we
arrived.

Calcutta's swarming crowds and endless streets frightened
the life out of him. He could find his way about the jungle
like a wild animal; but one minute on a pavement, and he
was lost for good. I had to bribe a hotel bearer to keep an
eye on him for part of the time and take him about with me
for the rest; which led us into some curious places and situa-
tions. I doubt whether the Ladies' Department at the Army
and Navy Stores ever really recovered. Even the hotel itself
bewildered him. He had never seen or heard of a three-storey
building before, and the ramifications of the Great Eastern,
in which, as he truthfully said, you could put some half a
dozen Zemi villages and still have room for a morung in the
dining-room, had him baffled from the start.

The very first night there, when I had gone out to dinner
and he was sleeping as a guard in the corridor outside my
room, he had occasion to go down to the courtyard. He
found his way down all right; but when the time came to
return, he climbed up only one floor, instead of two, and
began to roam round and round in the half-dark, in a state
of almost complete nudity, in a search for his own bedding.
All round the first floor servants woke and saw this terrible
figure stooping over them—hungry, it was to be supposed,
and in search of meat. They clapped their blankets over their
heads, fell on their faces, and began praying all they knew for
deliverance to their several Gods; and poor Namkia, more
and more lost, more and more mazed and helpless, drifted
on, convinced that he would be arrested as a suspected thief,
clapped into jail, and never seen again.

At last some bolder spirit suggested he go up one floor
higher. Looking in the dimness like an anxious tiger, he
padded away up the spiral iron stair. Then, on the second
floor, the harlequinade was repeated again, till he came round
the last corner (it would be the final one), saw his own bedding, and sank on to it with a groan of relief. He was still

lying there in a state of nervous collapse when I came home. From that moment on he insisted in sleeping in my room on the mat below the punkah. It was, he said, cooler; and, more important, his elder sister the She-Sahib could keep an eye on him.

Two years later in Shillong, an officer, seeing Namkia and Haichangnang waiting outside on the hotel drive, pointed them out to me as Nagas—he didn't suppose, he said, I had seen any before—and told me a highly garbled version of this story.

CHAPTER XIII

HGANGI

I FOUND myself faced that winter with a lone Christmas at Laisong. The Zemi New Year Feast of Hgangi fell directly after; so it looked as though we were in for a riotous time.

We were.

By dint of a great deal of scraping and stinting I had saved up enough to buy a small mithan. This was brought over from Tolpui, up the valley, killed by the cook and left at the water-point for the village blacksmith to cut up. I had arranged to go down and supervise this, but some domestic crisis intervened at the critical moment, and when I ran down there at last—alas! for the slate-grey hide I had planned as a bedside rug, for steaks, for sirloins, for any joint whatever! Hide and all, the carcase had been hacked to pieces with dao and axe, in the purest Naga style; nothing remained but a pile of tripe and a mound of bleeding hunks weighing a pound or so each. The cook and I went gingerly through the heap. After much gruesome Scotland Yard work, we found something which, by a stretch of the imagination, might once have been rather like a roasting piece. So that was chosen; and we sent it back to camp for my Christmas dinner next day.

At eleven o'clock on Christmas morning, the cook reported sick with fever. But, he said, he had arranged everything with Paodekumba. I was on no account to spoil my holiday by sweating over a stove myself.

When, that evening, Namkia entered the room with a triumphant sweep and my Christmas feast on a tray, he laid before me a sodden bone—a bone wringing, waterlogged; a bone from which depended in places ragged bunches of what seemed to be wet, brown string—my poor joint, warmed in tepid fat some time that morning, laid in a gallon of water, and boiled unremittingly ever since.

I opened a tinned tongue.

Hgangi began a few days later. This great feast marks the

turn of the year. It opens with the parting of the dead from
the living; with its main day, Hgangi itself, the old year
closes and the new begins; during its course, huge, stylized
wooden effigies are set up at the gates to the village, and
ceremonially speared by the men and boys—a relic of human
sacrifices; and the various religious ceremonies, omen-takings
and holidays run on for a full fortnight.

The week before the feast was almost entirely given up to
bringing in large slabs of stone to finish the graves of the
year's dead. It was astonishing what weights were moved,
and across what country. Only manpower was used, but
until one has seen what can be done by it, properly handled,
one can have no real conception of its efficiency. Once one
has seen it, Stonehenge and Avebury are comprehensible. I
always wished I could hear Namkia, who had dragged, and
superintended the dragging of, many stones in his time, give
his expert opinion on those two monuments.

The working rule is to carry uphill and drag down. To
take a stone up a slope it is built into a horizontal scaffolding,
an arrangement of stout poles lashed together on either side
of and behind and before the stone, allowing perhaps a hundred men to surround it to take the weight. The stone is then
lifted and carried as though in a litter, on men's shoulders.
To bring a stone down, or along the level, it is first jacked
on to a stout sledge made from a forked tree-trunk, and
then dragged by gangs of men heaving in unison. The Zemi
have a heaving-chant, a slow 'Ho—ho—Hoi!' with the time
given by a cheer-leader, who, if not alongside his team like
a tug-of-war coach, may stand on the stone itself like the
overseer in an Egyptian frieze.

The work is not without danger. Close to the bridle-road
between Asalu and Impoi, where the track curves round a
spur through high grass, they still point out to you a stretch
of twenty yards or so where the ground is 'bad'; accursed.
There have been two fatal accidents there, within a few yards
of each other. One concerned a large, flat table-rock, a little
way up the hill; the other, the shattered fragments of a big
stone, just visible in the grass a dozen paces below the lip of
the road.

The first tragedy had nothing to do with stone-dragging. In the old days of Impoi's glory, when it boasted a hundred and forty houses and stone walls, the bucks were out hunting. One of the stops, a young lad, overcome with heat and boredom, lay down to sleep in the lee of the table-rock. The hunt, in the forest above, started a sambhur, and the hunted deer, in full flight down the hill with dogs and men after it, leapt clean over the flat rock—and came down right on the boy.

The second occurred almost where the road runs now. In those days the path to Impoi followed almost the same line; you see it still as a hollow ditch above or below the shelf of the Government track. Impoi were dragging in a huge slab for a grave. The whole manpower of the village was there, with reinforcements from the other villages of the group; an immense, an unwieldy body, numbering, they say, three hundred men.

Suddenly, as they were crossing this short slope, the last man on the rope slipped and fell in front of the sledge. There were shouts, confusion, cries to the teams to stop. They were not heard above the din of chanting. An onlooker snatched out his dao and cut the haulage-ropes. Down went the whole body of pullers, flat; but it was too late. The man had gone under the sledge, and he was dead.

They cut the lashings and pushed and tumbled the great slab down the slope. Then they piled brushwood over it, and logs and dry wood, in a tall pile, and fired it. They let it burn for a day, stoking it till the stone was red-hot, and then like a line of ants they carried water from the near-by stream. This they doused until the cold water on the hot stone cracked it into the scattered fragments that are seen there today below the grassy furrow of the old road.

Laisong's biggest stone for that year stood about three-quarters of a mile from the village, rather above it and well out to the side. It was a good-sized slab, but it was the difficult country rather than the weight which made it a tricky job to bring in. A path had been cut out to it, and it was all that I could do to get there on my own two legs, carrying only a camera—over logs, over screes and rubble, over piles

of rock, through mud, and all across a slope of forty-five
degrees. It was impossible to drag the stone, so they were
carrying it, and something like eighty men were taking part.

About eleven in the morning they manned the scaffolding
and drag-ropes, two fore and two aft, and started out, lurching and straining down the steep drop from the quarry to the
cut path. The drag-teams came down flat to the ground like
anchor-men in a tug-of-war, belaying on every stump and
stub they met, till with a fearful flurry and stagger and reeling
to and fro, the stone and its human carpet of carriers checked
at the bottom and levelled out at the entrance to the cleared
belt.

The slope was so steep that not more than a quarter of the
carriers were taking the weight at any one time; the rest were
having all they could do to keep on their feet. Swaying,
rocking, lurching, now and then careering off down the slope
with frantic ho-ho-ing all round and every muscle cracking
among the men on the ropes, they progressed slowly and yard
by yard towards the village.

Three times the stone took charge, and the whole body
swung floundering downhill into the jungle, while the stone
itself hung unmoved and impersonal above all the frantic
confusion of human effort. But the last time there was no
check. Round they swung, down and down, the drag-teams
scrambling helplessly along the ground. Their feet tore
grooves in the loose mould, and found no grip. Down went
men under the feet of others, who were themselves about to
fall. There was a frantic note in the ho-ho-ing as they fought
to halt, to hold, to avert an imminent disaster. Every man
and boy among the spectators was running to the place.
Namkia was already in the struggle. I stood burdened with
heaven knows how many cloths and discarded necklaces, let
alone the camera; but the old headman caught me by the arm
and tugged. Down went all my holdings in the jungle, the
camera on top of the heap; down went his red cloth; and we
flung ourselves at the nearest empty places, at the head of
the starboard rope. The others on it were already heaving,
heels in, backs to the ground. Down the slope we went,
fighting and fighting, we belayed on a tree and were dragged

over it, we belayed again, we hung on, we lodged, we held —and the rear team took hold at the same time, and the stone, bobbing slowly down the hill like a juggernaut above its worshippers, checked and swayed gently where it was. The ho-ho-ing redoubled. The stone swayed up a foot. We took in a fraction on the ropes. Up again a little—and inch by inch and step by step we worked it forward on a long slant till it reached the path again with the village in plain sight not twenty yards away, and, sweating, strained and panting though we all were, we brought it in with a run under the water-pipes and swept it in a rush of victory to the head of the village street. And there it lay at last, lashed round and across with its ropes of twisted cane, its scaffolding spreading half the width of the street; still, grey and dead, as though it had never, a few minutes before, been crushing men against trees or bearing them down under one another's feet.

A day or two later, when the graves were completed, came Hkakngi, the parting of the dead from the living.

The Zemi believes in an after-life. The dead, he thinks, linger in their old homes until forced to go, and after a death in the house, food and drink are set out for the ghost at every meal until ceremonial separation is complete. On feast-days, sometimes, great bowls of pounded soap-creeper, thick with suds, are put out so that the ghosts may bathe, like the living, and join the celebrations. At Hkakngi comes the final parting. The last sacrifices are made. All that the dead will need is the next world, gourds, cloths, tools, seeds, anything else omitted from the grave-goods at burial, must be provided now. When everything is done, the priest goes up to the top of the village. Then, when his ritual there is complete, he moves down the street, and, calling aloud, bids the ghosts take their possessions and go. When the last of the invisible host has passed through the lower gateway and taken the Low Road to the land of the dead, the old man shuts the gate, and returns again to a village emptied of all but living men.

The village priest was a most gentle and charming old man. I had from him, during my stay at Laisong, more small kindnesses than I can ever remember. He always called me 'Daughter' and was wonderfully good in admitting me, a woman and an outsider, to watch the village ceremonies, and in answering questions about the ritual and underlying beliefs. So it was with Hkakngi.

The preparations were over by noon, and, with Namkia, I went to the village to see the final separation. The street was entirely deserted. We walked up it between rows of half-closed doors, round which, here and there, a woman peered. Not a child, not a dog, not a chicken was out; a few men stood concealed in house-porches, well back behind wood-stacks; and the whole, long, stony space was clear under the noon sun.

We were half-way up it when there was a long cry behind the upper morung. Namkia pulled me back at once to one side, behind a fence and a big boulder. The priests had finished their ceremony at the upper gate, and were coming down, telling the ghosts to go. The living must all withdraw; for souls are chancy things, easily drawn away into the passing crowd of spirits, and, when the soul goes, the body dies.

The old priest came into sight at the head of the street. He carried a smouldering brand; the grey smoke coiled gently up from it as he walked. There was not a breath of air. The old man's white hair glinted in the sunshine. His voice was unexpectedly clear in the hush.

'O all you dead! Go to your own place and leave the living here. O all you dead! It is time to part. Let the living remain, and let the dead go!'

There was something indescribably melancholy in the cry. There was something eerie, too. The old priest himself had lost a son that year. The earth was red and raw over the new gravestone, just across the street from where we stood. We neither of us moved. It felt cold in spite of the windlessness and the sun.

The old man passed on. He turned the corner by the lower morung, and his voice came back from behind it:

'O all you dead! Go to your own place——'

Still nobody stirred. The silence lasted, perhaps, for five or six minutes; and then we heard the priest's voice proclaiming as he returned.

'The dead have gone to their own place! The dead are separated from the living! The dead have gone to their own place!'

The tension relaxed. Doors opened, pigs were kicked squealing out, men laughed and talked, and all through the village life and movement came flowing back.

A day or two later the pigs destined to provide the feast were turned loose and caught in much the same way as the Pokpat mithan had been, except that the proceedings were on a smaller and informal scale. The pigs were simply chased out of doors by their owners in the early morning into a crowd of catchers massed a few yards from the house; some of the bigger boars were filled up with rice-beer first to give the chase more zest. The staff were, of course, in it up to the hilt. The Zemi have an engaging custom by which the winner of a contest is de-bagged, or rather, de-kilted, by any elder present, on the ground that anyone so gifted by nature can spare mere ornaments to those less favoured. The chase took place about six or half-past; and at eight o'clock, when I was wondering if any of the men would return, and when, if ever, I should get some breakfast, a small boy appeared with a message. Paodekumba, it seemed, had caught the big pig. He had been de-bagged on the spot by the senior priest, and was now in seclusion in the lower morung. He couldn't report for duty until we sent him something to come home in—a kitchen clout would do. A spare kilt was despatched. And ten minutes later, Paodekumba, rather sheepish, was washing dishes again at the kitchen sink.

His long absence, and the fact that the others all came back again drunk, upset from the start the never-stable cook. I could sympathize with him, for Namkia drunk was, as I knew to my cost, a holy terror, and for some reason he always vented his fury on the current cook. The more he drank, the more his rage piled up, till, at the height of his bout, he was screaming abuse and insults as though murder were imminent. Even so, it was all right so long as the wretched victim kept quiet; for Namkia would eventually rant himself to a stand-still, or go to sleep, or think of another enemy, and in the morning deny with indignation every act and word of the night before. Unhappily, the cook never did keep quiet. An hour or so of vituperation, and he would fly in on Namkia and scream hysterically back, and then the fat would really be in the fire, for Namkia was almost mad for the time being, and the cook had a brother in an asylum and was probably half-mad anyway; and I had to come scudding out and break up the party before the cook took the kitchen knife to Namkia or Namkia a dao to the cook. At any rate, on this particular day the cook's nerves troubled him from breakfast onwards; I could hear him snapping and squealing at Paodekumba like a peevish woman.

At ten o'clock there was a sudden confusion which brought us all out running. There on the slope between our water-point and the village the entire strength of both morungs was embroiled. It had started over the pig-catching—A, of one morung, had bumped or bored B—and somewhere in the middle of the mêlée were the two original combatants, each with hands locked in the other's thick shock of hair and tugging away till they were almost on the ground. Round them, in one reeling, kicking, struggling, punching, hair-pulling rugger-scrum, were all the friends who had gone to their assistance, the friends who had gone to the aid of the friends, and every other boy or buck able to kick, scratch, or bite; while round the outskirts danced the village elders, screeching shrilly and waving scrawny brown arms—not in any attempt to stop the battle, but shrieking abuse at the enemy and encouragement to their respective grandsons. The cook tiptoed out barefoot, long, lean and timid, took one look, screamed like a rabbit, and ran back to the cookhouse, sobbing aloud and stumbling in his skirt-like *lungi*, and there had an attack of the vapours in Paodekumba's arms.

By five o'clock that afternoon Namkia was in the village and fighting drunk, and I was praying he would stay there. The cook's strained nerves had snapped, and he had given a loud scream at some minor irritation and slapped Paodekumba. He had had enough of the cook, slapped him back, left him weeping, dismissed himself from my service, and doubled off up the village to get drunk with Namkia. There was not a soul left in the place except the cook, who, sniffing miserably, served my dinner. When darkness fell, I left him to any hysterics he cared to have, barred myself into the basha, and made a New Year resolution to celebrate all future Hgangis whatsoever in civilization.

Like most New Year resolutions, it was never kept.

CHAPTER XIV

THINGS THAT GO BUMP IN THE NIGHT

THE parting of the Zemi dead from the living and the various propitiatory sacrifices to spirits were not the only times when the unseen world impinged upon ours. One way and another, the supernatural was always with one in Naga life. Sometimes mysterious lights were seen in the remote jungle on the surrounding hills and the men claimed that they were 'spirit-fires'; sometimes there were alarms at night and half the household declared they heard cries and eerie whistling. But the 'spirit-fires' always looked to me like brushwood burning, and though I heard the cries twice, and couldn't identify the animal making them, I never managed to hear the whistles at all. My scepticism, however, received a sharp jolt when in January of 1941 we developed a poltergeist in the camp itself.

It began when Haichangnang complained of disturbances in his quarter, which was the last one, at the far end of the lines. The door, he said, was being shaken at night and sometimes flung down, and pattering noises were heard, as of a pig or dog running. I briefly suggested he drink less. But he found the trouble serious enough, and soon abandoned his own room and moved in next door with Hozekiemba the gardener, Samrangba's successor. Noises, however, continued, and when, a week or two later, I returned from a trip to Hangrum, both Hozekiemba and the old caretaker, who had been left in charge, asked me to leave more men on the place next time, as voices had been heard at night in the empty bungalow.

Whatever it was had, in the interval, moved several stages up the lines. Almost everyone had heard it by now, and it had taken—of all noises for a ghost to make!—to blowing 'raspberries'. Then the cookhouse became affected. There were fearful crashes at night as though a whole stack of pans had fallen, and when the men came running, there was nothing disturbed. The manifestations, too, were growing more frequent. There was one almost every night now; and, at the beginning of February, the thing spread to the bungalow.

I was sitting by the fire in the living-room one evening after dinner and reading peacefully enough, when I suddenly heard a pattering as of a heavy dog trotting down the outside veranda. My mind leapt to Khamba and the risk of leopards, and I caught up a flashlight, opened the nearest door, and jumped out to catch him. As I laid hold of the door-bar the noise was opposite me, but as I came out I stopped short, for there was nothing there. I thought he must have leapt out over the railing, and swept the torch-beam round the ground outside; but there was no sign of anything; and then I hailed the lines, and was told that Khamba was safely tied up there that minute, and hadn't been off the chain since dusk.

A few nights later exactly the same thing happened. The third time I heard it, I didn't bother to look out.

The next appearance in the bungalow was sheer farce, and rather vulgar at that. (Phenomena, by the way, were going on in the lines all this time as well.) It was at the usual time in the evening, about an hour after dark, and I was just starting dinner. The camp table was pushed up to the partition wall between the two rooms and was just beside the connecting doorway, and the hurricane lamp on it cast a ring of light round the table and myself and for a yard or so through the doorway into the bedroom beyond. I had a book propped against the sauce-bottle and was half-way through a plate of pumpkin soup, when off went a loud, explosive 'raspberry', as unmistakable and as concrete as a 'raspberry' can be, just beyond the doorway and within a yard of where I sat. I could tell the spot to a foot, and it was well within the ring of light. I put down the spoon and looked. There was the dog-bed, there was the doorway; there was the wall, there was the half-seen room beyond; and nothing whatever odd about any of them. Well, if a spirit wished to amuse itself by making rude noises in my bungalow, I could see no immediate way to prevent it; so I found my place in the book again and went on with my soup, and that was the end of that episode.

Piqued, possibly, by my ignoring it, the incubus next had recourse to more alarming methods. The incident occurred at the same time and place as the others, in the living-room and at about eight o'clock. I was reading after dinner by the fire, with the lamp on the table by me and my back to the two small windows. The shutters of both were closed, and were held shut by a bar across the frame on the inside. A string fastened the bar to the matting shutter, and the matting's natural springiness held all fast. A faint noise made me look round. There was the bar—which, being new and tautly-fastened, it took a sharp pull to dislodge—slipping out corner-wise through the window-space as though someone standing behind me were handling it, and, the next second, the whole freed shutter fell loose with a clatter which, I don't mind saying, startled the living daylight out of me. I yelled for the men, and we searched, but found nothing. I made Namkia sleep in the house at night, after that, by way of company.

The next manifestation was also a physical one. It came at an earlier hour than the others, at about six o'clock, the time sacred to my evening bath. At the exact moment, I remember, I was standing up and baling water over myself, and wishing the wind didn't blow so fiercely through the matting wall. At that minute there was a sharp creak from the door. It began to shake and quiver as though someone were trying to open it—it was a heavy door, slung from an overhead cane— and I gave a yell of outrage, grabbed a towel, wrapped it round me, and jerked the door ajar myself to see who it was and rate the intruder. But the bedroom beyond was empty. The cold grey light slanted across the bare floor, and I stood there, thoughtful. There had been no earthquake. One sharp enough to shake the heavy door would have set the house creaking. I saw clearly, too, what I had not noticed before, that no one could have reached the door, or left it, unheard. The bungalow floors were covered with bamboo matting. They were stiff and thick. The earth below them had packed and sunk with wear, and now when anyone, even the cat, crossed them, the matting sagged and crackled inescapably. There had been no sound either before or after the door moved.

A few nights later, when Namkia and I, after an uneventful evening, had retired, I to my camp cot, he stretched out against the far wall like a big dog, there was a rasping, scuffling noise from the small room used as a store. Rats had been very destructive recently; and I was certain they were making off with something, and called to Namkia to go and investigate. He merely hunched himself more tightly in his blankets, and said it was the spook, and he wouldn't.

There was an argument then, he maintaining that he wasn't afraid, but that the spook did not steal eggs or chew tea-packets, and there was no point in leaving a warm bed on a bitter night to paddle about in search of the intangible; and I declaring that until he had investigated, he couldn't possibly tell whether it was the spook or rats. He, however, insisted that he could; so, the noise still persisting (it sounded, say, like a brick on a piece of paper being drawn steadily across a concrete floor) I said I'd go and see for myself, and tumbled shivering out of bed with a flashlight. Namkia then reluctantly wrapped himself in a blanket and followed.

He was perfectly right. There was no sign of a rat in the store. The room was small, not more than ten feet square, with rough bamboo shelves on three sides and the usual matting floor. I searched it all, peering along the not-very-full shelves and behind the jappas, and nowhere could I find anything to account for the noises; which, maddeningly enough, continued the whole time at a point impossible to place. It was close, certainly within a few feet of us, but I could not locate it. Puzzled, and by then distinctly chilly, I gave it up and went back to bed.

An hour or so later the rasping grew so loud that it woke me up. This time I was determined to find it. There must be something solid to account for the row. Up I got and put on a coat, and, followed by a still-reluctant Namkia, searched the whole of the store, the back hall and the bathroom systematically and chink by chink. I looked in and under everything. I opened jappas and boxes; I ran a torch-beam along the rafters; I stamped on the floor, to discourage anything underneath; I routed with a stick in the rat-runs at the foot of the walls; and all the time that wretched noise kept steadily and imperturbably on. At the end of half an hour's intensive hunting, I had found nothing. I left it still briskly scraping and went to bed.

The fifth and last visitation was, perhaps, the oddest.

The cook and the rest of the staff had gone to a village party, but Namkia remained behind on his usual bodyguard duty. We sat up talking by the fire, and it was perhaps eleven or after when we both heard a low murmur of voices in the cookhouse, which was at the bungalow end of the lines and only about twenty feet in a direct line from us. Namkia, saying he wanted to have a word with the cook, jumped up and went out by the back door, and I sat on waiting, listening half-consciously, for the sound of normal conversation, for obviously the cook and the others supposed me asleep, and had been whispering. But there was no sound, though the murmuring had now stopped; and there, all of a sudden, was Namkia back again, to say that the lines were in darkness and quite deserted, and that everything, the cookhouse included, was fast barred from the outside and just as it had been left. We looked at one another for a moment, in silence; and then, without comment, turned in.

There were no more manifestations after that inside the bungalow, but the phenomena continued in the lines for another month or so. They grew gradually less, however, at much the same speed as they had increased, until at the end of March they ceased entirely. They never recurred. I offer no explanation. We had rats before the spook appeared. Rats and rat-noises continued during its activities, but, as Namkia rightly claimed, they were distinct from it, either at once or upon investigation, and, when the ghost had vanished, rats and rat-noises unhappily remained. There was no child, servant or villager who was even a candidate for suspicion. To take the case most susceptible of human explanation, that of the voices in the cookhouse, when Namkia came out of the bungalow door a few seconds after hearing the voices, he overlooked, at once, the cookhouse, the lines, and the cleared belt between them and the scrub, for they lay below him and to the right. No one could have got out and reached cover in the time available, and still have left the doors fastened tight behind him with strings tied and heavy logs laid against them, as Namkia found them all. The time-factor still holds good for anyone standing outside the lines and not in them. The cleared belt was steep, wide and rough, and I do not think a running man could have got across it both unseen and unheard. Had an intruder, on the other hand, run back past the bungalow out of Namkia's sight, I, sitting there listening, would have heard him; bare feet running on hard ground are not noiseless.

The Nagas' own theory was that the spur was haunted ground in any case. Laisong used it before we came as a burial-ground in the case of suicides or other accursed deaths, and claimed that curious lights were often seen moving there in the small hours. It was generally thought that in building the camp we must have disturbed a burial, or that the arrival of human beings had unsettled the supernatural powers in occupation. Nor was there an adolescent with whom the phenomena could be connected. The nearest approach was Hozekiemba's thirteen-year-old son; but he only came to the camp at infrequent intervals, while the manifestations pursued their independent and very definite course.

There was a parallel in another Zemi poltergeist, that haunting, or reputed to haunt, the rest-house at Hangrum. This, a violent sprite, had, too, no apparent connection with any human being and manifested itself in a bungalow and out-buildings; once, when we were there, scaring the men severely. The bungalow caretaker and his family had had to leave the compound and settle outside, the creature's activities proving so frequent and such a nuisance. It was a ghost of long standing, and its occupation went back over ten years more. Yet, though I stayed at Hangrum a dozen times, I never heard or saw any of the reported phenomena and have never heard of any European who has. The bungalow was, it is true, a creepy place after dark. All bamboo houses let off raps and bangs as temperatures change at nightfall, but Hangrum would at times go off for minutes on end in a per-fect fusillade—so violent, one night, that the walls vibrated and the shotguns leaning in the corner clinked together. And Khamba, oddly enough, though he never turned a hair at

Laisong, bogy or no, would never on any pretext sleep in the bungalow at Hangrum. He howled and whined from dusk onwards, till sent away to sleep with the men in the lines.

We ourselves never saw any of the moving lights on the spur, but there was one instance where the villagers claimed to have seen them while we were there. In the small hours of a dark morning a group of bucks were sitting in the porch of the lower girls' dormitory, which affords, I'm told, a clear view over the camp. They suddenly saw a small light, which came up from the col, moved over the hill till it reached a point behind the bungalow and there vanished. Although Namkia in reporting this told me he did so because all the men were accounted for that night, I still think the true answer was someone returning from an assignation.

Another apparition was certainly earthly. I was away, Hozekiemba was in charge of the camp, and one night he called in the blacksmith—a skinny, impoverished man who often did odd jobs for us—to bear him company. To cheer the long evening, the smith went off to the village to fetch a pot of beer. He was on his way back with it and nearing the bungalow, when he almost collided with a dark form which rushed on him out of the night. He clutched the pot to him and ran like a deer for the lines, convinced that he had barely escaped the devil; and the fiend no doubt ran just as fast in the other direction, taking half a tin of my best white kerosine with him—the only theft ever made from the bungalow.

One other happening is perhaps worth mention, though still without explanation offered. It occurred some years later, during our spell with the guerilla forces.

Namkia went off one morning on leave, to spend a few days in his village. That afternoon his porter came hurrying back to say that Namkia's small son had cerebral malaria and that they needed the military doctor at once. The doctor was out on tour, but he was due the next day at a village one march on the far side of Impoi, so I picked a pair of the best runners in Laisong and sent them off to intercept him. At cockcrow, just before dawn, I woke up. I was lying there wondering what had roused me when I heard a man's voice in the death-cry, the terrible shrieks a Zemi gives when a death has just occurred. It was a long way off, I imagined among the houses at the top of the village, and I was surprised to hear it at all, as we knew of no one ill. Speculation was idle; so I turned over and went to sleep.

The next morning, when I inquired, the men were surprised. There had been no death in Laisong.

At noon my two runners returned, with the letter to the doctor undelivered. They had reached Impoi late at night and had halted in Namkia's house to wait for dawn. At cockcrow, however, the child had died.

CHAPTER XV

VILLAGE JUSTICE

I HAVE said that the Zemi virtually administered themselves. Take, now, the case of Samrangba, once my gardener.

He had had to go. I didn't mind him personally; he was a harmless kind of waster, meaning no ill, but somehow never there when he was wanted. Scolded, he plodded remorsefully back to the potatoes (which, being love-lorn at the time, he planted in heaps whose shape made Namkia laugh till he cried) and then, somehow, was just not there again. So, after repeated warnings, he was sacked, and his periwig hair-cut, his swagger and his serio-comic face were of the camp no more. He went off sadly enough, but I don't think he was really sorry. He'd made his pile, and it was in any case his uncle, that senile old ass of a headman—ex-headman, he was now—who had pushed him into it. He married on the strength of his savings and set up house, and all was peace and domesticity till autumn.

His wife, by then, was expecting her first child. The event was so imminent that she had gone back home to her mother, who also lived in Laisong, which left Samrangba ranging alone at large. This would not have mattered, had Samrangba only been more gifted with sense and continence; and one night he was on a drinking-bout with a few old friends—not that that in itself would have mattered either.

The tale takes up again in the early morning. It was not yet dawn, but the sky had begun to grey, and objects—houses, trees—were just visible against it. Two early-rising bucks were picking their way down the street towards the gate. Suddenly, as they went, they heard a shriek in the girls' dormitory; a confused clamour, a struggle, gasps and cries. Then the door burst open and a man broke out and fled. Then a girl ran out. She was crying. She hurried past them and disappeared, still weeping, among the houses opposite. The two boys looked at one another; and, chilled and shocked, they turned back and sat down in the lower morung to await events.

There was in the lower dormitory a pretty girl who had long refused Samrangba's advances. He had courted her, everyone knew, for a long time, and would much rather have had her than the girl he married. But she was the daughter of a prominent house whose standards were far superior to those of Samrangba, whose family's record, as well as his own, was unsavoury. More than that, she disliked him personally. She could not bear him. On this girl, asleep, Samrangba had now in a drunken burst attempted rape; and rape is one of the three capital crimes in the Zemi calendar.

After the brief commotion, the village was still. But, in the girl's house, a hastily-summoned meeting of her male relatives was cross-examining her. Had she ever encouraged Samrangba?—had she ever made him a hint, a half-promise? —for if she had, no case at all could lie. Her story, however, held. Her aversion to and refusal of Samrangba were common knowledge among the young people, and probably, for these things travel, with most of the village as well. Finally, the two bucks (who were found in the morung, knowing they would be called) gave clinching evidence of identity. The girl could only guess that it was Samrangba, by his build, his ornaments and his shock of hair, for, though she and the other girls had grappled with him, he had broken loose and run before they could see who it was. But the two young men had seen him. They were men of his own morung, and in no other circumstances would they have spoken against him; but the crime was one which broke both the tribal law and the code, the set of conventions, by which the young people everywhere conducted courtship; it was not merely a gross offence against morality, but a breach of trust and privilege. They made no bones about it, they told. Afraid, dishevelled, with uncovered face, they had seen him plainly. The raptor was Samrangba.

With the first light, when it was possible to move about easily, her kinsmen took their spears and went to kill him.

The morning sun came clear and cold into the bungalow bedroom. The sun wasn't over the Nenglo hill yet; time enough to move when it came. The air stirred gently in the veranda thatch, where the long straws hung down, loosened by the constant wind. There should be, soon, the scrape of the back door opening and the careful steps of Namkia approaching with the ritual cup of tea. And then, shrill, hideous, appalling, came the yells from the village.

I had never till then heard a Naga roused for blood. I leapt for the window, thrusting the shutter back. There wasn't a thing to be seen; only the village, quiet in the morning chill, the shadow still on it, the sunlight slipping slowly towards it down the hill behind. Then, up the narrow path which led from the water-point, came Hozekiemba, plodding, his black hair bobbing. I hailed him through the window.

'What's the matter?'

'Boy and girl talk!' said Hozekiemba briefly. 'Boy and girl talk!'

He vanished, striding, round the back of the house, and I fell into my clothes and went to look for Namkia. From time to time, a shock at each repetition, those horrible screeches came tearing through the air.

Namkia, it seemed, already knew the story. (He had never approved of Samrangba.)

The scene in the dormitory, the struggle and screams, had sobered up the boy. He ran for his life, aware, by that time, of what he had done. He hid himself somewhere in the surrounding woods, where a friend found him and warned him that the avengers were out. He ran then, ducking from cover to cover to reach the village, with the idea of taking sanctuary. He didn't, thank goodness, come into the camp. He picked the last house in the street, the one at the very bottom, and they took him in.

He reached it only a little ahead of the hunt. (That was when they began to yell, when they found him there.) They raced back, shrieking, up the street, to where his mother and younger brother, the boy Ningchangba, had barricaded themselves in the inner room. They tried to smash in the door; they put two spears through the outside wall; and would almost certainly have broken in and killed Ningchangba had they not been stopped by the headmen and village elders, who intimated that the case was now in official hands. Nevertheless, they ranged the village for most of the morning, screaming for blood, stabbing the ground, and shaking their spears like a mob of lunatics; shrieking threats, and challenging Samrangba's family, till a village meeting drew off all but the quite insane.

Meantime, in his protector's house, Samrangba was in the inner room. A ceremonial meal was cooked and served to him, as the formal seal of sanctuary. His host, and as many friends and kin as he could in the hurry collect, were standing sentry at both the entrances. An armed attack was perfectly possible, should feeling run really high; an attack which, having given sanctuary, they were bound to resist. In the morung, the village council was in emergency session.

At all costs bloodshed, and the resulting blood-feud, must be prevented. The headmen were not at the moment concerned with abstract justice. To them, the point of Samrangba's crime was that it had opened a rift in the village, a split which might, if action were not taken, destroy the community. He was the erring party; he must go—at least till tempers had cooled (which, among Nagas, can happen quickly) and the case could be temperately reviewed. His wife's family, since his own dared not appear, tried hard for a stay of execution on the grounds of her condition; but his offence was rank, and the council adamant. He had to go.

Just before noon, then, we saw from the camp a long file of armed men, neutrals recruited as a village police force, descending the steep street with his mother, brother and wife escorted between them. They halted opposite the bottom house. From the top of the street, by the upper morung, came the last few screams of the frustrated killers. Out from his refuge came a dumbly miserable Samrangba. He was moved into line, the escort closed up, and off they went, to take him four miles away, to safety in Kepelo—that useful Alsatia, which accepted exiles no reputable village would take. His wife and mother, loaded with pots and clothing, wailed aloud. The young Ningchangba, who had more nearly met death than his brother, was still white. Down the wide path the party trooped, in a long line, spears blinking in the sun; the four escorted figures were dark and obvious.

The ex-headman, Samrangba's uncle, was standing near me when we gathered at the foot of the path to see them go. He was weeping, and tears streamed down his crumpled old face.

'My boy, my boy!' he kept crying. 'That this should happen to my boy!'

Seeing me, Samrangba checked, and would have spoken. But the guard behind him took him by the shoulder and pushed him on, and he submitted and went. They filed away through the gate and down the steep drop outside, and the lamentations of the women grew fainter and fainter till the hill shut them off.

The next day, tempers had cooled. The village court had met and two years' banishment had been decreed. To my amazement, Samrangba walked openly into the camp that afternoon to see Namkia—sentenced and sacrosanct; back to collect his possessions.

CHAPTER XVI

THE LOST FOLK

ALL through the Barail area, tucked away behind ridges, on precipitous spurs, at the heads of hidden ravines, were the lost villages of a vanished people.

The Zemi said they were the relics of the jungle-folk, the Siemi, who had preceded them in the occupation of the country. Tradition had it that the Kacharis had wiped them out; certainly the sites were, one and all, in places easily concealed and easily defensible, and most of them had, on the one spur or neck by which they could be approached, double or triple ditches, banks, and even complicated defences and walls of dry stone. Whoever built those villages had enemies.

Small settlements, recognizable by their house-platforms, which, sometimes stone-faced, cropped out on otherwise smooth hillsides, were legion. The Asalu bridle-road crossed one a couple of miles from Laisong, and the Nagas could lead you, if your legs were equal to the slopes and your hide to the prickly jungle, to a dozen others within a day's march. But some of the larger sites were of more interest.

There was one in the Jiri valley, on a spur two miles to the south-east of Nenglo village, where a strongly-defended neck between two gullies led to a level ridge. On this, beside some denuded house-sites and a peculiar type of bamboo, the *gareo*, associated, for reasons never fathomed, with most of these remains, were two large slabs, apparently gravestones, of which the smaller bore several engraved designs. Some were probably phallic. The others were the curious, crude outlines of bare feet.

The large stone had been tilted up by a tree which grew, a good yard thick, almost from under it. A man could crawl by now into the cavity below, and men had, if report were true, for legend said that from this hole the 'Nagas of old' had fished out some of the old, dull-golden-yellow *deo-moni* beads, which were to them of such immense value; beads of unknown origin, which looked like stone, and were, so un-expectedly, of primitive glass; beads which were in themselves a major mystery. Namkia and every Zemi of consequence wore a string of them. They were heirlooms, handed down from father to son, and a good string might, at a conservative estimate, cost Rs 200/-.

Zemi tradition connected the beads very closely indeed with the lost race, though with what accuracy one could not say. It might merely have been a case of two mysteries com-bined, for convenience' sake. At any rate, the Zemi believe that the Siemi made the beads, and that a bamboo container full of them—a fortune at present-day rates—had been buried as part of every Siemi's grave-furniture, each household of the settlement contributing a share to the hoard. For this reason, they hold, the Siemi concealed their graves. Being great magicians, they either split rocks, placed their dead inside, and then sealed them up again; or by means of incanta-tion they caused great stones to fly from a distance and pile up over the grave, so that its exact position could not be found.

Now it is worth considering these two stories in connection with the two known classes of pre-Naga funerary monuments. The urns of Bolosan and its companion fields are stones whose purpose was most definitely to hold the dead. Is the story of the split rocks a garbled version of burial in the great stone urns? I never, after seeing the Siemi sites in the Barail area, had a chance to return to the western plateau and search for them there. The Western Zemi I questioned said that there were none; but it is still possible that sites exist. The western hills are far less thickly populated than the main Barail, and old sites by no means obvious, unless revealed in the course of cultivation. Certainly, since the urns are there, one would expect some pre-Naga settlements, and, whether they resemble those of the main Barail or not, their positions relative to the urnfields would be interesting.

There are, however, no urns at all in the Barail, the only area where, at present, pre-Naga settlements have been identified in North Cachar. The probable graves there are covered with large stone slabs, as at the site at Nenglo, at one at Khangnam, and at a third near Haijaichak. I think they could be found at others. Sites are many; and the dense reed-grass, the thick bush-jungle, hide, on an uncleared site, anything not big enough to stand above the layer of leaves and mould, and everything more than a foot or so from you. To crawl round a promising site which you cannot clear is agony, an investigator's hell. These flat slabs, then, might perhaps be the 'stones which flew from a distance' and 'covered the whole grave up'. Not likely; but just possible. To those who would like a gauge for Naga tradition, with its wonderful gift for noting the salient fact and then providing a wholly marvellous explanation, I would quote just this. The first time that Nagas saw Europeans to any extent, and in any number, was the bustle's heyday. In 1940 it was still their fixed belief, an unshakable fact, that all white people had tails and wore clothes to hide them.

To return again to the question of ancient beads. The stories of these being found on the sites are most persistent. During my stay at Laisong Namkia acquired from the Kukis of Padhekot, where there is a well-known Siemi settlement, a string of quite undoubted *deo-moni*, which the seller claimed had been turned up one by one in cultivating over the old house-platforms. I am bound to say that their dull, rather brown appearance was consistent with this. Beads always in wear have a fine, high, greasy gloss. Namkia later sold them for Rs 40/- to a Hangrum man, I being far too broke at the time to buy them, as I wanted to do; and later on when I had the money, the owner would not sell. Their value as a specimen would have been greater had there been any valid evidence of their connection with a Siemi site; but even without they would have been of interest as *deo-moni*, which are by no means easy to buy.

About a quarter-mile east of Hange village, on one of those spurs which jut out from the steep Barail where it runs, like a black wall, directly above the railway, was another site. This was, perhaps, the most inexplicable of the lot. A narrow alley, twenty yards long and winding gently in the shape of a reversed S, started for no particular reason on the lip of a gully, ran down its outer slope, and ended, equally baldly, on the edge of a round, flat pan which suggested a dried pool.

The alley was two feet deep and two wide; it was walled
and paved with stone slabs, uncut, but set to form a smooth
face; and heaps of rubble along its lip suggested that walls
had once risen on either side of it above the ground. A few
worn house-platforms, a long way off up the hill, and more
traditions of the Siemi than anywhere else, were all that Hange
could provide as allied remains. The alley, they said, was
once a walled and roofed path down which the daughters of
Thang-grung the Siemi King came unseen to draw water.
But where the king and his daughters lived or why the
hidden path should begin so unaccountably some ten feet
down on the wrong side of a steep slope, were matters on
which tradition was silent. We searched, scrambling and
crawling, for an hour or more through the surrounding jungle,
Namkia commenting crisply, as usual, on my perverse insanity; and we left the alley as isolated, as inexplicable a relic
as when we came.

Hange had, too, an interesting story, echoed elsewhere,
that when the Zemi came they found a handful of Siemi
survivors with whom they intermarried. And it was in the
Asalu group next door—if anywhere—that one could find the
clearest traces of the ancient tribe. Not merely in the major
remains, the stone outwork and the huge settlement which
lay a mile from the village on the hill called Chilei, but in
the village itself, where there still survived a markedly negrito
type.

Its members were, of course, all Nagas in name and descent.
Nor was the type confined to the Asalu group. It could occur,
and did, in other Zemi villages, and in other Naga tribes.
But nowhere in the Zemi area did it appear in such a concentration, or in such purity, as at that time could be seen
in Impoi. In a village of light-brown complexions, straight
hair, and near-Mongol faces, the dark skins, steep foreheads,
thick lips, and above all, frizzy hair, were most conspicuous,
and when all these features met, as they sometimes did, in
an individual, the effect was startling.

The Asalu sites, the largest and most remarkable in the
district, lay almost due south of the village, on the Barail
ridge.

One climbed up to them from the bridle-road, through thick woods. At the top of the slope one bumped suddenly into stone walls, mounds, ditches; clumps, for no reason, of the odd *gareo* bamboo. Then you saw that the ridge was crowned by a square stone fortification—at first sight square; for, on investigation, the walls died out on slopes, in jungles of creeper, in cane-brakes through which not even a Naga could cut, and the plan which, accurately, one could put down on paper was only a fraction of what had been there on the ground, of what could still be hinted at and surmised.

Inside the double set of walls and ditches were more hummocks, more walls, lost, now, in a tangle of forest. Tucked in one corner, the south-west—if you risked a fall and clambered and crawled and clawed your way there through thorns and bushes and over the pits and screes of the tumbled masonry, all dry-stone work—was an oval pit; and out of this, on the north-east side, there opened at a higher level a curious, stone-walled lane, which, crossing the spur, became on the far side an unwalled shelf as broad and as made as a modern bridle-road. At the edge of the wood it stopped, destroyed by slips, for the hill was grassy and steep; but there was no doubt where it led. It pointed directly down to the second site.

By climbing a short way up the hill one could see below, in the thick, deciduous forest, great clumps of a lighter growth —*gareo* bamboo. A strange companion, this, of the Siemi sites; explained by the Naga legend, but fitting in no way into soberer archæology; and yet so often there that we used, when searching for a reported site, to look first for *gareo*. If we happened to find it, then sure as fate the remains would be somewhere near. If we did not, the search was that much more difficult; and the site, when found, was likely to be an uninhabited one, such as the fort or the alley. The *gareo* mostly appeared on the old settlements. It was so here; the ravine where the remains lay was thick with forest, and only from the *gareo*, so clearly visible from the opposite hill, could we find the site in the first place.

It was the biggest Siemi settlement we saw anywhere, an enormous village. There must have been, in all, between one and two hundred houses—as big as any Zemi site, old or new. In many places the stone facings to the house-platforms still survived. They cropped out here and there in the grass and bushes; on the steeper slopes, they might be ten feet high. The site lay spread round the head of a valley, concealed, but not defended. Perhaps the stone outwork on the ridge above was its sole protection. We found no other; and the Asalu men, who had seen the area cleared and under cultivation, said definitely that there was none. But there was, through the very middle of the village site, a deep ditch. It was a shallow gully sharply deepened (you could see the point at which the cut began) till, when men had done their work and the Rains had improved it, a twenty-foot chasm, a Devil's Dyke, divided the two halves of the ancient village. And no one could tell us why.

Now for the Naga legend.

The Siemi were, it is said, an uncanny race—magicians, 'small and dark'. They lived in the forested hills; and, by a secret process involving the use of fire, made precious *deomoni*, the 'spirit-beads', from slender, carefully-cultivated *gareo* bamboo.

One day, when the Siemi of a village near the present Guilong were making beads, the smoke of their fires poured up in such a volume, a smoky haze, that it was seen by the Kacharis in Maibong below. The King, his curiosity roused, sent men into the unknown hills to find out what was burning. When they came back with a group of captured Siemi, the King demanded who and what they were. They answered that they were a jungle-people; that they did not live by digging or cultivation, but that they made, and traded, the yellow beads, and from these derived a living. At this, the King insisted they tell him the process. The Siemi refused.

The King, in a royal fury, then ordered a metal pot to be made red-hot. He had it set on the head of one of the prisoners, and kept it there till the man's skull burst. Then he turned to the others, and, on pain of a similar fate, again demanded the secret. But he could not daunt the Siemi. Each clamoured to be the first to suffer. And so, horribly, one after another, they died without revealing a word.

Then the King, determined to have the process, sent men out again and again to hunt down the jungle-folk. By every torture, by every horror he could devise, he tried, from each successive batch of prisoners, to drag the precious information. But his victims died infuriatingly dumb, and the few survivors fell back into the hills, concealing their settlements, hiding farther from the Kachari grasp, until at last there were no more; and the Nagas filled their place.

The Kacharis have their own version of the story. So far as I know, it does not mention the beads. The little people were a nuisance; that was all. And so they wiped them out. One can think of parallels. A handful, though, concealed themselves in a cave. From that they came out at night to raid and loot Kachari settlements, returning home before daylight, like bats, to their lair. At last, however, the Kacharis tracked them down. They did not attempt to attack the cave, a deep, defensible tunnel. Instead, they cut great armfuls of scrub and brushwood, filled up the cave-mouth with it, and fired the whole. So the last of the jungle-people perished, suffocated, in their last retreat.

Naturally, ever since the area had been administered the story had attracted the attention of officers. Almost everyone who served there, I think, had tried to find the cave, but without success; either the cave was there, and the Kacharis would not tell the secret; or, as was often claimed, an earthquake had shaken down the cliff and closed the cave for good. But still one kept on wondering—was it there?

In 1945 Mr Perry, then S.D.O. at Haflong, met, on one of his tours in the Kachari country, an elderly villager who said he knew the secret of the cave. It still existed, he said, and he himself had been there as a boy. It was superstitious fear—fear, probably, of the ghosts of the slaughtered Siemi—which had for so long kept its whereabouts a mystery. Indeed, no man had entered it from the day of the massacre.

It lay, he said, in the side of a hill to the west of the railway-line, between Haflong and Mahur stations. It was in dense forest, and quite invisible unless one knew the trick. The entrance was some way up from the ground and concealed by the upper part of a big tree growing in front of it; only by climbing up could the mouth be seen. Once there, it was quite accessible, and there should be no trouble in getting in, were one inclined to do so. He personally had never been farther than the mouth. He had peered in with his two companions (one a Naga) but they had no lights, and were much too scared to enter. He felt, he said, that the old things were now dying. Nobody really cared for the old traditions. However, Perry was a kindly officer and genuinely interested in the old beliefs. These he respected, and he never attempted to remove the relics. Therefore this old villager wanted to show him the cave while there was still time.

Perry, in great excitement, let me know. It was the chance of a lifetime. An expedition was prepared, a date was fixed; and just before it the old man fell ill with malaria.

There was a postponement. The weeks dragged on. The man was a little better; then he relapsed, and was ill again. Perry went down to see him. There seemed little doubt that his wish to reveal the secret was perfectly genuine. Unable to come himself, he sent his son, and swore that the boy knew the place as well as he. Path-cutters were mobilized, they and the boy were sent out, and with ropes and lamps we stood by for operations as soon as they reported success.

But either the cave was in truth lost, or, more probably, the young man would not take the responsibility of telling. It was all right for his father, not long for this world, and more or less exempt from tribal reprisals. The first party returned after a mere day's walking, and were chased out again by the indignant Perry. This time they were gone longer; but returned again to say they could not find it. Would not, was, perhaps the better phrase. And a few days later, the old man, who alone could have settled the matter, quietly died.

The problem still remains. Does the cave exist, with the relics of the jungle-people, their weapons, their pots and tools, their beads, and, for the physical anthropologist, their skulls and skeletons? Or did an earthquake truly bring down the hillside over the cave in the half-century since the old man's boyhood visit? The facts as we know them fit both theories; and which is the answer only God and the Kacharis know.

CHAPTER XVII

FIRE, FIRE!

THE camp's position on an open spur, with a grassy cliff below it and an open valley in front, had certain very obvious advantages from the point of view of light, air and space; but it had one major disadvantage—the danger from grass fires. We found this out our very first spring there.

Much of the Zemi country, whose natural vegetation was certainly forest, had, by over-cultivation, been reduced to grass; and not for nothing did every village on an exposed site have a thick belt of woodland round it. In the late spring, tinder-dry weather combined with high winds to make deadly danger, and it was no uncommon thing then to see a whole village's possessions, most of them shut up in stout cane jappas, standing or heaped in some comparatively safe place on the edge of the site for days on end.

The risk was first borne in on us when Laisong had a scare. The drums were beaten—the emergency signal, to call the men back from the fields—and, in a fever of ant-like activity, men cut firebelts in the ravine below, women and girls ran scurrying down with water, old men evacuated the valuables and livestock, and the most complete alarm and confusion reigned for the rest of the afternoon. I inquired, a little tentatively, whether our spur was safe.

'Oh!' said the headman cheerfully. 'The flames go sweeping right over it every year!'

The obvious course, on that, was to cut a firebelt. The trouble was the cliff. One could only get down to cut for thirty yards, and after this, though a boy could clamber down, and the whole of the slope was covered in grass and scrub, inflammable as they come, the ground was too steep for a man to stand and work. When the men had cut the scrub by hand as far as they could, we held a consultation. It was decided we'd have to burn off the cliff. So operations were suspended till sundown, when the wind was likely to drop, and when the men of the village would be there; and we started to carry water and prepare wet sacks.

Sunset found us ready. Some twenty men of the village had come to help. Two were perched on top of the bungalow ridge, armed with wet sacks and ready to beat out sparks; two or three more were astride the men's lines. The main body was massed with fire-brooms in front. On the right flank, towards the village, Zhekhuingba the caretaker and his two sons presided over the water—several buckets, some bamboo tubes, and a tin bath. The wind had dropped, dusk was falling, and all was still. Namkia looked at me. I nodded. Old Hozekiemba went running off to fire the foot of the hill.

For a disappointingly long time, several minutes, in fact, nothing happened. Then the air in front of us began to quiver. Whorls and vortices appeared. The hills beyond, still in the afterglow, dissolved in a thin film of coppery smoke. Specks of ash and dry leaf came up, dancing. There was a dull murmur, the coppery smoke increased.

'It's coming,' said Namkia.

And by gosh, it did.

We had not reckoned on the cliff, a good hundred feet of it, creating its own draught. With a whoof like an explosion, a roar like the Day of Judgement, a sheet of flame rushed boiling in front of us into the evening sky. I saw the men in the firebelt running for safety, little black specks against the scarlet wall. Then Namkia grabbed my arm and I turned to face the bungalow. The whole was bathed, was bright with a fiery glow; snowstorms of sparks were falling on the bone-dry thatch; the men on the ridge were flailing away like maniacs; and as I looked up, I saw the tip of the great flame, wind-blown, curving directly above us and twenty feet over our heads.

'The house—the house!' Namkia was shouting. I could hardly hear him through the bellow of the flames. 'There isn't a chance—we've got to get the kit out!'

We had to a certain extent put things together, but they were by no means packed. We raced into the house, where, as usual, the lamps had been lit and the table laid for dinner —an incongruously ordered and tidy scene; we flung books, clothes, papers, cameras and bedding higgledy-piggledy into baskets and boxes. Ramzimba, the caretaker's eldest son, dashed in after us, his face white. He snatched up each bale as we threw it across and rushed with it to a dump in the wet scrub behind. Chairs, tables and beds we hurled out any-how, as they were, Ramzimba bolting out last with a bundle of spears, and Namkia and I went into the veranda.

The fire was in full fury. It was, in spite of the danger and the imminent risk that we should lose the camp, a marvellous sight. The whole space between rail and eaves, where nor-mally one looked out at stars and a dark valley, framed a rushing, pouring, licking wall of rosy-copper. The roar was incredible. The flames must have been forty or fifty feet high. Sparks and burning leaves were spattering like hail on the veranda matting, and we stamped and stamped, Namkia regardless of his bare feet, till Ramzimba came back and began to beat them out with a piece of sacking. Then I ran out by the back door to see the lines.

Rows of black figures, beating and gasping, were on the roof-ridges. Others, like imps in hell, dashed about below, carrying goods to safety, hauling water, or flinging up new-damped sacks to the men above. Tongues of fire were licking over our heads as the wind caught the monstrous flames. I saw the men on the bungalow wince and duck when one bent down and snapped within ten feet of them. I looked to see the bungalow go in a matter of seconds. And over it all there was a red snowstorm, a whirling shower of burning debris. It swept in tourbillions over our heads, in glowing, dust-devils which broke and fell; and, where the air was stiller, it floated down like a cloud of crimson blossom, dim and soft.

Then, at that critical moment, the water ran out. I heard the men on the roofs begin to yell. They had been sprinkling the thatch, which otherwise would have caught, and now it was dry and the flames were leaning over. I fled at the nearest figures, grabbed them, pushed, shouting: 'Water, water!' Namkia was doing the same. They heard us, turned and sprinted. All in a moment, everything was redoubled—it was like a movie trick-shot, when everything goes twice as quick. And just then, the cook saved the house. A spark fell on the back porch, caught. A small flame stood up. The cook, who alone was tall and near enough to see it, gripped the edge of the main thatch, jumped, hung for a second, and beat at it with his hand. A smack or two—it was gone, and he tumbled down, gangling, long, unhappy, and wrought-up nearly to tears. I sent him off to sit on the baggage and watch.

The water came. And as it did, for no particular reason the fire-wall fell. It lost a third of its height, it veered off; the shower of crimson sparks almost ceased, and what remained was falling outward now, on the uncut jungle beyond the camp perimeter. The men on the ridges sagged. On the ground, the black, sweating, exhausted figures sat down where they were, with sacks and buckets beside them, and stared at the receding fire.

It must have found at that moment a clump of dry brush, a patch of elephant-grass. There was a violent crackle. The flames shot up. They towered, boiling, in licking dragon-tongues, in a whirling column of sparks. A small night wind had got up. It breathed across the hill. The flaming tower tilted, bent; and it and its pillar of sparks swept down on the old hen-house.

We heard, above the roar, the shrieks of the forgotten geese.

I shouted for help and sped like a thing demented down the narrow passage at the foot of the garden. The sparks were hailing. I beat them out of my hair, was aware of the flames over me, and dived, in eddies of smoke, into the old shed. The two geese, flapping with terror, dashed under the broad bench. As I ducked after them, I dimly perceived that someone had followed me in. I grabbed the gander; the goose flew screaming out and was seized and removed by my unknown helper. The gander, apart from a startled flap, gave no trouble. I tucked him under my arm and fled, one hand over my head, and the sparks catching my shirt.

Before me, in the long passage, I saw the cook. He was running as hard as he could in his tight *lungi*. It was he who had followed me in and saved the goose. He had her clasped to his chest; and her large wings, flapping with agitation, waved on either side of him, as though he were an angel with a tractor air-screw. We threw the geese into the cookhouse, where they were moderately safe; and all sat down on the turf to watch the hen-house go.

But it didn't. The flames, an instant before they took it, bowed aside. They fell, they flagged. In half an hour, only a dull glow down the slope of the hill showed where the last fire was burning out in the jungle.

And, no one could tell us why, the camp still stood.

CHAPTER XVIII

THE FIRST RAINS

IT began to rain that year, 1941, on May 7th. From that day till the first week in September there was hardly a break at all. Twice, only, I saw Nenglo on the opposite hill.

Day and night, mist swept up out of the valley. Standing exposed as it did, the bungalow took the full blast of the south-west monsoon; for weeks at a stretch we couldn't open the front doors for the rain which drove against them. Cloud filtered through the walls and damped everything. Mould spread greenly over books, clothes, furniture, all I had; and I spent my days in the small space under the windows, where at least there was light to read.

I turned to recording folk-lore, for which there had hardly been the time before. Namkia himself had a fair collection of stories, but when I had pumped him dry there were only a few examples to be had in Laisong—just two or three good beast-tales from a junior headman. I collected one vivid Naga story, with the true ring and tone of old Zemi life in it, from Hangrum; and with that, the immediate neighbourhood seemed to be exhausted.

Then Namkia brought in a man from Impoi.

He was elderly, poor, and, I imagine, rather shiftless, but he was the nearest thing to a professional story-teller the area possessed. I wished to take down the Asa-Munsarung cycle, a vast corpus of linked stories about those two familiar figures of Naga tales, the clever trickster and his simple friend. The Impoi man sat down by my hearth and day after day for three weeks he dictated the cycle. Never, before or since, have I heard such crisp and lucid Zemi spoken. I could take the material down on the typewriter as he talked, without preliminary transcription. He was superb as a story-teller. The stress, the balance, the skilled suspense, and particularly the use of rhythm and repetition, were the very voice of folk-lore. One who has merely read such stories and never heard them told, knows only the shell. The eye slips too quickly over the printed page, missing the *leit-motifs*, the subtle variations and harmonies, of which a teller and hearer are so keenly aware. Written folk-tales are to the spoken as a musical score is to a full performance.

Since the Rains are always the sickly season, there was a great deal else to do besides taking notes. I had run a dispensary at Laisong from the beginning, for it was much the best way of winning confidence. At first they only came with infected cuts, days, weeks, even, after the initial injury. But, in time, they realized the value of first aid; and when they did, it became routine for men to arrive panting and dripping blood in the front veranda, have a gash dressed, and trot off again to resume their field-work, which might be anything up to a mile away. Quinine they wanted too, for malaria was rife, but in all other illnesses they preferred their magico-religious ceremonies. I am bound to say that the only time that one was done for me, it was an immense success. I went to bed a groaning cripple, and I got up and walked next day.

We were weeding the spinach, Hozekiemba and I, and when we reached the end and I straightened up, my knee went suddenly click. The cap had slipped, an abrupt and complete disaster. With Namkia's help I just reached the bungalow. The knee swelled as I watched it; it hurt like sin. There wasn't a doctor for miles. I strapped it up with elastic plaster to hold it still, and then, in pain and despair, I went to bed.

The staff gathered round me in grave concern. They wanted to fetch a skilled Zemi to manipulate it, but I refused. There was nothing else that I myself could do. The only thing left, then, was an appropriate sacrifice.

They fetched a dao and a piece of ginger and old Hozekiemba sat down to divine the trouble.

Now ginger, the Zemi say, is the one instrument of divination the great healer Herakandingpeo had time to reveal before the spirits killed him; for spirits live by eating the souls of men, and as they eat, so the body wastes with sickness; and Herakandingpeo, by his marvellous skill, was robbing them of every soul they seized. The spirits therefore killed him by a trick and took care that he passed his knowledge to none—only the few words concerning ginger survived, whispered to his youngest son in the last few seconds, when the boy, misled by the spirits before, arrived at last.

Old Hozekiemba cut the ginger in half. He laid the two halves carefully on the flat of the dao, and then addressed them.

'O ginger! Tell us the truth and do not lie. Of old, men turned to you for truth, and so do we now. Is it black magic which has attacked our mother? If so, then come down odd; if not, then even.'

With that, he tossed the ginger up from the dao. Both halves fell the same way, with the cut side down—that is, they were even. Black magic was eliminated. He took the pieces up and started again. At the end of fifteen minutes of trial and error we learned that an evil spirit had seized on me in the garden, and would, in return for a cock, release its hold.

Namkia went off at once to fetch a suitable bird and call the village priest. He found the bird, but the priest was not available, so he returned with the old ex-headman, Samrangba's uncle. Like many elders, he earned extra income by performing such minor ceremonies for the sick.

The house was cleared. The old man, accompanied by a helper with rice and beer, came in and settled down at the living-room hearth. He first offered the cock, with invocations, to the offending spirit. Then he killed and cooked it. A few scraps of the liver, with a little rice, were laid on a leaf plate and set out for the spirit. Then some similar scraps were given to me. Next a libation of beer was poured for the spirit. Some more, in a leaf cup, was handed to me. Lastly, the old man rose and pronounced a blessing. The ceremony, he told me, had been correctly done; I should most certainly be cured. Then he went off home, his friend following with their joint perquisites, the rest of the food and beer, and left me feeling not one jot worse or better.

As I turned painfully over in the small hours of the morning, my knee gave a click and went back. I could limp about next day.

It may, of course, have been the elastic plaster. But I never tried to tell the Zemi that.

CHAPTER XIX

DOGS, SNAKES AND LEOPARDS

THE animal kingdom was always well represented in life at the camp.

First of all, of course, there was my dog Khamba himself. Then came his two wives, Lassu and Nagi; Lassu arrived as a tired little thing with the same Tangkhul dog-pedlar who sold me Khamba, and Nagi I inherited from a guerilla officer. She was heralded by a signal describing her as 'bitch with escort' and everyone in Haflong made facetious remarks about it for weeks. Then there were waves of pups, who rolled and staggered and growled and yelled, chewed the furniture and slept on the bed, until they were given away and peace returned; but they were pets as babies, with their fat, white, pudgy paws.

Considering that we lived in a semi-tropical climate we were really very fortunate with snakes. There were, it is true, two hamadryads which nested in the bamboos at the foot of the hill, a few yards from the main path to Laisong; but the villagers used to put up a knot of grass and a railing there during the nesting season, to warn pedestrians against stray-ing; and we never bothered them or they us. The only snake of which the Nagas were really in awe was, strangely enough, the python, and that was a superstitious fear and not a physical one.

Once upon a time, in the very beginning, the great spirit Bangklawong—who was at that time king of all things on earth—had a sister. Miraculously conceiving, she went away to the source of the Barak River, and there in the dark jungle at the foot of a waterfall, she gave birth to seven eggs. One by one, after she had left them, six spirits hatched out. Only the seventh egg remained; and when they had waited a long time and nothing had happened, they decided among themselves that it must be addled and pushed it down into the running water. Then they went away to find their mother.

When she saw them, and learned there was no seventh, she wept and wailed and tore her hair and lamented, crying: 'Alas, alas! Oh, for my youngest child! He would have been the best, the greatest, the wisest of you all!'

But the seventh egg hatched out in the deep river, and out of it came the python.

The Zemi believed that the creature could draw men down by magic into the water and there drown them. Several deep pools on neighbouring rivers were supposed to be pythons' lairs; there was one where the gorge began below Laisong, and another, against which I was always warned, right down on the lower Jenam below Baladhan. There a grey rock overhung deep, golden-green water, and it would have been a perfect diving-pool. The Zemi wouldn't hear of it. If I even walked too close to the edge to look over, watching the fish down there in the lovely, lucent cool, anxious voices behind me would call me back.

The python's markings, too, were believed to have significance. One of the few men left who were skilled in their reading was Zuingpeo, Namkia's maternal uncle, a delightful old gentleman of Impoi. The only person who had recently divined from a free and living python, he had met one on the Impoi path some time in 1940. In accordance with the Zemi belief that the python understands human speech, he asked it to stop, which it did. He then examined its markings, judged therefrom the coming luck of the village, told the python to go, and went home himself. But the Zemi had an even odder ceremony than Zuingpeo's simple encounter. Young men used to bring in python alive.

Namkia, as a buck, had helped to carry one in. He had taken the head, the post of honour, and so was able to give a complete account. When a python is found, all dogs must be taken away and weapons hidden. The sight of either infuriates the snake. The bucks then move in close to it, the leader telling it that they wish to take it up to the village for everyone to admire. When he has finished his speech, they step up alongside it, one to the head, one to the tail, and one in the middle. The leader drops a stick across the neck and holds it down tightly, while the other two seize the body and stretch it out. That done, they lift it up and over their shoulders, and off they go with it slung between them like a length of cable. The buck in the middle has the easiest time. The lad at the back has the tail twisting all round him, the boy in front has the head against his cheek—and the tongue, Namkia said, never stops flickering the whole time. To the clothes of all of them, and to their bodies, there clings a horrid and peculiar smell which they cannot wash away for days after.

Somewhere on the way up to the village they stop and make a patch of soft earth. They draw the snake across this and then go on. In the morning they all come down to look, and by the marks in the earth they know their fortunes—a girl's footprints, success in love; a tiger's pugs or a bear's prints, success in hunting.

On arrival in the village, the python is taken straight to the bucks' own morung. They have already announced what they carry by a special chant, and half the village will be there to see them come in. The python is released, and for half an hour or so allowed to slither at large about the hall and in among the spectators. During this lull, the old men—if there are any present who have the skill—look at the markings and foretell the future. Then a man chosen for the job comes up to the python slowly, a dao carefully concealed behind his back. At the last moment he whips this out and strikes off the snake's head at a blow. The tip of the tail is also cut off, and put with the head on one of the morung benches; the body remains on the floor, writhing slowly, the bloom dying on the gorgeous scales, for two hours or more. Its flesh is finally eaten by the old men, the only people to whom it is not taboo, and the skin is hung up in the morung porch as a trophy.

Occasional snakes, often but not invariably harmless, used to fall in the hot weather out of the bungalow rafters or hide themselves in holes about the place, but only once or twice were the encounters alarming. I was one day picking dead blooms off the zinnias in the little strip of flower-bed along the garden fence. The men loved flowers for their ears. Bathed and arrayed, they would wander at four o'clock along the bed, matching scarlet here with yellow there, and a touch of white to set the whole thing off, fitting the final bouquet— with squeezings and stretchings, and screwings-up of the face —into a distended earlobe. I grew cannas there, scarlet and yellow for them, and pinks and whites and flame-colours to please myself, with a front line of zinnias and white verbena. I was, as I have said, picking dead blooms off the zinnias, a thing Hozekiemba never troubled to do, when all of a sudden there was a sharp twitch, a smooth ripple, close by my hand, and I leapt a good yard and shouted for Namkia.

He came running, armed with a large hoe. I backed off out of the way, to the bungalow wall. He tiptoed carefully up till he found the snake—a long pit-viper, wound well into the clump—swung up the hoe, and brought it down in the most imperial welt, destroying the corner zinnia completely. As he swung it up again for a second blow, I saw the live and lashing remains of the snake fly off the blade and shoot through the air towards me. It was coming straight for my face—I hadn't time to duck. It hit the wall with a crack a foot from my head and fell on the ground, writhing. I made for the step and sat down: Namkia, when he came across, was most intrigued. Had it hit and bitten me, he remarked, it would have been a most unusual accident. He was quite proud, in a way, that he had nearly caused it.

Of all our local animals, far and away the most notable was the leopard. What happened when it met the Army, though, must be told in the proper place.

It had its lair somewhere in the rocks of the upper gorge, in the deep cleft down behind us. It once mauled Lassu, and we were lucky to get her back. The pigs and dogs of Laisong were its nearest prey; its nightly route to the village lay over the spur, and sooner or later, as the jungle grew up, it took the short cut through the camp itself. When the major incidents occurred, however, I think the beast had been hurt in a Kuki trap and was lying up in the scrub on the spur itself.

The first of us to see it was Monsieur Coty, who was the face-powder-coloured kitchen cat. He shot into the lines one night through the cookhouse drain with such a violence that he left fur on the top edge; took a flying leap straight on to the cook's bed; and dived under the clothes with uncatlike noises. The cook, whose close companion he was, immediately realized that he had met a leopard. For all I know, they spent the night shivering together under the bedclothes.

The first human contact with the beast was made by Hozekiemba two nights later.

It was just growing dark, the hour when all was usually most quiet, when the whole camp was electrified by four shrieks, each one louder and nearer. Then came the most infernal hubbub of lights and voices. Ramgakpa was serving dinner (Namkia was away) and he dumped the dishes and I my spoon and we both leaned out of the windows and called for an explanation. There was a long lag before we even managed to make ourselves heard; and then two or three people answered together: '*Makao, makao!*'

(That means 'Something, something!' If you ever mention a great cat in his hearing, he comes to take you.)

We continued to dangle out for a minute or so, waiting to hear the story; and then we saw the staff in a body come over, with all the lamps, spears and daos the lines could muster and poor old Hozekiemba, gasping and stuttering, in their midst.

He, it appeared, had gone to the jungle in the course of nature. Though it was almost dark, he was not alarmed when he heard a gentle rustle coming towards him, supposing it merely to be a belated pig. But, to his alarm, the bushes suddenly parted; and out within fifteen feet of him stepped a full-grown leopard, which stopped in some annoyance, and stood there as disconcerted as Hozekiemba himself, for it had apparently mistaken him for a grazing goat. For a few seconds they both stayed still. Then the old man rose and ran shrieking for camp; and the leopard, presumably, slipped back disappointed into cover.

The very next evening the cook was taking a breath of air at dusk. There was, beyond the garden, the run and hen-house. Glancing at this, he noticed a village dog, some miserable yellow cur, creeping up belly-flat on robbery bent. He picked up a pebble, and running, flung it as hard as he could at the dim, grey blotch. The blotch stood up as the leopard and walked away.

Two nights after this, Ramgakpa was on bodyguard-duty, Namkia being still on leave. As we sat by the fire after dinner, we suddenly heard, in the stillness, a click of gravel outside. Then, quite clearly, came the low, coughing grumble of a leopard talking to itself. Twice round the house it went, close up to the walls, and then we heard it no more. But it wasn't nice to hear. We were alone in the camp. The others were in the village. There wasn't a gun in the place, and very few spears. Nor do well-mannered leopards which mean no harm walk round and round houses and grumble —the odds were that it was a wounded animal, hungry, and with a mind to break in. It wasn't a pleasant thought.

A few days later Namkia came back from leave and flatly refused to believe in the leopard at all. I could only hope he'd meet it, and face to face.

It wasn't Namkia, though, that the leopard met.

One night I, like the gardener, had cause to go down the hill on my affairs. I took the long way round by the front of the house. The path ran level at first, and then turned right, and the small latrine was some yards down the slope. I had reached the turn when I saw, or thought I saw, something ahead. There was a half-moon to confuse the issue, and the slope was dotted with shrubs and tufts of grass. But I was almost sure there was something there, a kind of grey shadow of a shadow, hunched half-way down the path and ten yards from me. I had no torch, and only a hurricane lamp; and as I hesitated, I suddenly saw that the shadow was looking at me with large, green, luminous eyes.

'Now,' I thought. 'If that's the leopard, and it should charge, I've had it. I can't do anything but throw the lamp and scream. If, though, I give a yell and run from a village goat, I'll never live it down. I must have a look.'

With that, I hove up the light. The two great shining eyes went out like lamps. The shadowy blot swung round. It slid away, with an indefinable, flattened cattiness, along the path to the edge of the bushes. There it turned, stood up to its full height—it was a big leopard—gave me a long, green glare, and went like a ghost.

I stood where I was and shouted for Namkia. He was a

good way off down the village path, in conversation, and shouted back: 'Hold on!' He came up, strolling gently, some minutes later, and found me still waiting and watching the edge of the scrub.

'My sister, what's the matter?'

'I saw green eyes.'

He stiffened.

'One eye, or two?'

'Two.'

'If it was one eye,' he said, with emphasis, 'it was a demon. If it was two, then it was a leopard. And either way you're safer in the house!'

Grabbing me by the shoulder, he spun me round, rushed me before him up the stony path, thrust me indoors, barred everything fast behind us, and slept with his spear beside him all that night.

It was perhaps three nights later that we had the last alarm. He and I were sitting by the fire, gossiping, when we broke off as though shot. Outside, in the long veranda, we heard the slow, cantering pace of some big beast travelling down the length of it, *lumpety-bump, lumpety-bump*. He leapt for a spear, and I for the flashlight. It was opposite the bedroom door now. Cloth thrown off, muscles tense, spear ready, he slowly opened the door a fraction, while I stood close behind him and shone the beam through the chink.

There, in the circle of white light, was a large rat (*lumpety*) fleeing full speed from a pursuing Coty (*bump*).

CHAPTER XX

THE LAND AND THE PEOPLE

Although I lived at Laisong, most of my staff and friends came from the Asalu group. This was dwindling fast, but was the best and kindest community in the Barail.

First there was Namkia's Impoi, up the hill. It perched on a ridge with a wild background of peaks behind it, a grandly theatrical setting. The Chiku ravine, a black and eerie cleft, cut so closely under the village that you could almost toss a stone down into the gulf. A multitude of water-demons and beasts of the night could have laired in the cold Chiku. On the other side, foothills and hazy plains were spread away like a blurred green carpet, and sometimes far to the north above the dun dust-cloud covering the Assam Valley, one saw the snow-peaks of the Himalayas. Impoi was cool. Day in, day out, a wind came down from the hill and kept the thatch of Namkia's morung rustling. It wasn't a big building, as morungs go, for Impoi hadn't the manpower for major works, but it was a *kamarum-ki*, a house put up at a feast of social merit, and conferred a definite status on Namkia. *Kamarum-ki* was a house of the lower grade. *Hekwi-ki* was the upper, to which Namkia, having done the first, could go on, but the building ceremonies cost a thousand rupees and nobody was rich enough to perform them now. Since the last specimen fell down some years previously there wasn't a single *hekwi-ki* in North Cachar—even the ceremonies were being forgotten.

The other Impoi morung lay down the street. Beyond it, the track crossed the stone sill of the old walls—the steep and narrow gate, its once-precipitous steps now a rain-worn gully, lay in the high grass above the path—and zigzagged down through giant bamboo to the bridle-track. A mile and a half away along this and several hundred feet below Impoi's level was Asalu.

Tired and shabby, the blight of malaria on it, much of its

young blood gone up the hill with Namkia, it stood on its long spur in the open parkland. Strewn in the grass around were ancient relics, stone rows and monoliths, the weathered remains of a century's occupation, and, perhaps, of settlements earlier still. Beyond the village the spur levelled, and here was the site of the John Company outpost, for forty years headquarters of North Cachar. There was almost nothing left of it now—only the old stone guardhouse, earthquake-cracked and split apart by trees, a broad stretch of gravel, where, they said, the parade-ground used to be, and, in the thick grass, a bungalow plinth. It was uncanny to go to the site with Namkia in the dusk, when the hills were blue-grey and the sunset an orange band along the western plateau, and hear him pointing out in the barren waste where this and that had been—there, by a stunted bush, the clerks' quarters, there the sepoys' lines, there the rifle-range, there the Sahib's big mango-tree, which had lasted long and at length had perished too. It was all so sharp a reminder of death and decay. The Sahibs, the clerks, the station all were dust, the village was failing. Only the wide, clear arch of the sky remained, the dulling sunset, the night wind coming down from the quiet hill.

The blight which had fallen on Asalu, reducing it from a powerful group to a scatter of poor hamlets, was an advanced stage of the North Cachar Barail's general economic trouble. This was of such importance that it is worth considering in detail. It was a tragedy for which no single person was to blame; a series of circumstances had built it up.

Its cause lay in the soil. The Zemi is an agriculturalist; he turns to trade and outside work only when crops fail. From boyhood on he goes to the cultivation—clearing, weeding, harvesting, when, as a buck, a rich man hires his *kienga*; then as a married man working in his own little family patch. His feasts are set by seasons and harvests, his religious ceremonies and days of rest and abstention are designed to secure good crops. Anything affecting the fields will necessarily be felt throughout the social structure.

The staple crop is rice, though millet, maize and vegetables are grown as sidelines. The method of cultivation is that known as 'jhuming', and is practised by most of the Assam hill-tribes. By it, a different block of jungle is felled each successive year, burned, cleared, planted, and cultivated for two or perhaps three seasons. Then it is left to lie fallow, and the longer it stands, the thicker the jungle grows, the deeper is the humus and the better the next crop. If, then, a village controls sufficient land, and each block in turn can lie fallow for years, the system continues indefinitely without loss to the soil.

Now the North Cachar Barail is extremely steep, a tract of extraordinary complexity. Cliffs and crags abound, the spurs lie close, and in between are gorges and deep ravines. Land suited for 'jhums' exists only in scattered patches, and to maintain itself in such a terrain a village must control an abnormally large territory. Of this, a part will be widely-dispersed jhum-land, and the rest—by far the greater part—wild rock and forest on which cultivation is either uneconomic or physically impossible.

Because of their intensely difficult country, the Barail Zemi were forced to develop cycle-migration. Each stretch of jhum-land was by itself too small to maintain a village indefinitely, since, to feed large settlements, it must be cropped at intervals too short to allow complete regeneration. As the Zemi lived then (and for most of their history) in a state of war, the community dared not subdivide and send a colony out to each parcel of land. When in the course of years, therefore, a stretch became exhausted, they left it, village and all, and cultivated a second and distant tract while the first recovered.

What of the Zemi *kadepeo* system, on which the village polity was based? The village sites they left, and the land attached, were not abandoned. The ancient site-land, the ancestral graves, the hallowed *haʒoa*, the rights and powers of *kadepeo* and 'citizens'—that is, the descendants of the original colonists of the site, men who were 'of' it, who had rights in its site-land—were, and are, most potent influences in Zemi life. To give them up was unthinkable. When the land at the first site had recovered enough and the second was becoming exhausted, the movement was reversed and the community returned. Some of the larger settlements, such as Hangrum, exhausted their patches of land so rapidly that they had to make three, four or even five removes before their first site was ripe for re-occupation, but however many sites a community possessed, each had its own *kadepeo*, the first founder's descendant, and its own 'citizens', heirs of the colonists, and, as one site was left and another resettled, the proper *kadepeo* and 'citizens' took up their duties—laid down by their ancestors, perhaps half a century before. In the same way, each time a site was left, its 'citizens' prepared it for their descendants' re-occupation. The *haẓoa* was marked by a standing stone, boundaries were traced and landmarks memorized; individual householders sometimes buried property by their hearths to identify the house-site for future generations. Lifetimes might pass, it was true, before the group returned to the place, but what was that in the rhythm of tribal life?

For more than two hundred years the cycle continued, a slow progression round acknowledged sites—we may disregard the mergings, the abortive colonies, which here and there disturbed the regular pattern. So slow a cycle was it, measured in generations rather than years, that a Zemi would have had difficulty in defining it. Enough that when harvests declined, when a village decayed, when the land of a site was old and full of graves, it was time to move to another elsewhere.

Then, in the early nineteenth century, the British and the immigrant Kukis arrived almost together. For the first time the Zemi came under another's control. They had so far successfully resisted attempts at immigration into their territory; the second Zemi wave, that driven out by Angami pressure, had been deflected past the Barail and on to the emptier western plateau.

When the Kukis settled the fallow land, the Zemi protested to the administration. But no officer had an inkling that a cycle-migration system existed (the Zemi are still the only Nagas known to have one) and the Zemi were incapable of explaining. The tracts of land they claimed seemed to the Government fantastically large; the authorities concluded that the Zemi had abandoned their ancient sites and were taking a dog-in-the-manger line. To the Zemis' rage and dismay, their protests were overruled. Their claims were disallowed; and all that they were not currently occupying was awarded to the newly-come Kukis. Only the Zemi knew that two tribes were now living on land enough for one.

The political consequences were unfortunate. The alienation of their treasured land, unwitting though it was, set the Zemi against the administration from the start. The more the Government tried, as it thought, to hold a just balance between the tribes, the more it seemed to the Zemi to be tilted unfairly against them, and the more it seemed to the Government that the Zemi were difficult and intransigent. No matter how they valued—and they did—roads, markets, and protection at last from the Angami terror, still the land, the lost and needed land, was a rankling thorn.

But if these effects were bad, the economic results were even worse. There was bitter competition between Zemi and Kuki for the means to live, since neither side had enough land —squabbles, boundary-disputes, trespass, and sometimes more serious troubles—and, of course, since both tribes must eat, progressive over-cultivation. As the years passed, the damage became apparent. Forests receded, grassland-areas increased; fallow intervals grew less and less; villages split and shifted restlessly in a vain search for space; jhums were cut on steep and impossible slopes from which the monsoon washed away soil and crop. Throughout the area the level of prosperity fell. There were no more *hekwi-ki,* no more great feasts. First the annual surplus dwindled and then the grain reserves, until, in the worst-hit parts, there was no safety-margin at all. Year by year more and more households could not grow enough to feed themselves, and a grim insecurity began.

Had the area only been under Naga Hills, the story might have been different. There the administration was of an extremely high standard and tribal problems were studied and understood. Despite his disaffection towards an abstract Government, the Zemi liked and respected the individual European officer, while his mistrust of the plains Indian was considerable. Over a term of years an experienced man could have done much to save the position. But unhappily, by an accident of geography, the area lay in the 'Cinderella of Subdivisions', mixed, nondescript North Cachar, and North Cachar was tacked on to Silchar, a plains district with which it had no connection except by proximity. North Cachar's officers were often temporary, holding the post for a while between better jobs; they seldom had hill experience; they were not always of the best type. Hardly ever did it enjoy such skilled handling as Naga Hills next door. The few periods when it did are spoken of to this day as Golden Ages. It was in one of these that Mr Mills, then Deputy Commissioner, Silchar, visited the Barail and realized what was wrong, the first officer to do so; and his discoveries and efforts to clean up the mess are recorded in a series of caustic tourdiaries. Clean up a very great deal of it he did, and took immediate steps to deal with the economic problem.

Since there was not enough land for shifting cultivation, it was necessary to change to permanent fields, by which the same population could live on a fraction of the acreage needed for 'jhuming'. An excellent system was to hand in Angami wet-rice terracing; funds were allocated, demonstrators engaged, and a start made with experimental terraces. Although the Zemi believed that to have water in one's fields caused death by dropsy, the economic position was such that they took to terraces gladly. Within a year or two a number had been constructed at Thingje, Haijaichak and Asalu.

By far the worst sufferers in the decline were those Zemi villages caught at the end of a cycle. The hardest hit of all were the Asalu group. They had been on the Asalu site, the unhealthiest of their three, for more than a hundred years; while disease had reduced their numbers by just a half, they had lost no less than five-sixths of their former land and were left to struggle along on a worn-out fraction. When harvests began to decline—about 1920—they would, in the normal course, have moved away, but all Gareolowa's and most of Impoi's land had passed to the Kukis.

When terracing seemed a solution, several men tried it. But by then Mr Mills had returned to Naga Hills as Deputy

Commissioner at Kohima, and North Cachar was sinking back again into its old neglect. The Angami wet-rice demonstrator scamped the work on the channels for Asalu's fields, and, in the first Rains, they broke repeatedly. Most of the Asalu experimenters lost their crop and were ruined. Grain was dear and wages small; they went to work in the fields of neighbouring tribes, Kacharis and Kukis. These made the most of the chance. A day's wage in grain was a pittance. To keep his family alive, an Asalu man must work all day and every day in his employer's fields, never seeing his own, and so in the following year had no crop and must work again, unless some wealthier kinsmen could redeem him.

Then, just about that time, a Thingje terracer died of dropsy. Right and left, the superstitious abandoned their irrigation. When coaxing failed to make them resume it again, an impatient officer tried to use compulsion. He fined some men who had let their terraces go, and that was the last straw. Wet-rice—if they had known it, their one hope—was damned for ever as a racket, a trap. There was nobody to resolve the misunderstanding. The Zemi retired, bitter and hungry, behind their glass wall. The Kukis, unimpeded by any such mistake, went on with irrigation, and took over, in many cases, irrigable land which the Zemi—fearing Government action—were only too glad to let go. While Kuki wet-rice demonstrators were trained and made available for their own people, the vacant Naga post—the Angami had been sacked —was given to Masang and turned into a political sinecure, and soil-destruction on the Zemi land continued unabated.

Let us return once more to the history of Asalu. They, when terracing failed them, had recourse again to the ancient remedy. Namkia's contingent left to resettle Impoi, where a little rested land remained round the site. When once Asalu's unity was broken, the whole community collapsed. It resolved again into its component parts, the 'citizens' and *kadepeos* of the several sites. Impoi and Gareolowa had gone off together, Impoi drawn to its old home, Gareolowa following its *kadepeo*, Namkia; now Hakaokhang—a tiny alien group, forced to seek shelter in Asalu from Angami raids—moved off a mile away along the hill. Asalu stayed where it was, decaying away among its graves on the half-dismantled site. In the days before administration, pressure from raids would have forced them all to Impoi. But, under the Pax Britannica, they could scatter at will, and so was the ruin completed and their poverty sealed; for each of these little settlements was below the economic size. Only Impoi, with its greater numbers, its healthy site and strip of good land, had any reasonable chance, though there was nowhere to go when the strip of land was finished. Year after year in the Asalu and Hakaokhang granaries, the piles of grain were less; and more and more men went daily to work in Kuki and Kachari fields.

Out after pigeon once in the Asalu parkland, Namkia and I stepped out of the high grass into a patch of cultivation. The crops were ripe, but the sparse and wretched rice was barely a foot high; a few thin ears topped it. It was a typical Asalu harvest. A few days before, in a field far to the east, rice in a jhum had dangled on my shoulder.

'If I could find a demonstrator who knew,' said Namkia, as we looked at the field. 'I'd terrace that bit of land of mine up at Impoi. It's a good piece, and the Kukis are asking me for it. I've got my own savings, too; I wouldn't need Government money. But who is there who really knows the job? Masang is useless; he doesn't know a thing.'

'What about the Kuki demonstrators?'

'Do they really know? And what sort of a job would they do for me, a Naga? These streams are steep. We want a man who knows. Why can't we have someone good, a proper Angami?'

But war-time inflation had by then begun; and though a new S.D.O., alive to the danger, was searching everywhere for an able man, no skilled Angami now wanted to come at thirty rupees a month. Rescue must wait till after the war—if ever.

We walked on home at the edge of the tragic crop.

CHAPTER XXI

MASANG

IN November, on a cool, clear day, when the forests were dry and sun-dappled, when the air was crisp, and the sky a sheeny, unflecked blue; when the streams were running bright and low and rods of light slanted into the green rockpools, Masang died.

I had seen little of him for a long time. At first a constant companion, he later found, when we were settled in at Laisong, that Namkia's hostility was too much for him. If Masang came into the house, Namkia walked out, and left Masang to talk as best he could—and he spoke no Hindustani. So, gradually, he came no more; and I had almost forgotten him.

He had lost his job as a wet-rice demonstrator, his irregularities having at last become more than the S.D.O. could bear. Dikheo, his old ally, had, that year, after a hunt which had lasted far longer than that for Gaidiliu, been surprised in his house at Bopungwemi and shot dead in a scuffle. So nothing now remained to Masang of his old ties, the old alliances, which, I am certain, he had done his best to maintain. A plain Zemi, an inconspicuous villager, he dropped clean out of sight. Nevertheless, it was a shock when his brother came and asked me to go to see him. Masang, he said, was seriously ill.

Namkia poured scorn on the idea that I could go over and back in the day, though Kepelo was not four miles off. Did Masang, then, think that the She-Sahib was a village woman, to trot here, and trot there, like a dog at heel? Let Kepelo take the trouble to build a camp and the She-Sahib would be over there quick enough. Masang's brother retreated, apologetic.

But I did go over. I couldn't desert Masang. I had an innate sympathy for the rascal—he had been my mentor before Namkia. Namkia or no Namkia, the appeal had been made to me; it had to be answered somehow. So, as he wouldn't go, I took Haichangnang, and early next morning, with a wallet of drugs, we took the eastward road to Haijaichak.

Kepelo lay in the U-shaped pass, a little way up the side from Haijaichak. We turned to the north from the road, and climbed steeply, through graves and stones and gullies and all the litter of a village; through a belt of wood; and then, up a steeper slope than ever, between the granaries on their bamboo stilts, into Kepelo's wide, bare village street.

As soon as the villagers met us, memory flew back to the time when first I came to this district. They seethed, they surged, they fell on me, as they had at Guilong. They clamoured, they cried out, they thrust gifts on me, they touched my clothes, they begged my blessing. Then Masang's brother came out and brought us through the mob. He led us into the house where Masang was lying and closed the door in the face of the crowd outside. Soon I was to understand what had prompted all these repeated and embarrassing demonstrations since my arrival in the Zemi country.

The house, as all Naga houses are, was pitchy dark. A fire burned on the hearth, between three stones; behind it the family sat, the firelight catching them; behind them again was a rich, brown shadow, a smoky darkness, with glimpses of mats, clothes, gourds, beds, baskets, leaping for an instant out of obscurity as a flame briefly rose.

At the near side of the fire, on a mat on the floor, was Masang.

All doubts and fears I had of the wisdom of coming, of seeming to patronize him, were gone in a moment. Masang was dying.

Of the old, hard, stocky ruffian, tousled and tough and brutal, there was nothing left. On the long cane mat, under a cloth or two, was a skeleton. Caked with soot and grime from a two months' illness, his powerful muscle gone; his bones—the skull-like shape of his face, the thin, thin arms, the legs like stalks—alone showed now, under the tight-drawn, leathery skin. And, from the skull, the little, yellowed eyes looked out at mine. A hand came up, a hand all bones—

a dry, harsh, dead, black hand, like a bird's claw—and groped for mine.

'My mother. Goddess. Save me,' said Masang. 'I am afraid to die.'

I looked across the hearth at Haichangnang. I saw his face, his look; and I understood. To Masang I was, and always had been, re-incarnated Gaidiliu.

I sat there most of the day. It comforted Masang. He hardly spoke at all, except to reiterate his pathetic appeal, but he lay, half-seen in the dark, his hand on my knee, or holding mine, like a child. When I moved away, as I once or twice did, there was a sudden moan, and that dreadful hand, that crusted, skeleton's hand, came feeling over his head to pull me back. I was glad I had Haichangnang and not Namkia. He didn't interfere with the dying man, rate him, exult, as Namkia might have done. His face convulsed with pity, the little man sat, and watched the two of us from across the fire. When he spoke at all, it was with sympathy, comfort and a human gentleness which I loved in him.

Then there was time to think. In the quiet house the whole mysterious jigsaw fell into shape.

From the very first moment he saw me, I later learned, Masang believed that I was Gaidiliu. Why, Heaven only knows; for, as far as I can tell, there is not a single point of resemblance between us, except our sex. But she had promised, it seemed, to return in another form, one in which her enemies would not know her; and what disguise could possibly be better than the shape of a European woman? At all events, he up and announced my godhead publicly, in Laisong village, at the meeting there; and while the steady element, such as Namkia, recoiled, and the main body sat tight and awaited events, the mad and faithful, such as Guilong, fell for it hook, line and sinker. So that was why I had been mobbed as I was. That was why strangers appeared from the back of beyond with presents. That was why the Bopungwemi party stripped their youngest member and made me an emergency gift. That was why headmen had fallen at my feet and called me 'Mother' and 'She-Spirit'. And oh! how right she had been, when she told Mr Mills it was hard work being a goddess, and she never had time for a bath! Oh, the bleating inanities of Guilong! Oh, the clutch of hands! Oh, the clawing, the thrusting, the arrogant claim to worship, to derive benefit, at any hour of the day or night! Oh, anthropology! Oh, shades of *The Golden Bough*! The strain, the misery of being a God!

And after that, there had been the second visit from Bopungwemi. While the others, whom I had seen before, distracted me with chatter and gifts laid out, the fourth man of the party, a big, tall, hulking brute, had leaned against the veranda-post and stared and stared. And later, somehow, the rush of visitors had declined. I never asked Masang; but I was almost sure—he had been down, they said, and been to Maibong—that that was Dikheo; come at the risk of his life to see this re-incarnation Masang was talking of; and that he failed to pass me. So only Masang believed, and the few he led. Namkia, knowing—they all of them knew, but me—had kept him away from Laisong, cut short his visits, till, with his job gone, Dikheo dead, he fell ill, and sent for me—sent, Haichangnang said, by the name of Gaidiliu. And here we were by the hearth, on a dirty mat, Masang's black hand in mine, and Haichangnang looking at us across the fire.

From that moment, I think, I became a Zemi. I understood them as I had never done before. Their faults, their follies, their sincerities, were all so clear. I would have said before that Masang's recognition of me, based, it would seem, on no good reason at all, was just a device to regain his former power. Given a goddess, he could be her prophet.

But what to make of this? Masang was dying. He knew it, and so did we; I could do nothing for him. He was afraid of death, but he was not asking me, myself, to save him. He was asking Gaidiliu, his queen, his goddess, in whom he so believed, in whom he trusted, whose hand he now, half-conscious, held and held; she for whose sake he had been beaten and jailed; she to whom, dying, he clung. I sat on and on there, quiet, the dry paw lying in mine.

It was evening when we left. The village mobbed us. For the first time consciously, but for the last time, I went down a village street as a divine being. They crowded and clung to me, as when I came. Now it was all simple and comprehensible. When Masang died, I knew, there would be an end of it all. Haichangnang caught my eye and knew that I understood, and, leaving the village gradually, patient at last with the crowds, we reached the bridle-road and went slowly home with a strange new sympathy and understanding between us.

A fortnight later, we heard that Masang had died. I doubt if Gaidiliu had a better servant.

CHAPTER XXII

THE COMING OF WAR

WHERE lay the taste of Laisong, its special flavour; what brought us back, aching for it, after ten days away? There was the square bungalow, with its sagging thatch and its latticed railings; the infinite grey and brown tones of its matting walls and woodwork; the morning light slanting steely and sharp through the shutter cracks; the hills behind, with the pale, clear colours altering on them, on grass and wood and forest, as the sun climbed across the Jenam valley. There was the jungle which merged into the camp, creeping up in a green tide till cut and driven back to another temporary boundary; the men's bare, copper backs lifting to the rhythm of the cut, as they worked in line across the slope. There was the garden, a small, fenced patch; ridged brown beds dotted with clumps of dull green, with blossom-dotted beanstacks, peas loud with insects; where the men came in at that slack hour just before dusk, to stand and appraise, and patronize the gardener, white cloths and black heads passing between the rows. There were the clouds of swallows which swooped and swept, like midges, above the village; diving to their nests in the morung gables; flickering over in rapid flight, flashing by at ground-level, or hardly visible in the high, soft, tinted evening sky. There were the rock outcrops below the bungalow, where one could sit and look over the whole great bowl of the Jenam; the river little and bright, the patch of Rangalang's field, the sheen of the big pool where Namkia and I fished, the complexities of the gorge through which the river wound, doubling back on itself again and again between the interlocking spurs.

But chiefly it was an atmosphere. A barrier lay between us and the outer world. One could, by walking over the hill to Asalu, pass it; for there below was the railway, the shriek and clatter of trains and the stink of travel. Here, behind the Barail, was an ageless calm. The smoke of evening drifted out of the morungs; the last few stragglers came trudging up the path; the last sun left Nenglo, on the farther hill, and the short twilight gathered the village in.

Life itself was hard and uncertain. One never let a quarrel linger. A bout of fever, or a falling tree—who could be sure of surviving to make it up? One lived entirely in the present, with a directness, a simplicity, which produced a great content. The lack of material wealth, too, accentuated spiritual values, set them, rather, in higher relief; they were seen more clearly, without the irrelevant clutter and distractions with which, in a more complex society, they are overlaid.

Life might be short, but it was rich and human. I think the Zemi were a great deal happier than we. There one derived pleasure from small and transient things, from kindnesses, friendships, loyalties and the like, which because of their simpler, barer state were more deeply felt and of greater meaning. Then, too, there was always the sense of mortality and impermanence to quicken appreciation. Death was never very far from anyone in that malarial, doctorless country, and thinking back, I believe it was chiefly that which held one so firmly in the present and prevented too great building of hopes for the future. Certainly, to enjoy every simple pleasure as though it were for the last time sharpened the sense and gave life an extraordinarily rich texture.

Security there was, though, in a wider sense. There was an immense feeling of temporal unity, of a past reaching back into the mists, but very little different from the present; of an inevitable future stretching forward in time. A man could plant and build for twenty years or for generations hence. If he did not live to enjoy it, his children might, and if not his own children, then his brothers' or cousins' sons, linked to his own line far back in the ramifications of the clan, children of his own kindred and his own descent. Men often spoke of their clan or family as of themselves, 'I'—'I founded Gareolowa', 'I killed an Angami down there by the river, before the British came.' It proved on inquiry to be some ancestor, not always a direct one; they would speak of ten or fifteen generations back in such an intimate tone. So closely were past and present linked in one long continuity that the individual life was almost lost in them, for they were one. And if the individual were mortal, the clan, the tribe, of which he was a part for ever, went eternally on.

Inner peace might be of the Zemis' own making, but external peace, which they valued in spite of themselves, was nothing more or less than the Pax Britannica; which was already threatened.

I went to Calcutta again in December, 1941, on my annual holiday, and once more took Namkia. This time he insisted on bringing Haichangnang for company, chiefly because last year the villagers had not believed Namkia's all-too-sober accounts of the Second City and had called him a liar. Haichangnang, he felt, would be a safe witness, for the little man hadn't the brains to tell a lie. His mind worked slowly, on the most literal lines.

There was the episode of the garden peas. We had raised a crop of an imported strain, and Haichangnang loved them. He was always begging a few as a treat. One day he was discovered among the pea-sticks, carefully and methodically killing off all the bees which were visiting the blooms. I stopped him in horror. He said in an injured tone that he was 'killing the flies which are spoiling the peas, because I like peas, you see'.

I called Namkia and asked him to explain. He drew Haichangnang away to the end of the garden and there expounded slowly, in simple words, why, if it were not for the little bees, there would be no peas for Haichangnang to eat. There was a long, anxious silence while the little man's churning brain tried to make sense of it. Then came the dawn—a radiant spreading of comprehension and a long-drawn: 'Ohhh!'

I had my own reasons for taking them both to Calcutta. The war was drawing nearer the Far East and I knew only too well the kind of talk which was going on among the disaffected Zemi. I wanted to show them the War Weapons Exhibition which was then on—not very much, perhaps, but still something to quote against the irresponsible elements. So, arrived in Calcutta, off we went to it at the first chance, the men in all the glory of tribal dress.

We were a third of the way round before anyone really noticed them. Then things happened. Cameras appeared, a solid, blinking row, at waist-level, eye-level, held against cheeks and chests; cinés whirred, officials hurried up—they were the two most-photographed men in Calcutta.

In return for publicity-pictures, they were allowed the run of the Exhibition. A friendly sergeant-major took charge of them, and when sightseeing palled and the sun grew hot he ran them off to the canteen and filled them up with ices.

'Whenever you want to park them, miss,' he said (I still had to tail them round when I went out shopping), ' you bring 'em along to me. I'll keep 'em happy.'

Day after day I did; and they waxed fatter daily and loved him more. In later years, whenever we met British troops Namkia used to go over and look for his sergeant-major.

We came back to Mahur to find the former S.D.O. gone and the new one, Mr Perry, encamped at the bungalow. I went to meet him with some trepidation. To a woman alone, as I knew to my cost by then, district officers were mostly hostile.

A slim, very tall man came out of the house to meet me. We shook hands. Even today, very many years later, I can still say that there are few who have shown me as much kindness as Mr and Mrs Perry.

With the first post to reach Laisong after our return came the news of Pearl Harbour. All through the winter of 1941/2, however, the war still seemed to be a long way off. There followed the blow of Singapore and the invasion of Burma. Still it didn't seem to touch us, remote as North Cachar was, and Laisong remoter, shut off behind the high wall of the Barail. It was all far off, something happening in the infrequent newspapers, not concerned with our immediate affairs, the risk attendant on jungle-fires, milk for a motherless baby, the blacksmith's illness, the urgent necessity of rethatching the house. Then in March I went to stay with friends down in the Plains. I found everything prepared for evacuation at twenty-four hours' notice; the men ready for call-up; and an SOS out for women to help with the Burma refugees.

The war was on us. There was one thing I didn't intend to do, despite the general confusion, and that was leave Assam —whether there was a general evacuation or not. Returning to Laisong, I recruited, not without difficulty, a team of Zemi volunteers, and offered our services to the Government on any of the refugee routes where we could be of use.

Our luck was out. They had stopped sending women workers up the roads, because the conditions there were so appalling. In the last days of March, 1942, we received orders to go to Lumding Junction, to run a canteen at the station there. Swearing a little, for we had formed an efficient unit for jungle-work, we reorganized ourselves and prepared to go to Haflong and collect equipment.

This abrupt upheaval, involving myself at least in the fringes of world catastrophe, threw sudden strain on relations with the Zemi. We at Laisong, that little group of half a dozen or so, had become a team, a *kienga*, a matriarchal family. There was no telling what its ties, which were delicate and undefined, could stand. One couldn't expect too much; but, though the others remained behind with the house and dogs, Namkia, Haichangnang, Ramgakpa and Dinekamba were all going to Lumding, which they feared much more than the Manipur refugee routes.

When it became generally known that we were going, there occurred an unexpected incident.

A deputation of headmen suddenly appeared to protest against the Governor's orders to me to go. This was no time, they said, with invasion imminent, and the country in a disturbed state, for a young woman to be about alone. If whatever Europeans were responsible for my safety (and they supposed that the British, like the Zemi, took care of their own people) were not prepared or willing to look after me, then, they said, the Zemi would. They as a tribe would take full responsibility. And, as a first step, they forbade me to leave the shelter of the hills.

I said that whatever happened, orders were orders. They stopped my porters, left the camp in a swirl of red blankets, and went off to Haflong and Perry. He only got me away at all by promising them that he personally would see me back, come hell or high water. And then we left Laisong at last for Lumding.

Namkia was strangely silent on the way down. On our last night in the hills, in the camp at Asalu, he drifted to and fro, hanging about—wishing, it seemed, to say something, and yet not able to nerve himself to the point. A little after dark, when the lamp was lit and I was sitting writing, he came abruptly in. Before I could move, he dropped on his knees in front of me. His arms went round me, his head went down on my lap, and suddenly, bitterly, he began to cry.

This was so completely unlike Namkia, so shocking a collapse, that for a few seconds I did nothing.

'Namkia, Namkia! Whatever is the matter?'

I shook him and tried to raise him. He didn't move. I tried to quiet him. He went on weeping. I pulled myself free and stood up, and his head and arms fell on the empty chair, where he went on crying. There was some rum in the stores. I hunted for it and found it, gave him a stiff tot, and bullied him into taking it medicine fashion. In a little while it worked. His sobs grew less, and he sat up gulping, regaining his self-control.

'Well, what's the trouble?' I said, after a little.

He got up and perched himself on the edge of the bamboo table, always his favourite seat.

'It was all right before I left Laisong. I didn't mind a bit and I wasn't afraid to go. But now my wife and mother have been at me, and I don't know what to do. Suppose Assam is invaded, and abandoned without a fight, as they say it's going to be?' He looked across at me. 'Suppose we can't come back? Suppose raiding breaks out again in the hills when the British go? Who'll look after my wife and children? I was in the village today, and heard what they're saying. They say this isn't our war and we ought to leave it alone —we aren't Japs, we aren't British; we're Zemi. What's it to do with us?' There was dire trouble in his face. 'We've been together now, you and I and the others, for two years now; we are like a family. How can I leave you?—What about my children? Oh, my sister, my sister, I'm being pulled in two! Which way shall I go?'

I sat down at the table.

'Well,' I said, 'I don't know what's going to happen, either. But my home's here in Laisong, and I'm coming back to it whatever happens. After all, Lumding isn't far; we can walk home in four days. As for the rest, I don't think you Zemi will be able to stay as neutral as you think—certainly not if the Angamis and Kukis take sides; and I doubt if you'd find the Japs a fair exchange for the British. From what I hear, they're rather more like the old Kachari Kings you talk about, who made men lick knives, and flayed the soles off their feet and made them walk along thorny logs.'

'That's likely,' said Namkia.

'Meantime, there are all these people coming through from Burma, in the devil of a state. I've been told to go down and help; and I'm going, with anyone I can find to go along with me. If you people won't come, it's my bad luck—I've had the orders, not you.'

Namkia got off his perch and wiped his eyes.

'*Asipui-ghao*,' he said. 'Dear elder sister—don't be afraid, we're all in it together.'

We shook hands on it, and he went off to the lines. Three days later, in vile discomfort, by fits and starts, half our kit adrift on a line already disrupted and chaotic, we landed up on a hot, dark night at Lumding.

CHAPTER XXIII

REFUGEE CANTEEN

L UMDING was unique, in that it was pure junction. It had no other *raison d'être* whatever. It had originally been built, in a clearing hacked in the steamy green Nambhor Forest, at the point where the proposed Hill Section Line was due to meet that running up the Assam Valley. Unhappily, when the Hill Section was completed, the actual junction came at a point about a mile and a half west of where they had already constructed Lumding. So there the two were; the station, platforms, signals, sheds, yards and town, as isolated in the jungle—except for the railway—as an island-universe in space; and, beyond it, a mute divergence in the heart of the forest, where one bare line went one way, and one the other, each disappearing into a green channel of vegetation like two friends cutting each other dead.

The place was in the first throes of that confusion which would undoubtedly have swamped Assam had the Japanese come in. The yards were choked with wagons—loads of bamboo, of building materials, which, in the panic, no one had claimed; consignments left lying about unforwarded till the siding overflowed on to the main line, and mail-trains had to wait at the outer signals while, in a sudden frenzy, the trucks were shunted up into a temporary jam elsewhere; to be de-compressed again, and left re-blocking the through tracks, as soon as the immediate crisis had passed.

Had it not been for the providential Mrs Rankin of the railway, there wouldn't have been a canteen. For there was nothing; no shed, store, hut, space, cookshed, food or fuel; not even a place where we could sleep. All was panic, a dusty confusion, like an anthill dug out into the light of day. She it was who conjured table-tops from nowhere and com-mandeered girders on which to put them. She it was, by virtue of her husband's authority, who found us charcoal stoves from the engine-sheds, and a room at the Institute for our apparatus; who badgered someone, somewhere, into doing something about the promised buildings for us. Money, food, equipment and helpers, supposedly there, were not. In those first two weeks we had exactly as much as we could collect for ourselves, and we lived on Mrs Rankin's local knowledge.

Early each morning the refugee-trains rolled in loaded to the roof. In theory, they passed through during the night, reaching Chaparmukh or Pandu in time for the morning meal. In fact, they spent the night in sidings while troop-trains went up, so that it was into our arms that, hungry, thirsty, exhausted, numbed with shock, the refugees fell out at any time between five and eight next day.

To all of us, I think, the main impression of those weeks was one of physical exhaustion. Let no one suppose that dealing with thousands of uprooted and demoralized human beings, against time, and with improvised equipment, is a kind of Church Tea. It is a dirty, sweaty, frantic navvy's job; one is hewer of wood and drawer of water, coal-heaver, stoker, scullion, constable, nurse, all by turns and all at once, and dustman to wind up with. One's taskmaster, the hardest I know, is the crying need of hundreds of fellow-beings, displayed daily in all its nakedness. But, as conditions improved, both on the railway and in our own organization, and our hours dropped from eighteen a day to sixteen (a very great improvement, believe me), we had time to notice something of what passed.

In spite of an initial coolness we joined forces early with a Nationalist organization which was running an Indian canteen at the far end of the platform. We arrived at an active, though unofficial, co-operation. Where the serving staff were concerned, it amounted to integration, for latterly supplies were drawn impartially from both kitchens and their workers, in their off-time, sometimes gave us a hand in serving troops.

Mrs Rankin left ten days after we came, her husband being posted elsewhere. We moved then from her house into the vacant half of the small rest-house. There was no quarter for the men, so they came in with me. There was a tiny extra bedroom, which Namkia took, a bathroom, which I had for a dressing-room, and one bed-sitting-room where I ate and wrote and where I and the three remaining Zemi slept at night, in a complex maze of mosquito-nets hitched to bed, table, chair and any projection which offered. It was hard on the men, for they had no privacy; waking or sleeping, they were under my eye; but it was undeniably convenient for getting promptly to and from our work.

Our day began at half-past two in the morning, when a messenger knocked on the window and gave me the day's figures. Generally there were two thousand or so all told— so many Europeans, six to sixty of them, for whom sandwiches must be cut; so many Indians—the other canteen would feed them, and tea would be drawn from both. At 3 a.m. I roused the men, and, in the only cool hour of the twenty-four, we made our way down in the dark with loads of kindling and the bread for the sandwiches. Here were the tracks, shining a little in the starlight. Over them we trudged —here and there was the familiar glow of red or green lights; we came to know the night aspects of Lumding well—then the small bulk of our newly-built canteen, a little thatched shed, and a cookhouse behind it. (The Yenangyaung contingent, I remember, came through when the cookshed was building. They sat about on the half-built fireplaces and ate sausages fried over our stoves; asked the day of the week; and decided it was 'the second Sunday after demolition'.) Then there were sixty gallons of water to carry, at eight gallons a trip, the fires to light and the water to boil, and while it heated we cut the sandwiches and set out the mugs.

Somewhere between four, when the first smell of dawn came in the air, and five, when the birds were waking and the night cool fading away, there came, with any luck, one or two of our faithful contingent of helpers—usually the Hogermeer family, the only Europeans to tackle the early shift. Then day came. And with it, clanking in over the points, the expected train—dull, brownish paint peeling and sun-bleached, the high, old-fashioned carriages packed, jammed, with weary people.

The next two hours were one whirl of serving and pouring, of fetching, washing, dishing, handing out; of crises and scalds. We leaned at last on the counter among the dirty cups and debris, the crumby plates, the spilt tea, the stains, the odd, wet tea-leaves, to watch the train pull out, and then washed up, swabbed, cleaned, swept, and went home in the growing heat to breakfast.

Ten o'clock, and, armed with baskets of bread and buns, we came down to open again for the wounded.

For some reason their train always stopped at the far end of the platform, giving us a hundred-yard dash with each lot of tea. Most of them, too, were stretcher-cases, unable to come to the canteen. Others, whose wounds were foul or clothes bloodstained, would not, from an innate delicacy, come up to the shed for fear of upsetting the lady helpers. They were amazing. Tired, thirsty, in rags, some with reeking wounds, some with first field-dressings still on, packed into filthy compartments, often without a doctor, an orderly or a bedpan on the train, they grinned, and said: 'Please', and 'Thank you', and 'Take it easy, miss', and carriage after carriage went out with windows solid with waving men: 'See you on the way back, miss! Thank you for the tea. See you on the Road to Mandalay!' The Naga is an emotional creature, quickly responsive; to see the men who, in Namkia's phrase, were 'putting their bodies for a shield between us and the Japs' brought the war home to them suddenly. It became a personal matter, a debt to be discharged. Instead of following me, they began to work furiously at the canteen on their own account.

By twelve or twelve-thirty the wounded were gone. The station baked in the heat, in a glare of sun. A pi-dog or two wandered about the glinting metals, sniffing and scavenging. Behind the sidings, the *gul-mohur* trees were in flower. But the sunlight swallowed their colour, ate it up in yellow heat; one had to wait till evening to see them in all their blaze of scarlet, of bunches of bloom floating against deep, cool, green leaves. We washed up and closed again, and went back to lunch.

The little house was stifling by then. It was too hot to sleep. The men bathed; so did I. Then at three o'clock, when the heat was at its thickest and most stuffy, we went down to the third shift, for the Up Mail, and those stray trains, loaded with trucks, ambulances or mules, which trickled through from time to time on their way to the front. Generally, we were through with that by seven or eight. Then there were accounts to do, and correspondence, while the fan clacked overhead and the men slept on the floor round me. At nine or nine-thirty I switched off the light and rolled into bed myself.

And at half-past two in the morning it all began again.

CHAPTER XXIV

FAMINE

Not till the middle of May 1942 did we see Laisong again We came crawling back over the Tolpui pass, exhausted, a shadow of the party which marched off. We were worn out, worked to a standstill.

When my relief took over at last—she, brave woman, was a grandmother, the only person who could be found to come —and we fell into the Haflong train, we lay on the narrow benches and just slept. Back at Laisong, we went on sleeping for a week. The Burma Army was falling back then, fighting, to the Manipur border. Imphal was bombed; invasion was imminent; children were being sent away, women were leaving; and we lay like logs on our beds and made up six weeks' arrears. Had Assam been abandoned, had invasion come, had India itself fallen, still we couldn't have staggered as far as Mahur.

Then the Rains broke. Invasion was halted till autumn. A wall of falling water, a grey screen, shut us and our eyrie off from the rest of the world. Three weeks later, on the first clear day after the downpour, in walked the Zemi problem in living form—three human skeletons, which, with horror, I recognized as Asalu men I knew. I ran for Namkia. He admitted at last that there was a famine in Asalu, and that they were keeping it from the Government's knowledge.

It was all as tragic a misunderstanding as one could find. A generation before, in another scarcity, a Haflong clerk who was gifted more with dramatic than common sense had come out with bulging grain-bags, opened them wide, and told the hungry villagers to help themselves. Quite a number did; but only years later did they learn what the clerk, at the time, had omitted to tell them; that the grain was a long-term loan, to be repaid. Brothers, descendants, heirs of dead-and-gone men, youths who had never even tasted the borrowed rice, found themselves liable for its repayment. In the end, the headmen had to resolve the hopeless tangle by a house-to-house levy throughout the village. Not unnaturally, the Zemi took the whole wretched mistake for calculated cunning. They swore that never again would they accept help so mean, and allow their distress to be exploited for usury.

Now here were the fruits of that twenty-year-old stupidity. When, the August before, a plague of grasshoppers ate up the flowering rice, Impoi and Asalu had lost most of their crop. Whether through their concealment or through the negligence of the man sent to inquire, nothing of this appeared on the Haflong records. Both villages had launched out unsupported on six months' scarcity. There were no grain reserves; it was years since they had had any. Now an epidemic had laid out the able-bodied men, on whose daily earnings everything depended, and there was nothing left. The people were starving. Everyone who could stand, grandmothers, even, was out searching the woods for roots and edible leaves.

The headmen arrived to see me that same afternoon. They were a tragic sight, lean ghosts of my old friends. Their hair was lank, they were pitiably thin; the dry skin was tight over their ribs and cheekbones. They wanted me to keep quiet about the famine and make them a private loan to see them through.

I argued with them and Namkia for a long time. There seemed no way to clear up that clerk's mistake. They wouldn't believe for a minute that, though loans were the normal thing, they could have free relief in real trouble. They were convinced that if anyone once knew an avid Government would be down on them to squeeze out every penny it could —it was heartbreaking. I gave it up at last and paid out the loan. But I sent a letter in to Perry next day.

The crust of Zemi secrecy so rarely cracked that when it did, what emerged was startling. One moment all was peace and silence in the Barail, and the next a shocked Perry, still new to the district, was faced with a full-grown famine sprung out of the ground. There wasn't a thing on the books, not a hint from his predecessor—he couldn't believe it. He sent a man out hot-foot to confirm or deny. His report was enough—things happened. As soon as the stuff could be sacked and put on porters, twenty loads of Government free-relief rice were on their way up the road, while Perry himself, with the ample balance, was hurrying up behind. Like the clerk before us, he and I opened the bulging sacks and called on the people to take—and they looked at us long and dumbly, and turned away.

Arguing, cajoling, we persuaded the urgent cases to take a little. My Asalu friend Miroteung, whom I had seen a few months back lying laughing on his porch bench, tossing his fat, gurgling, golden-brown baby up in the air, came in fresh from the baby's burial and almost too weak with hunger to stand. He sat against the doorpost and shook his head at all my entreaties—talking exhausted him. He wouldn't touch the rice.

'But, Miroteung, you must! You've been ill, so has your wife—if there's any catch in it, any interest to pay, I'll make up every last anna myself, I swear I will.'

He nodded at that; but he wouldn't take more than ten pounds. I had to send one of my own men to carry it down for him.

When Perry and I met again at Laisong a week later the worst sufferers had been fed and immediate tragedy prevented; but only just. It had been a near thing, the Asalu headmen said; deaths from starvation would have begun that week. Comparing notes, Perry and I were agreed on one thing in heart and soul, and that was that something must be done about the Zemi. We couldn't let this horrible misunderstanding continue. But what were we to do?

Perry was a just and able officer and well-liked, and already was as freely accepted by the Zemi as I, indeed as no officer had been for a dozen years; but the trouble was far too deep-rooted for our individual influence to cure. Something much bigger was required. True, confidence might be built up only to be thrown down and destroyed again by the next twist of the political wheel, but that risk had to be taken; things couldn't go on as they were. Perhaps, if we were lucky, we should get the chance, the opening we could use.

Perry went back to Haflong, and we stayed on at the camp. Over and above the famine it was a bad Rains. Our nerves were still in rags after Lumding and we snapped and squabbled like bad-tempered children. Then I went down with malaria.

No woman could have been more gentle, no nurse more devoted than Namkia was to me then. I was very ill for a time and quite helpless. For a day and a night he never left my room; every time I roused, he was sitting by me; at night he lay beside the bed and woke at my least move. There are no words for his tenderness, his delicacy and his care; this was a new Namkia.

In July came the dysentery outbreak in Nraitsak. This tragedy, like the famine, sprang directly from Zemi conservatism and isolation. Like the famine, it was preventable, but unlike it, it was discovered too late.

The dysentery was a new and virulent kind brought in by the refugees. Their trains infected the line as they passed down it, and thence it spread outwards into the hills alongside; all that summer and in the two succeeding years it sprang up here and there in deadly outbreaks. When it appeared in Nraitsak, which it did early, before its danger was known, the elders decided that, as medicine could not cure at one magical stroke and must be carried on over long and tiresome periods, and as a doctor would need feeding and housing all that time, they would economize, keeping the outbreak a close secret and ending it by the time-honoured sacrifice of a monster pig.

Alas, for their mistaken piety! When, a month later, a man we had treated once before developed symptoms and sent over for help, the whole thing came to light. Of their population of sixty, twenty were then dead.

As if to match the confusion in human affairs, the Rains were the wildest and windiest we had known. The short bushes on the south cliff shook day after day to a lashing south-west gale; rain rattled like bullets on the outer walls. Inside the house, strings of wet clothes hung in a perpetual haze of wood-smoke. Only the fiercest and most expert blowing roused the damp logs to a flicker. Out in the garden the very soil was swept away; the top beds were left as gravelheaps, while the rich silt banked on the lower fence. The fence itself blew down, and the few flowers were mashed to pulp. Believing, in my innocence, that what had withstood that first hailstorm was still safe, I went on sleeping like a child in the end room. I was unmoved when first the front and then the side matting was whisked off the roof and the thatch scattered over half the spur.

Then came the third gale.

That night the rain was battering at the walls, water was cascading in through the cracks and chinks, and the whole house creaked to the gusts like a ship at sea. Lying there in the draughty dark, I could hear Namkia shifting restlessly in the far corner. Now and then, when a glare of lightning lit up the room, I saw him looking up at the roof above; but I snuggled down in my camp cot and hunched the blankets tight with that extra pleasure of being warm and dry with a wild, wet night shut out. I only turned a little, half-asleep, when a sudden crackling over us made him sit sharply up.

'It's only hail,' I said.

'Quick, quick!—the house is going!'

I reached the living-room floor in one electric leap. I stood with my heart thumping somewhere high in my throat till the ripping and rending stopped, and we heard instead the splash of water on the matting floor.

We ventured back step by step into the sodden room. Half of it now stood open to the sky. The thatch was stripped clean off. The rafters were splintered, the ties were gone; and purplish lightning flickered evilly behind the naked beams.

I could never sleep through a gale in that room again.

Lastly, there was the atmosphere of those three months. The Japs were just beyond the border, there was tension everywhere; rumour and counter-rumour rippled through. The Zemi were afraid. Talk magnified our defeats; Jap prowess was exalted. Invasion in the autumn seemed certain, and what to do when it came was a problem for all of us. Some time in July I had a message. Over in Manipur, the Kabui, Zemi and Lyeng had held a meeting to decide on joint action should the administration withdraw. They asked whether, in that event, I would stay behind as their leader.

I sent back, for the moment, a non-committal reply. But, if invasion came, I meant to stay.

CHAPTER XXV

THE COLONEL

IN early August I heard from Haflong that a Colonel Rawdon Wright was coming to see me.

One could, from the bungalow, see a strip of the road beyond the village. It must have been about noon or a little later when we saw a shirted figure, unmistakably European, descending it with attendant Nagas in front and behind. I sent a man down with a note to ask the visitor to lunch.

He returned in an hour, with the note but no guest. Scribbled in the note's margin was:

'So sorry, but I've got a gammy leg. I'd better go straight on down to the rest-house.'

The messenger, who was Dinekamba, confirmed. The Sahib was very lame, and going slowly. I called Namkia, and we went down by the east path, expecting to meet the party at the bottom. They weren't there.

We looked at the road for tracks. There weren't any. We followed it back towards Asalu. Turn after turn we passed, and still no sign. We weren't far from the mouth of the western path when at last we saw them. Then I understood why. The Colonel's leg was straight; he couldn't bend it. There was a broad stretch of bandage showing between stocking and shorts. Nor was he young.

We shook hands in the middle of the road and Namkia and I led on down to the rest-house. It was late by then, so instead of my lunching him, he lunched me. We ate sardines and bread in the long, cool, concrete veranda.

'I've heard a lot of you,' I said. 'You knew Mr Jeffery, didn't you?'

There were a host of mutual friends, Mr Mills not least. The Colonel had met my parents, too, casually, in the country at home. He'd had a job joining up again when war broke out. He'd retired, and there was his gammy leg, which he'd collected in the Kaiser's war. There was an open wound in

164

it still. He got into the R.A.F. in the end, in a ground job. Then the war came near Assam, his old stamping-ground— he'd been in the Assam Rifles between the wars. He began to raise heaven and earth to get out again. He did, in the end —but, only for desk-work, when he'd wanted to get back to the hills and his men. And as to what he was doing now——

I heard about that next day.

He belonged to a guerilla organization, a unit known as 'V' Force, whose job it was to recruit the hill-tribes for service as scouts. It was now nearly the end of the Rains and the Japs were standing along the length of the Burma border. Behind us, in India itself, the Congress Party had stirred up widespread internal trouble, apparently to coincide with a Japanese invasion in force in the near future. It was only to be expected that the Japs would press forward as soon as they could. The fact that they had not moved yet might be because they were watching the Congress Party's rising. If it scored more success than it had at present, or even if it did not and they felt themselves strong enough, they were likely to attack India at the first chance. 'V' Force was therefore actively interested in the border areas, and among them North Cachar and that part of Manipur which lay in front of it. Several tracks crossed this stretch, converging at Haijaichak and thence running to the railway; the district would be of importance if invasion came, and meantime it was as well to stop spies and agents from reaching the enemy through it, as they could easily do from the wayside stations. What did I think about recruiting a Watch and Ward?

We brought out a map and spread it on the table. There were the tracks; the road from Kohima, and the Naga paths from Maovom and Impuiloa, meeting at Haijaichak in the eastern end of the pass. The only other route, that from Hangrum, came out at the west end of the pass by Laisong rest-house, and Laisong itself covered it. There was a possible route from Hangrum up the stream-beds and by Tolpui, which cut out these; but it was difficult, and would need local guides. Hangrum covered that. One thing was clear. Nothing could be done without the Zemi.

Not only were they in the great majority, but their villages lay at every strategic point. The Luki villages were small, scattered, and tucked away in corners of the hills. Only one village, Khuangmual, near the Naga Hills border, occupied an important position. The Zemi had everything else which was going to matter.

As a former Commandant of the Assam Rifles, the Colonel knew, at first hand, all about Gaidiliu and the political situation.

'What d'you think they'll do?'

'I don't know. There's a sound element; that interpreter of mine, Namkia, is one of them and he carries quite a bit of weight. Asalu and the Impoi group could be relied on— that's where he lives. Then there's a big group, much the biggest, I'd say, which doesn't want to get mixed up in any-thing; just wants to be left alone. Then there's the old crowd, Gaidiliu's lot. There aren't many of them now, not that one knows of, anyway, and it's hard to say what influence they've got. But all the Zemi are really pretty sticky.'

And I told him about the famine, and a good deal else that I knew.

He said he'd like to go on by Hangrum and out that way to the Plains, to see the country a bit for himself. I said I'd go along with him as far as Hangrum, as I knew them by then. They knew me, too, and they wouldn't hold aloof from me as they would from a stranger alone. We arranged to start at eight o'clock next morning, and I went back to raise porters from Laisong.

I didn't realize until we came to keep pace with him on the bridle-road how desperately slow his leg made him. We were making barely a mile and a half an hour. On the steep climb which leads out of the Jenam valley to the Nenglo ridge, there are short cuts; narrow Naga paths, for a hundred feet or so, which leave out several hundred yards of road. To get down a steep slope, the Colonel had to use a man's shoulder; on the short cuts, where none of us could get alongside him, he dropped on hands and knees and crawled up. He didn't complain. There was no doubt that his leg hurt him.

Before we reached the top of the hill I asked him outright

why he had taken on this trek with his leg as it was. (This after he had apologized, for the fifth time, for holding us up, and pressed me to go on.) He said he'd spent many years in Assam, and more than anything he loved his Assam Rifles. And, too, the hills, the rivers, the life in the open. He'd come back full of hope, and joined 'V' Force. But it was manned by young men, who laughed at him, he felt, as a desk-bound crock. Therefore he'd begged himself this reconnaissance, and he was going to do it if it killed him. For, he argued, so long as his leg would carry him, he wasn't a crock.

So we went on slowly towards Hangrum. After the steep climb to Nenglo, two thousand feet or more of it in a couple of miles, the road humps itself along a pinnacled ridge, five miles of ruckles and pleating, till it climbs the big, camel-hump hill which hides Hangrum from Laisong. And this road we travelled, in the August steam-heat; a man's shoulder for the Colonel, step by step, on the down grades; and on the other the step by step climb up.

On the halts, we didn't talk about the road any more. We talked about fishing, and people we'd known in Manipur. He was superb. We might have been sitting in a Club veranda.

When we came to the last summit, the one which overlooks Hangrum itself, I saw the headmen waiting at the village outskirts, by the upper morung. I knew they'd be in a panic at a Colonel Sahib arriving—anything scared Hangrum—so I did go on then, Namkia with me, leaving the others to bring in Rawdon Wright. The Hangrum headmen came on to greet me and we met in the middle, at a turn in the road. Before I could open my mouth, Namkia broke in—I had never seen him so excited:

'That Colonel Sahib—he's not a man, he's a tiger! He's got a wounded leg. He got it in the German war. His bearer told me. He goes up the hills on all fours, like a bear. He comes down the hills like this, on a man's arm. And not one word, not one!—the courage! Anyone else would be weeping aloud by now. I tell you he's not a man—he is a tiger!'

We all stood, and watched the little group of figures, the thick-set Colonel conspicuous, descending the dozen zigzags of the opposite slope. When he joined us at last, it was in a hush greater than any words.

We halted next day at Hangrum, and went round it. There was a silence on the village, as there generally was with strangers; but not this time the silence of hostility. They all looked at him in the same way as did Namkia, or, for that matter, as I. His was not a courage on which one could comment. One could only watch.

Sitting over our drinks in the veranda at sunset, we looked out over the hills of Manipur—their infinite ridges, all green with forest, lifting, locking, melting, merging; reddened now with the sunset reflections behind them. I said something of them.

He looked at me.

'I think you're in love with the hills.'

'You're right.'

The Hangrum headmen came in that evening with a deputation of elders. They wanted him to have a litter. They'd have one made; they'd arranged the porters. They would provide men free of cost, as a gift from the village. Namkia translated. The Colonel shook his head.

'I'm a soldier, tell them. I'm not going to be carried about the country like a woman.'

This was translated back to the Hangrum headman. He said:

'The Sahib got his wound in the war. It's nothing to be ashamed of. Nobody questions his courage. He ought to be carried—he shouldn't go on as he is.'

But Rawdon Wright wouldn't have it. He went on next day, over Hemeolowa, that mounting, narrow scramble, on foot. The headmen and I stood outside the bungalow, watching the white shirt climbing slowly, painfully, with the aid of the interpreter's shoulder, over boulders, gullies, and slippery red soil. At the last turn of the road he stopped and waved. We waved back. Then the white shirt was gone. Nobody said anything, because there was too much to say.

He fell, the porters told me, three times, coming down the steep descent to the Plains from Baladhan. Perry was shocked when he met him again on the return journey to 'V' Force H.Q.

I heard from him once or twice later; he left 'V' Force, and was busy organizing a Porter Corps. Then he fell ill.

The reconnaissance, that last gesture, had been too much. His leg was amputated at the end of November.

He died in December, after a three weeks' fight, just as the scheme he had started, North Cachar Watch and Ward, came into being.

CHAPTER XXVI

RECRUITING

NOTHING much happened till October. Then, quite suddenly, another 'V' Force Colonel dropped in. A young and extremely tall one it was this time. Critchley, who had been Wingate's adjutant in Abyssinia. I had an interview with him, too, in the veranda of the rest-house. I came back from the discussion with a sheaf of miscellaneous papers, a credit of Rs 1000/- at the Haflong Treasury, and instructions to go ahead and recruit the Zemi and Kukis for Watch and Ward.

I managed to meet Perry a few days later. Here was the chance we'd been waiting for to reconcile the Zemi with the Government. But there was one thing we must do, or it would make things worse than ever, irretrievably bad. Every promise we made must be kept to the letter. Here was the means, here was the opportunity; and now it was up to us.

With the perversity of the female I chose to start recruiting at Hangrum, easily the hardest point.

It was about a week before Namkia and I went up there, as I had a bad leg and wasn't fit to march. In the meantime Paodekumba, lately my scullion, called in at the camp; and, hearing of the scheme, volunteered as a scout at once. For the next fortnight he was our one and only recruit.

The Hangrum headmen, when the scheme was put to them, registered disapproval and consternation. But they didn't say no outright; they said they'd put the matter to a village meeting. So Namkia and I sat at the rest-house for a week and nothing happened. Then Hangrum called a public meeting at last and invited us to come and thrash it out.

The meeting-place was the open space in front of the headman's house. The audience, of whom there were about forty or fifty, mostly householders, many with babies on their backs, sat, stood or squatted round it. Namkia and I sat together on a bench facing them. The headman was beside us, acting more or less as chairman of the debate.

It was a clear, cool day, such as one gets in the hills in the early autumn; a sky like pale silk; all dust, all haze dissolved out of the atmosphere, so that the farthest hills stood out crisply. Behind our opponents was the village street, sloping here in a broad fan, and on the far side, towering over us, so that with the sky behind it looked like an operatic backcloth, was the sweeping, smoky-grey prow of the lower morung.

The headman stood up and briefly announced why we were there. Then Namkia rose, and, in a short, forceful speech, stated our case.

To me, sitting there largely as a spectator, the whole procedure was ridiculously like an opera. There was the sweep of the street upstage to the morung, on which even the sunlight looked like a stage effect. There sat the male chorus opposite; and the debate itself took oratorio form. We leapt up one after the other, hurled accusations and denials at each other and as abruptly sat down.

A Hangrum man up:

'You'll take us away! It's a trap!'

Namkia up in answer:

'No! It's an honest offer!'

'Why should we fight for the Sahibs? We didn't fight for the Kacharis, we didn't fight for the Manipuris—why should we fight for the British?'

Namkia again:

'Why shouldn't we? Did the Kacharis or the Manipuris stop the Angamis raiding? Haven't the Sahibs done that? Haven't they given us roads and salt-markets? Haven't they given us protection and peace? Don't we owe them something for that?'

'I tell you it's a trap! They want to take us away! What about the Lushai War? We sent porters for that. How many returned?'

(He was right. Most of the Zemi porters had died of cholera.)

Up went Namkia:

'That was fifty years ago! They've got new medicines now. You can get injections now against these things. Don't quote the past at me! You won't be taken away. It's all for service here. Here, in your own village. You'll be paid. You'll get guns. This is our country, isn't it? Why shouldn't we look after it?'

Opponents were hopping up like fleas now, one after another, as the debate grew hot; Namkia and I jumping up in turn to reply.

'Lies! Lies! Lies!' A man with a child on his back, stepping up to shout it at us.

'It's no lies, but the truth!' (I was up now.) 'If you Zemi won't do it, then the Kukis will! Or else there'll be troops here to do the job for you, and how will you like that? I'm offering you guns—guns! Where are your own guns? When did you last have them?'

'Bring your troops in! Let them do it!'

'All right! You didn't like it before, did you, when the troops got off with your girls? Don't squeal at me later if things go wrong! Fools! We've got guns for you! You've been disarmed for ten years. If you do the job well, you'll have a chance to keep them. Fools!'

'Lies! Lies!'

'Truth!'

'You'll take us away!'

'You'll serve here!'

'Lies!'

'Truth!'

'You'll take us away!'

'We won't!'

It was developing into a nursery shouting-match.

'Lies! Lies! You'll take us away!'

'Truth, truth! We won't!'

The meeting ended, as Zemi meetings do, by everyone just getting up and going home. We hadn't carried our point. There had been nibbles privately to Namkia, but the main body of the village was all against it. They weren't going to play unless they were forced to.

Asalu and Impoi, on the other hand, were eager to do so. There were so many candidates we were able to pick and choose. The pay offered wasn't high, only ten to fifteen rupees a month, but the two villages were still almost destitute and the work offered a heaven-sent escape from economic bondage in the Kachari fields. Not only that; since we had helped them in the famine and kept our word to them about the free relief, they trusted us. If Perry and I said that this scheme was a good thing and they ought to join it, why, then, they did, for what we said was likely to be true, and if the Government had helped them when they were hungry it was up to them to turn to and help the Government.

By the time I went back to Perry to report, the smaller Zemi villages were all co-operating and so was each Kuki settlement we had approached. Only Hangrum and its satellites—the two Shongkais and Baladhan—were still holding out.

'H'm!' said Perry. 'I'll talk to them.'

We went back to Hangrum, Perry with us. We found them in a state of mental turmoil. It was a profound shock to them that the smaller villages were supporting the scheme. For years Hangrum, because of its great size, had dominated the area; now the little settlements had shown that, given a strong lead such as Namkia's, they could defy the colossus. It was unprecedented, it was unheard of. Hangrum didn't know what to do next. They abused the recruits who had come with us for not doing what Hangrum had decided was right for the tribe. The recruits said, to the devil with the Hangrum dictatorship. Perry talked to Hangrum like a Dutch uncle, and in the middle of his speech Hangrum's last vassals revolted. Shongkai and Baladhan had arrived at the meeting with their recruits, so to speak, in their pockets, ready to produce them or not, according as the cat might jump, and, seeing the balance tilted for Watch and Ward, the headmen leaped up suddenly, dashed out of the meeting, and returned, voluble, with their candidates, whom they punted into the arms of the astonished Perry in the very middle of the council. After that it was all over bar shouting. Hangrum, though, that big and unwieldy village, was still in such a state of argument with itself that it was incapable of deciding anything, so Perry gave them a week to make arrangements in and we all moved off down the ridge to Baladhan.

When I and my party came back on the way to Laisong, the first people we met were the Hangrum headmen, who greeted us with that over-effusiveness which always means that something's gone wrong. Had Hangrum found its recruits? Oh, yes, it had! The two elders fell over each other to offer us beer. I caught Namkia's eye across the lip of the cup, and found it eloquent.

The headmen arranged to bring the recruits along to us that evening. Hangrum was large, and had a hundred and twenty houses; it had a goodly number of bucks and husky young men, the type of scout and runner we wanted; one or two of them had already, through Namkia, who had relations there and so a quiet finger in the pie, said they would like to join if the village council agreed on co-operation.

And then, at four o'clock, we met the recruits.

The headmen ushered them in with distinct nervousness. It was justified. The village council, determined to fulfil its quota but not to let us have a man whose loss could possibly matter, had swept the place of the lame, the halt and the blind. Out of the ten candidates, only three had two good eyes. None was under forty; most of them had no teeth; and one was crippled. It wasn't really the old headman's fault. He was a decent old chap in his way and the village was rather much for him. But, drawing a breath, I spoke my mind.

The headman looked distressed, but it was quite plainly no more than they had expected. The candidates didn't mind in the least. In fact, they perked up. I sent the whole lot packing and told the headmen that they must find us something which at least was all in one piece.

They came back again next day with a fresh selection. One or two of the old ones were, it is true, still there, but the more noticeably damaged had been replaced. There was, too, a new tone apparent in this consignment. They were more or less volunteers and they had not the resignation of the other crew. They were apprehensive, certainly, but they were going to take measures to protect themselves. I could tell by the way Namkia wrapped himself in his scarlet blanket and stood aloof that he disapproved of those measures *in toto*. The old headman was in such agitation about it (he must have had a bad quarter of an hour with Namkia) that he couldn't, for stuttering, make me understand what it was they wanted. I had to call Namkia into it, and, disgustedly, he explained. They were asking me to take an oath on all I had said, to swear formally on my life that in no circumstances would they be sent away.

'Sahibs,' said Namkia sharply, 'don't take oaths. A Sahib's word is enough. If a man is a liar, then he isn't a Sahib. An oath—tcha!—the idea!'

'I don't mind,' I said. 'What I've said is true.'

Namkia conveyed this to the headmen and recruits and then dissociated himself from the proceedings entirely, leaning up against a veranda-post and looking distantly on.

Immediately they heard that I agreed, a tall, fair man—his name was Tseva—who had the Caucasian face and warm skin, like a sun-tanned European, which one sometimes sees in the higher villages, whipped an egg out from under his cloth and handed it to me. Namkia came out of his detachment sufficiently to tell me what to do. I should have to repeat the words of the oath, calling on earth and sky to witness that what I said was true, and offering my life as forfeit if I lied. The egg would then be flung down and broken.

Now among most Nagas, and particularly the Zemi, an oath is an exceedingly weighty thing; so much so that it is avoided as much as possible in village-court cases. The death of the forsworn is so certain, so inevitable, that if one of the parties to a dispute takes an oath he wins the case outright —there is no further argument. So, whatever Namkia might think, an oath was clinching proof of our honesty. I had to step out on to the gravel path (one must swear the oath outdoors, in the presence of earth and sun), and there I took the egg from Tseva and repeated the formula. Then, as I am not accustomed to throwing eggs and this was an important matter, I gave the egg to Tseva to fling away.

He did me proud. He took two strides and dashed it on the ground. It hit a knob of rock and burst like a hand-grenade. Shell, yolk, shot into space like bullets. Trotting anxiously, the party piled down the steps to the lower level and started looking for traces. They found them anywhere in a twenty-yard radius—outside the kitchen, on the old gravestones, on the gravel—tiny atoms, shattered, disintegrated.

They came back looking respectful. There could be no doubt, they said, from the egg's complete dispersal, that what I said was utterly, wholly true.

They went off back to the village.

'Huh!' said Namkia.

CHAPTER XXVII

THE SCHEME BEGINS

By early December Watch and Ward was in operation, though, pending invasion, it had not been extended forward to its scheduled frontier along the Barak from Henima village down. It covered, for the time being, a triangular area whose base was the Jiri River from Khuangmual south to the confluence with the Jenam and whose apex touched the railway at Mahur. Its main object now was to pick up spies or agents, eastbound or westbound, who might try to pass through the hills on their way from, or to, the small and unfrequented Hill Section halts; and it covered that key-area in which the three main cross-country tracks converged.

In every village covering an entrance or exit to that triangle we had a small group of scouts, usually five, and, where necessary, a pair of runners. Runners were stationed, by arrangement with the morungs, at every stage along our main routes, so that in emergency news and orders could travel immediately. The scouts' job was to bring to H.Q. all strangers passing through who were not hillmen, or Government servants, or otherwise accounted for; to report crashed aircraft, and generally to keep us informed of what went on.

The difficulty now was to put into the Zemi, so long trodden on by everybody, a little backbone. After the first week or so they came back complaining bitterly that without red cloths, the outward and visible sign of official status, they had no authority. They must have red cloths.

The civil supply was in any case strictly limited, and had now been stopped by the war. We sent an SOS to 'V' Force H.Q., by then located down at Barrackpore. They immediately ordered red blankets from some woollen mill on the other side of India.

Some two weeks after, an officer strolled into the A. & Q. office, and remarked:

'Lovely grey blankets those are for North Cachar! Wouldn't mind one myself.'

'*Grey?*' said the A. & Q., with a stack of 'Urgents' from us stacked up on his desk. 'Did you say *grey?*'

'Good Lord, yes!'

They rushed to look at the bale. The blankets were grey.

A captain jumped into a jeep and drove to Calcutta. He went the rounds of the military hospitals, and, by some sleight of hand or other means peculiar to the unit, came away with nineteen scarlet British Military Hospital blankets, which were despatched at once to Mahur. That gave us one per village group of scouts, and some over for the H.Q. staff at Laisong; and wrapped in these, vested with their brief authority, Watch and Ward embarked on its true career. I believe our own red blankets went by mistake to Kohima, where 'V' Force H.Q. kept them and made them into arras for the mess—at any rate it was draped in blood-red and looked like a setting for the Black Mass, or worse, when I happened to call there a year later.

Our connection with H.Q. was not always close in the very early days. Drafts and the Haflong Treasury's opening day failed so signally to coincide in the first weeks that at the beginning of November I found myself, when all commitments had been allowed for out of Critchley's initial Rs 1000/-, with exactly thirty rupees to keep myself for six weeks. I did it, touring hard the whole time and losing thirty-five pounds in the process; but when I went to Shillong for Christmas, directly after, Mr Mills, when he saw me, guessed what was wrong. I think he wrote to 'V' Force—I hadn't dared to complain, for, as a woman, I was a freak in the job, and I was always afraid that they'd find an excuse to fire me. They always said that sooner or later they'd send a British officer to take over. However, in the New Year they gave me a rise in pay and allowed me rations, a very great help, for things were growing scarce by then and prices were soaring.

Then Colonel Scott, A.Q.M.G. 'V' Force, came up to see us himself, and our teething-troubles were over. We lacked for nothing at all from that day on, and I particularly had cause to be grateful to him.

'Tough for a woman,' he said. 'Always wrong twice—once for being wrong, and once for being a woman.'

In January Colonel Binny, our immediate C.O., who commanded 'V' Force Assam Zone with H.Q. in Imphal, arrived to inspect and brought the promised guns. The Zemi had never had a great many firearms, though most Kuki villages had at least two; what Zemi guns there had been were confiscated in the 'troubles'. Namkia had one still, but his family had been hard put to save it. It belonged to Rintening, his aged father. The S.D.O. of that day—1931—had been searching for a Zemi interpreter. It was impossible to find a candidate. When he began to ask in some anger whethei Asalu could produce a man, Namkia's elder brother rushed home, seized the young Namkia, and crying: 'Go on, you be the interpreter—we might save the gun!' hauled Namkia miserable and protesting along behind him and handed him over as prospective interpreter to the S.D.O. That was how Namkia entered Government service, and how the Rintening family saved their gun.

With the issue of the first few weapons to scouts you could feel a wave of confidence pass over Watch and Ward, confidence in us because we had fulfilled the chief and apparently most impossible of our promises, and confidence in themselves because they were now armed. I myself felt that it was most unlikely that they would ever, in Critchley's phrase, 'stand behind a tree and poop off at Japs'. The guns were muzzle-loaders, of a type and vintage I wouldn't have fired if you'd paid me, long-barrelled, Last-of-the-Mohican guns, taking two minutes or longer to re-load. In some the barrels were of sheet-metal coiled and were not solid at all, and one or two scouts arrived back at Laisong looking very put out, with weapons which looked like a stock attached to a spring —the barrels had burst and simply unwound themselves. But most of all, civil guns, which were chiefly used to protect the crops from game, had had no powder-rations for two years. We were able to give our men powder and shot 'for practice', and so the scouts became, overnight, almost a privileged elite encouraged to spend their leaves in any village where game was doing damage. It was excellent target-practice and the effects on morale were immense.

Binny had devised a system of passes by which people moving through the area on lawful business could carry a paper, issued either by Perry or myself, rubber-stamped with a mark which the illiterate scouts knew. Some time that spring Binny sent up from Imphal a British signaller with a convoy of stores and rations. He came to Mahur direct, not through Haflong; he had no pass, and didn't know he needed one. I was right away in the southern spurs of the Barail, one of the most inaccessible parts of the district.

The signaller managed to find himself some porters and marched his loads up through the bewildered screen till he reached Laisong itself. On his tail, padding along in their red blankets, were the leading scouts from Asalu and Impoi. They knew their orders—no, he had no pass; but how on earth could they arrest a Sahib?

Paodekumba was in charge at the camp. Harder than ever, tough as a rubber ball, he would have arrested anything. But he didn't like to make a mistake. He sent Ramgakpa across to give the man tea while he and the others conferred in the men's lines.

They decided in the end that he was a Jap spy. They had never seen a Jap, but the signaller (who was, I believe, Welsh) had black hair. They had never seen a European who wasn't either fair or brown, and they didn't think that any such existed. They sent up the village for reinforcements, looked out a piece of rope, and, while Ramgakpa was serving the signaller's supper, Paodekumba, off-stage, was briefing his raiding-party. At that moment, fortunately for the signaller, a runner came in with a message. I had reached Mahur and would be back in two days.

Paodekumba regretfully postponed operations.

The signaller was very glad to see me when I turned up. He said he'd been well looked after by Ramgakpa, and that the Nagas had given him porters all right to come up; but they didn't seem to understand when he wanted to leave again. So here he still was. He wasn't at all happy about

Khamba. Khamba, darkly suspicious of him, had kept on prowling round like the Hosts of Midian, expressing opinions to himself in a sullen growl. I'm not sure the signaller was really happy about the Nagas, either.

Paodekumba met me with a rush outside the back door.

'Who is he? Why's he here? Is he a Jap spy? D'you want him captured? I've got the men here!'

He had, too. They came scrambling out of the lines, full of hope, bringing the rope with them.

'I would have captured him before,' said Paodekumba. 'But I thought I'd better wait till you came back. Can we do it now?'

He was quite upset when I explained.

'I did hope he was a Jap,' he said.

CHAPTER XXVIII

THE HANGRUM INCIDENT

ON the south of the Barail, a series of the steepest, highest spurs possible fanned out from the central peak of Katsingpeo-ki. On the far tip of one of them, almost hidden in deep, green woods, was a Zemi village of fifty houses— Khangnam.

I had never been there before 'V' Force affairs took me. It was so remote, so tucked away, so fortified by precipitous steeps and Naga paths like ladders, that even touring officers rarely came there. It was a lovely spot. One looked down between cool clumps of bamboo to the plains simmering below, or back to the north-west, where the Hangrum ridge and the lower Jenam gorge formed a wildly unfamiliar and Himalayan landscape. Alone of the Zemi villages, it had kept its stone defences. The others had let theirs decay into mouldering heaps of mossy rubble. Its shadowed approach path ran along the foot of a steep bluff crowned and plumed with the village bamboo-clumps, like huge and graceful bunches of ostrich-feathers. Suddenly the path ended, at a battered pali-sade; and on the right one saw the village entrance, a flight of a hundred and forty sheer, narrow steps, which rose to a stone wall and a gateway. Even the gate was in position. Pivoted at the top, its upper edge heavily spiked, it swung inward, leaving just enough room to pass through. Every night still it was closed, and wedged in place by a heavy beam whose butt was sunk in the ground.

Khangnam commanded no route, covered no ford. It was on the ground, as remote as ever. But far out beyond it on the Silchar plain one could see a raw, red oblong with a pale strip down the centre—the big new airfield at Kumbhirgram. Aircraft had been added to the excitements of life. Daily they cut through the Barail passes, sometimes finding a safe and straight one such as the Nengte gap, sometimes lifting the thatch on Namkia's morung at Impoi and sometimes skimming the Laisong garden fence. Sometimes they lost themselves altogether and we received a message through the Haflong police directing us to 'search for an aircraft'. The directions given were so inadequate, the information so poor and the effects so disruptive on the main network of Watch and Ward that a special set-up was called for. From the hill just above Khangnam one could command not only Kumbhirgram but almost all the face of the south Barail, so Khangnam became an observation-post and search-party base.

The camp stood on the ridge beyond the village. From it too one looked both ways—south into the heat, north into a swooping green gulf with the mounting spires of the Barail behind it. To reach the village, one went along the ridge between dusty rocks, and down over an outcrop into the broad street with its two big morungs facing one another.

We were just at the outcrop, Namkia and I, at nine that morning, when there was a deep, insistent, piercing hum—growing louder, vibrating all round us; the throb of massed engines, high.

'A lot,' he said.

'They don't sound like ours.'

The whole village was listening, standing at doors and staring up. Then we saw them. Two big formations of bombers were flying high, the attendant fighters hardly visible, seen only as tiny winks as one or other turned over and caught the sun. The two formations passed over. They were above the plain.

'They must be ours, Namkia—but they don't look——'

A little mushroom smoke-puff appeared below them. They sailed on. There was another and another. We heard the boom of gunfire. Then, suddenly, from Kumbhirgram, there was the deep *whoomp* of bombs.

You couldn't see the airfield from the village itself. The nearest viewpoint was a quarter-mile up the road. We all began to run. In ten seconds, the male population of Khangnam was strung out along that road—small boys scudding in front with a horde of dogs, bucks overtaking them, elders shedding their cloaks to run the faster, while girls and women shrieked and dashed for home. Namkia was gone from me in a flash, at a pace I wouldn't have believed of him. In a minute or two I was panting along alone, and one of the headmen, with perfect tact, slowed down to a trot to keep me company.

When we reached the viewpoint, a haze of red dust hid the airfield. We could just hear the moan of the receding bombers. From the dust-cloud came intermittent reports—whether gunfire or exploding ammunition one couldn't tell. When the dust-cloud fell, tilting and blowing away over the wide plain, we could see smoke rising from buildings; there was a fire of sorts, but it was too far to see more.

Namkia pushed through the crowd to find me.

'The guns hit one! We saw something falling. We couldn't see where it went because of the sun.'

'Was it in our area?'

He wasn't sure. He thought it was more over Manipur way.

Then, some days later, after we returned to Laisong, the Kuki wet-rice demonstrator came panting in. He had a porter with him who carried a knobby sack. Out of this he tilted, over our feet, a load of aircraft wreckage—of splintered, grey-painted plywood. Ferreting through it, I found a varnished strip with Japanese characters.

'Where'd you get this?'

It was down in the jungle, he said, near the Jiri-Jenam confluence. There was a lot of it. It had come down burning. The local village-people had all run—they had been terrified by the gunfire, anyway, and had all hidden under their houses for fear of bombs, which, they believed, could blow whole mountains away.

I sent a note to Perry to say that something was down, and then called Paodekumba and sent him out post-haste with a patrol. He was to find the wreckage and look for survivors. He went off as though shot from a gun. It was too good to miss, and Perry and I, coming up by divers routes, met in Baladhan the day the patrol came back. Our luck was out. It was only a shot-off wing.

'Bother,' I said. 'I thought we had something there.'

Namkia, like a spectre, appeared beyond the fire.

'There's a Hangrum party in to report,' he said.

It was Tseva and his co-leader, the wild, wall-eyed hunter of the lower morung. That afternoon, they said, a party of ten men armed with rifles and one man who seemed to be their officer had arrived suddenly, without pass or guide, at Hangrum. He didn't know who they were or where they came from. They were camped at the rest-house.

We looked at one another.

'It wasn't a whole machine——'

'Well, perhaps the rest of it came down somewhere——'

We sent off Paodekumba with all the men we could raise. Perry gave him a written order; if the strangers tried to clear out after seeing that, they were to be stopped—somehow. Paodekumba left with his torchlight patrol and we packed ready for a dawn start. Next morning, marching along the ridge behind Hemeolowa, we were met by two bucks with a note. As Perry opened it——

'That ends the Jap theory,' he said.

It was from a lieutenant of a Railway Operating Unit, sent out to look at the wreckage.

He met us outside the bungalow half an hour later. He was a small half-caste in a very large hat.

'Hallo!' said Perry, startled, looking past him. 'What on earth's all that?'

In the hollow where Tseva had flung the egg, ten men in uniform, with rifles, stood beside half a dozen loads of baggage, and round them were nearly fifty Hangrum men. There were the headmen, there was Paodekumba, there were the scouts, and there was a goat and two large fowls in a basket. Most unusual of all, there was, right in the middle, a long-poled bamboo carrying-chair.

'Why the litter?' asked Perry. 'Has one of your men gone sick?'

There was a hesitation in the reply which made us both look at the small lieutenant.

'My Naik's got fever,' he said.

We sensed something suspicious about the whole affair, not least the little lieutenant's haste to go. But it was then too late for porters to march and return, so Perry persuaded him to stay the night (he was most reluctant) and we all went into the bungalow for a cup of tea.

A few minutes' conversation with the lieutenant were a revelation. Never had we heard such a tale of muddle and ineptitude. He had been sent out to report on the aircraft wreckage, but was wholly misinformed as to the route and conditions prevailing on it—so grossly misinformed that we thought his C.O. had been joking, though it turned out later that this was not so. He had had from the start no mind to fulfil his mission, and, not knowing that we were ahead of him there, would have turned back as soon as he reached Hangrum, leaving any Japs there were to take care of themselves, had not the Nagas delayed him. Worse than that, he was in a state of sick alarm at the thought of being out among Naga head-hunters. By his own confession, he spent his service life in a state of transfer, flung, one imagined, from unit to unit by one disgusted Colonel after another. It was all such a mess that we were shamed and sickened. Seeing Paodekumba waiting outside, I left the rest-house and went off with him to hear his report.

He had arrived in the small hours and delivered the note, but the lieutenant, next day, ignoring Perry's message, had badgered the headmen for porters. They procrastinated as long as they could, but at last, fearing he would use force, they apparently agreed while actually putting Paodekumba's plan into operation. What we had come upon—in the nick of time—was its penultimate stage. As soon as the officer laid his hands on the farewell gifts, that is, the goat and chickens, the supposed porters, carefully briefed, were to jump the whole party, one man of each group wresting the rifle away while the others seized the sepoy. A hand-picked set and Paodekumba himself were all ready to collar the lieutenant.

'Good work,' said I. 'But weren't you scared to tackle the Sahib and his men?'

'Sahib!' said Paodekumba. 'Call that a Sahib! He's the laughing-stock of Hangrum! Didn't you know he was carried up in a litter? He told the headman he was over forty, and too old to walk.' (The headman was over sixty, and could out-walk me.) 'He's too scared to sleep in the bungalow, because of the ghost. He spent last night in the kitchen, with his men. What d'you suppose the disaffected are saying? They've been asking me how the Sahibs will beat the Japs if their officers are like that. What am I to answer? Tell me that!'

'But he told us the litter was there for his sick Naik!'

'His Naik's sick all right, but it's not his litter. That man was carried, and the Naik walked. Since Perry Sahib asked, he's ashamed to say, and he's just asked the headmen to make him a second litter for the Naik.'

I went back to the rest-house, got Perry aside, and told him what Paodekumba had said. As far as propaganda went it was a disaster, a wicked destruction of all that Rawdon Wright's courage had done. We had not been so bitter and angry for years.

The poltergeist manifested twice that evening, with a little help from Paodekumba and Namkia.

The lieutenant, his face a light grey, spent the night lying fully clothed on his bed with a loaded revolver beside him, and an electric torch, which he switched on whenever the bungalow creaked or rapped; which, after its custom, it did frequently, even without assistance from 'V' Force.

When he marched in the morning he left the house on foot, but the Nagas told us later that he had the two litters waiting out of sight. He stepped into one, his Naik took the other, and so, on active service, was borne away. Even then I think we'd have called it quits, but on following up we found he'd cleared the country of produce at his own valuation. Perry sent him in a bill for the difference, and somehow, in a very few days, the story of the poltergeist was known to every other unit on the line.

He was transferred again at the end of a week.

CHAPTER XXIX

CRISIS

ON March 28th, 1944, the midday news which came over on the amenities radio was not good. The Jap attack along the Manipur front seemed to be making progress. The news bulletins, however, didn't say much.

I had had in the last mail a brief scribble from Perry, warning me to keep my eyes skinned. But no more. I wished there had been. Perry had access to better information than I, though he wasn't always able to pass it on.

We could look back now on eighteen months of North Cachar Watch and Ward. This last year had been on the whole a good one. There'd been a bad smallpox outbreak in Khangnam and Peisia, just when those villages were cut off by the Rains; a vaccinator's negligence had contributed. The deathroll had been 20 per cent of the village strength. But what, before, would have been a major tragedy, famine coming straight on top of disease, had been mitigated by 'V' Force relief. Rice, salt, medical help—we had had all these, Perry and I disbursing them at discretion.

Never before had the Barail known such assistance. There was a full-time medical officer and all the drugs we wanted, all the quinine, all the mepacrine—guns, red blankets, powder and shot, everything we had promised and much more. We had had experience, too, in handling guerillas. I think it was Dundee who said that no one could lead a Highland Army who had not shaken every man in it by the hand, and much the same is true of the Assam hillman, to whom any leader is first among equals and nothing more. His attachment is not to the unit, but is entirely personal, and you cannot count on any man unless that attachment exists.

Namkia came into the room. I could tell by his look, as surely as though the dogs had barked, that strangers were coming.

'Who is it?'

'Two Sepoy-Sahibs.'

Boots clumped on the matting in the veranda and I went to the door. There were two British sergeants.

'Hallo,' I said. 'Come in. What's up?'

'Well——' said the first. There seemed a certain constraint. 'It's like this. Fifty Japs crossed the Imphal road at Kangpokpi about a week ago, and they ought to be here by now. We wondered if you'd heard anything of them. We've been sent from Silchar to see.'

The familiar hills visible above the veranda rail—Nenglo and the Hangrum hump—seemed, momentarily, to get up and revolve.

'Well,' I heard myself saying in a bright voice, 'you might as well have some tea while we talk it over.'

When they went on, half an hour later, they left me wiser, but shaken.

For eighteen months we had lived behind a belt of defences a hundred and fifty miles deep. We were the farthest back of all back areas. Now, suddenly, there was nothing. The belt had been swamped and rolled up. Boxes remained at Imphal and Kohima, and the rest was a vast expanse of country filled with advancing Japs.

What front line there was lay on the railway, twenty miles behind us. We were the only thing between it and the Japanese. The sergeants had asked me what force I had to meet them. I'd told them—a hundred and fifty native scouts, one Service rifle, one single-barrelled shotgun, and seventy muzzle-loaders.

We had arranged that I should put every man I could along the line of the Jiri, to give warning of enemy approach. The two sergeants would return to report, and do their utmost to send me help from Silchar. And so we parted.

The first thing was to send the scouts forward without starting a panic. I called up Namkia and told him some of the news, adding that troops would be up at any minute. Paode-kumba and anyone else available (the little man was unmoved) were sent out at once, and runners went back to call up the best men from Impoi, Asalu, Pangmual, Hange, and the villages to the rear.

The frontier was more or less manned by the second day. When I saw the effect which this cold gust of war produced, I could only be thankful they didn't know all that I did. For myself, I had just realized that the camp, with its steep-sided hill and one neck, was a perfect trap. I should have liked to sleep in the jungle. But I daren't; that would have set off a panic in good earnest. So I cultivated an easy air and slept in the house, as usual. They seemed very long nights.

I'd had a brief note from Perry by then, summoning me to Mahur on April 1st for a conference. I found him at the rest-house. Any troops that anyone could lay hands on, sections of this, platoons of that, Railway Maintenance Units, Railway Defence Troops—anything that could march and hold a rifle was being pressed into use. Mahur Station was full of dim groups, shapeless droves of men, standing, or stumping off to some place allotted.

We conferred in the rest-house, in a tiny lamplit room. Numbers of officers, all strangers; perfunctory introductions. The sum total was that the Japs were probably coming, but we didn't know where. We'd got to find out, as there weren't enough troops to protect the length of the line. There was no wireless communication, either. We used the railway telephone, with code-words, as the clerks all down the line listened. 'One elephant' meant 'ten Japs'. Then somebody caused confusion right and left by turning up on the Silchar border with forty genuine elephants.

It was decided to send out a patrol at company strength next day, to see if we could find those fifty Japs. If they were coming at all, they ought to be near by now. Finding the enemy was 'V' Force job. Though my immediate C.O., Binny, was out of touch in Imphal, I could still communicate with main H.Q. in Comilla, where it had gone along with Army Headquarters. I hadn't the least idea whether Colonel Scott would back me or order me out forthwith. I thought the odds in favour of the latter. I signalled to say I was going with the patrol, and asked H.Q. to send me thirty rifles, with which I proposed to arm the pick of the Watch and Ward scouts.

Namkia and I went back next day with the patrol, a com-

pany of the Chamar Regiment. We reached Asalu the first
night, instead of Laisong, as planned; the men were straight
up from the plains and out of training. The following day,
there were four men down before we crossed the pass. The
company commander was carrying one man's equipment,
Ramgakpa the second's, and Namkia the third's—Namkia in
a netted tin hat, with a Bren gun on his shoulder. When the
fourth went down, there was no one spare but myself. Willy,
the O.C., was a tower of strength, ramping up and down the
line, coaxing, cheering, scolding and keeping the men moving.
He bent over the fourth man and shook him.

'Come on—'tisn't far.'

A groan.

'Can't.'

Willy reached for the fallen equipment.

'All right—the Miss-Sahib'll carry your kit. Up you get—
come along.'

The sepoy had his equipment again before Willy had
finished speaking, and marched on the rest of the way to
camp.

All was quiet at Laisong. There was no news from the Jiri;
no word of Japs. Willy camped till sunset in the rest-house
and then moved off to sleep out in the woods. I gave him a
Laisong scout as guide and runner. As they were moving off
by the old road up the valley, the Zemi stopped short,
plucked Willy's sleeve, and pointed up at a tree.

'Jap sniper!' thought Willy. 'Damned if I can see him.' He
ducked and peered. The Zemi was pointing and gesticulating,
whispering excitedly.

The whole column had stopped by now. It was dusk, the
dim, creepy dusk of the dense woods. No one could hear a
thing; no one could see the Japs.

The Naga, with a cluck of impatience, raised his gun and
fired.

The company flung itself down and sideways into the scrub
and ditches with a frantic rattle of rifle-bolts and looked
wildly round for the enemy. With a loud thump a dead
squirrel fell almost on top of the prostrate Willy, and the
scout, with a pleased smile, picked it up.

I spent all next morning soothing Willy.

We went out to Thingje next day—baking heat and a road like concrete; no Japs. Then to Hangrum; no luck. On the 6th, back to Laisong again, still with no information. I left the Chamars to camp down by the river and trudged the weary eight hundred feet up the Laisong hill.

Zhekuingba came from the camp to meet us, and said: 'There's a "V" Force Sahib here.'

I tramped down the veranda and looked through the door. A fair-haired captain was sitting by the table. He got to his feet.

'Hallo. I'm Albright. Scotty sent me along.'

On the floor in the corner, where I hadn't seen them at first, were long cases, rifles and tommy-guns, boxes of ammunition, grenades and rations. 'V' force was backing me up.

Albright gave me the news. 2 and 3 V Ops—that is, Imphal and Kohima areas—had been dispersed and scattered all over the map. A large number of their scouts had been Kukis of those groups involved in the 1918 rebellion. Most of them had been playing a double game, and, when the Japs came over, they joined them openly and led them to every camp and cache set up by their 'V' Force officers. These were mostly missing. They were coming in by ones and twos, and it was hoped that most were safe. Murray, of 3 V Ops, had made a fighting retreat from Shangshak and beyond, ambushing the enemy a fantastic number of times. Ruther had reached Kohima. Someone called Betts was still missing. H.Q. staff had been sent out right and left to fill gaps (Albright was a Staff Captain) and down at H.Q. Scotty laboured almost alone with the clerks.

Our orders were to hang on as long as we could and watch the roads for the enemy advance. As soon as contact was made we should warn Haflong, and then get out as quickly as we could. We took stock in the light of these instructions.

No one had bargained for such a sudden swamping as had in fact taken place. There had been no time to organize a screen between the Barak and Jiri, as set out in the original scheme, and as was urgently necessary to our position. From our doorstep onward there lay an awful blank, a complete obscurity, where we had no contacts and could learn nothing. With our front line where it was, in the Haijaichak pass, we could hope at the outside for an hour's warning. We were far more likely to have no warning at all. There was no field-telephone and no W/T.

We first of all laid on a chain of beacons, supplemented by runners, from the front line to Laisong and on to Haflong. If they went up, it meant contact with the enemy. Haflong had some bad moments with spring grass-fires.

We ourselves lived like gazelle with lions about, ready to leave at once with the utmost speed. If we went to pick tomatoes, we took our tommy-guns, and worked glancing alternately at beacons and exit. At night we left the camp, and slept out in the thick, low scrub to the north, in shelters hollowed out below foliage-level. One man was left as sentry in the camp, to fire a shot and bolt if the Japs appeared, and the rest slept in holes in the jungle warren. We honey-combed the scrub with tunnels and little chambers beaten and cut out, and every night changed round from one group to another, so that no outsider ever knew where exactly in the wide spread of bushes we were hidden. There were cattle-trails, pig-paths, game-runs, our own tunnels—every shape and condition of bolt-hole—so that the chances of trapping us all were few. We had food-caches buried along our probable route out, one on our likely road, and the other in the ravines behind Impoi, the best spot to lie up if for a time we had to.

To me, the worst thing of all was the horrible feeling of treachery in the familiar. To creep back to the camp of a morning, scouting to see if it had been occupied during the night—the old, friendly camp a potential enemy; all those green tunnels of roads, where I had walked and where the dogs had run, known to the last twig—tunnels where we now went in single file, scouts out, expecting ambushes, looking ahead for danger.

Then there was Watch and Ward. Frankly, I never expected it to hold. The men had not been trained for active service. They were flung at it overnight, willy-nilly, without preparation, weapons or support. Had they broken and gone to their homes, nobody could have blamed them; it was never intended that they should face this.

At the height of the crisis, all my personal staff came and asked for leave, and, thinking this was the finish, I let them all go. But within twenty-four hours they were all back.

Later I noticed that Namkia no longer wore his old and valuable *deo-moni* beads. On inquiry, it appeared that the men had all gone home at that time, made their wills, arranged for their families' keep, and, believing that we couldn't survive, had returned to meet the end with us. Their heirloom necklaces had been left to their sons; they now wore only their beads for burial.

'After all,' said Namkia, when he saw me staring at him, 'which was the better thing? To desert and live, and hear our children curse us for the shame we put on them; or to die with you, and leave them proud of us for ever?'

CHAPTER XXX

LOOTERS

WE didn't have leisure for long to worry only about the Japs. In a few days they were merely incidental.

Bodies of Bengali and Madrassi Pioneers, evacuated from Imphal before the siege began, were being marched out across Tamenglong subdivision under their officers. The first company through lost more than forty men by desertion on the trip, though losses from later companies were much less. We spent most of the next fortnight in rounding the forty up. All the Pioneer companies were short of food, and we hadn't a grain to spare. We could only send them through to the railway as fast as we could. But no one, it seemed, though their coming was planned in advance and ample warning given, had thought to send up food for them to Mahur; so they camped there, hungry, in the market sheds.

With one batch appeared an R.A.F. man, from a Vultee Vengeance. The aircraft had got into difficulties over the hills and gone into a spin. Seeing a crash imminent, he baled out, and the aircraft disappeared, still spinning, behind a hill. He landed unhurt, ran to the top of the ridge, and saw a fire down below in the valley bottom. To this he went, tearing and fighting his way through the jungle to help the pilot, but when he came to the spot, he found it a jhum-fire, with no sign of any aircraft at all. Then he met some Nagas and asked by signs if they had seen the machine. Oh, yes, they said; it had come spinning down, like this; and then straightened out and gone off whirr!—like that.

He hadn't the faintest idea whether he was east or west of Imphal and which way he ought to walk. The Nagas took charge of him and led him up to the Tamenglong bridle-road, where the Pioneers were coming through, and here he was, walking out, and swearing he'd never do it again if he lived to be a hundred. We heard the sequel later. The Vengeance got safely back to Imphal, and the pilot jumped out, shouting:

'Hi, George, that was a near thing, wasn't it?'—and found there was no George. It was ten days before they heard where he was.

Worse than a few Pioneers was soon to come. When the big camps at Kanglatombi and other points along the Imphal road were overrun by the Japs, there was little or no ordered evacuation of their personnel. While some formed bodies marched off in good order, a large number left by ones and twos, with their arms and ammunition, and came trekking westward through the hills in a hungry and broken flood. They were not regular troops, but drivers, mechanics, water-carriers, artisans, men of every kind of auxiliary service, drawn from every creed and part of India, and for the most part newly-recruited and ill-disciplined. With them were handfuls of Naga refugees, mostly pastors and teachers from the mission stations, Indian road-contractors, Gurkha graziers with their wives and children, and stray, half-naked prisoners escaped from Jap hands—chiefly men of the Gurkha Parachute Battalion. All these had to be collected, questioned, helped, fed, clothed, doctored, disarmed if necessary, and sent to the rear. In a few days the armed stragglers were a serious problem. Over in Manipur, in the belt between the Barak and Jiri, the situation was already out of control. Though the Nagas started out by giving every assistance, their only rewards were assaults and lootings. Villagers took to the woods, normal life came to a standstill; and as the tide spread westward and reached us, it became increasingly hard to maintain order—the whole intelligence network was threatened.

Our only force, apart from the twenty scouts we had so far armed with rifles, was an under-strength platoon of Mohendra Dals, Nepalese State Troops. One day a British officer had appeared suddenly in the doorway, with the heated look of one who had just come up Laisong hill, and said: 'Are you Miss Bower?'

'Yes.'

'Well, I've got a platoon of Gurkhas for you.'

Albright demurred. I was a civilian—there would be reper-cussions. But the stranger didn't care. His orders were to

leave the platoon, and leave it he did, and it wasn't for us to
look a gift-platoon in the mouth, especially just then. They
hadn't been with us more than a few days when the main
surge from the eastward came. I could do nothing with the
stragglers without rank-badges. We split Albright's. He wore
captain's pips on the left shoulder, I on the right. It was most
effective.

'If anyone kicks,' wrote Scotty, when he heard, 'I suppose
I can always laugh it off.'

One morning we were down in the Jenam valley, practising
ambushes along the old road. A thunderstorm came over, and
we took refuge in the rest-house, Albright, I, the six Gurkhas,
Namkia, and a couple of Naga scouts. It poured, it cataracted.
The water fell off the eaves and we leaned up against the
veranda-posts and gossiped with Khuala, the stout-hearted
Lushai doctor, who was doing yeoman work for the people
coming through.

'Here comes someone,' said Albright, suddenly. 'Gosh,
they're wet!'

Running in through the puddles were two Zemi. One wore
a red cloth. Though by their hair-cuts they were of the
Thingje group, their faces weren't familiar. They jumped up
on the concrete plinth and in out of the wet. The taller stripped
to his soaked and ragged kilt, and stood there, wringing the
water out of his cloth as he talked to Namkia. He was very
angry about something.

Namkia translated. They were the headmen of Impuiloa,
a village just across the Jiri Valley. Four or five of these
ragged walkers-out had just been through the place and looted
the headman's house, among others. He and his friend had run
ahead by a short cut and were here before the gang, which
ought, he said, to be at Haijaichak by now.

We called the six Mohendra Dals and set off up the road.
The Naik and five sepoys were armed with rifles; Albright
and I had automatic weapons.

It was about four miles to Haijaichak, by a pleasant, winding
road along a stream. We were nearly there, and trudging
through the trees of the village copse, when two Nagas
rounded the next bend like running deer. They slowed when

they saw us and came up at a trot. One was Hailamsuong, head
of the Haijaichak scouts; the other Gailuba, his lieutenant.

Hailamsuong had the worst job in Watch and Ward, and
the most responsibility. Whichever way the Japs came,
whether from Kohima, Kangpokpi or Tamenglong, he would
certainly be the first to meet them. On him and his young band
(they were the youngest group of scouts we had) depended
the warning-system of North Cachar. Till the stragglers came
he was managing pretty well, but now his men were getting
beaten up by the looters almost every day. Each time it happened they left the observation post and resumed their watch
for Japs from the hillside scrub, while somebody ran down to
call us along. Evidently it had just happened again.

'H'm,' said Albright, echoing what I thought. 'That party
must have arrived.'

'It's more of those stragglers,' said Hailamsuong, breathless.
'They drove us out of the look-out first and then went into
the village. They started to loot the place, and the people ran
for the woods. They're all in the village still, with what they've
taken. There must be thirty of them! Come and get them
out!'

Thirty of them. That wasn't quite so good. We went on
round the bend and out of the woods and slowly along the
path below the village. There was no one about. An old Zemi
came out of the woods above and shouted something, but
whether entreaty or warning we couldn't hear. Everything
was quiet. We halted just below the col, at the foot of the
short path leading up to the village. One or two of the scouts,
who had been lying up in the surrounding bushes, came out
and joined us. And at that moment an armed man strolled out
of the village and looked down at us all.

There was a moment in which not one of us moved. The
man walked off again, taking us, I suppose, for another band
of stragglers. His tin hat bobbed away between the houses.

Albright pushed me behind a big standing-stone.

'You and the Naik and all the Nagas stay here. If we get in
a jam—well, use your head and join in.'

I didn't like being left out of it at all, but this was no time
to argue. I, the Naik and the Nagas waited in cover by the

look-out hut. Albright took the five sepoys and walked up into the village. We could see the Gurkhas rootling among the empty houses with fixed bayonets, perfectly happy to take on five to one.

I heard Hailamsuong's anxious voice behind me.

'Will there be shooting, my mother? My wife and child are hidden in my house.'

'The Captain Sahib is very clever,' I said firmly. 'He will take them without shooting if he can.'

We all stood there, waiting for shooting to start.

Then there was Albright, walking back down the slope.

'It's all right,' he said. 'We got them in the morung.'

As his party were searching the nearer houses, a Zemi had appeared and pointed them to the morung. Albright had tip-toed up and looked in through the window. They were all in there. They had cooked a meal and were eating it in the middle of the room, with their weapons stacked along the walls. He and the Gurkhas had stepped into windows and doorways, covering the men inside; and that had been that.

The prisoners were sitting there glumly when we arrived, thirty nondescripts from any part of India you choose. Another two were being brought down from the upper morung. As we entered, the Zemi came flooding back, having watched the proceedings from the hill above. We recovered a certain amount of looted goods, but there wasn't much else to be done. We impounded their arms and ammunition—twenty-one rifles, nine Stens, and three thousand rounds. They went off under escort in a depressed file, elated Gurkhas marched ahead and behind and Zemi porters carrying the collected weapons in firewood-baskets.

We gave Hailamsuong a Bren gun post after that. There were no more incidents at Haijaichak.

CHAPTER XXXI

INTERLUDE

THEN Kohima was relieved. The story of its amazing defence has never been properly told yet, and should be.

The relief removed the Japs from one of the roads converging on us, and it added to Laisong a half-section of the 3rd Assam Rifles, fresh from the siege and in tearing spirits. Lieutenant Tibbetts, a 'V' Force officer who had also been through the siege, brought them up and left them, and they took their boots off and went to bed for forty-eight hours. When they had done that and emerged again, they cleaned everything till it glistened and then looked round for some more Japs.

Lance-Naik Supbahadur Rana and Rifleman Riki Ram (commonly known as Mickey Mouse, whom he much resembled; a thin boy in large boots, with a heroic tenacity; be it feet or fever, you never lost Riki Ram—he always came up in the end, still limping, still game) were Gurkhas. The other four were Nagas, three Lhotas and one Ao. Their morale was most heartening. They knew they had the measure of the Jap, and all they wanted to do was to go and kill some more as soon as possible.

We had rather the same idea ourselves, but unfortunately there were no Japs. By that time we were not only in touch with a few of the Zemi villages beyond the Jiri, but were in wireless communication with Tamenglong, and knew, through them, that the Japs were now well back of the Barak and in the area behind and about Kangpokpi.

Our W/T was a gift from 14th Army. Scotty had thumped on desks at Army H.Q., and they had created—this with the invasion in full swing, the siege of Kohima in progress, and every possible commitment on their hands—out of bits and pieces and reinforcement camps, a W/T net with stations at Silchar, Tamenglong, Nungba and Laisong. That 14th Army could find the time in such a crisis to help an outlying side-show like ours was an index of what it was.

Then the Laisong forces were further augmented. The Mohendra Dals, who had been increased to a full company under their own officers, were withdrawn and sent to Nungba, and in their stead came a company of Mahrattas under Captain Archer.

We were at that time training as many scouts as possible to use rifles, and Namkia was being taught to use a tommy-gun by Archer's Havildar-Instructor. One day in the middle of rifle-practice on the miniature range, which lay between the bungalow and the garden, we were suddenly visited by a low-flying Jap fighter. In the rush for cover I drew the cookhouse drain. After the excitement was over, I, like the hero of Kipling's poem, 'flushed that four-foot drain-head, and it never choked again'. Archer, who was looking for a new camp-site, decided as a result of the fighter's visit that he must have one well-concealed from the air, and one of the few places which answered this requirement was a point on the east face of the hill. Platforms could be cut to hold the buildings, and the bamboos and jungle afforded fair cover. He and I went to reconnoitre, crawling up a well-trodden game-trail which ran in from the main path.

'This'll do,' he said, surveying the place as far as one could from the all-fours position. 'We'll have the platforms along on either side and the path'll do nicely through the middle.'

I saw just under my nose, immortalized in the hard, baked mud of the path, a large, feline pug-mark.

'You may get trouble with game,' I said. 'This is a main run.'

'Oh, they won't come when they smell humans about! After all, it won't be a small camp.'

So on that site it was, and we called in men and cut plat-forms and built huts, and the Mahrattas moved in. They were good company. They had a field-telephone which linked us, Archer, and their outpost at Haijaichak, and from it we derived all the exercise in exasperation which a field-telephone can provide.

On one occasion, when Archer was taking a small patrol across the Jiri, his Naga porters, who were Haijaichak men, laid down their loads at that point and refused to go farther. He had no interpreter with him, but didn't want to use force, so he went along to the 'phone and rang us up.

It so happened that Albright and I were out, and only Namkia was there. He had some slight experience of the telephone, having played with it twice in Calcutta in George Gemmell's office at Balmer Lawrie's, so he answered it, and Archer explained the trouble.

'Oh!' said Namkia. 'Well, put the Haijaichak headman on to talk.'

Archer fetched up the old man, another of those unfortunate asses who were so often figureheads to tough villages, and the Havildar held the receiver up. The old man took it and cautiously pressed it, as they told him, up to his ear.

'Is that the headman?' said Namkia, at the other end.

'Uh.'

The telephone made a noise like a burst of fire-crackers. The old man dropped it and backed off. The receiver hung, still firing intermittently. He was with difficulty re-connected to it, and even then held it out at arm's length.

'Yes,' he said. 'Yes, yes. Oh, at once, yes!' He dropped the receiver finally, scrambled out of the trench, and doubled off shouting at the recalcitrant porters; who picked up their loads and made off with the patrol and stuck to them like glue till they all came back to Laisong again three days later. Archer had hardly time to thank Namkia before he had to run to catch up with the patrol and porters. When we returned to camp, some three hours later, Namkia was sitting smiling beside the 'phone. The headman of Haijaichak was one of his pet dislikes.

One night about nine o'clock Archer's quartermaster-havildar, passing the store, which stood across the path from the quarter-guard, noticed the three goats which had just come up as rations standing shivering and looking beyond him up the central path. Looking that way himself, he saw, only a few yards from him and right in the middle of the track, a leopard, crouched, intent on the shaking goats. He dashed into the shed, expecting at any moment claws in his back, untied the goats, swept one under one arm and two under the other, and crossed the track at a staggering run to the quarter-guard where he threw the goats into the lock-up and turned out the guard. When they reached the path, the leopard had disappeared. They hurried up the path, where presumably it had gone, but there wasn't a sign of it. They went on, searching about, until they came to the next cross-roads, where a path led down to Archer's hut, just below the road, and up to another, I believe the Subedar's, a little above. There they stopped, debating.

At that moment the leopard walked very deliberately out of Archer's hut, pushing out under the door-curtain, mounted the steps to the road, looked at them once with a ghostly, green contempt, and vanished away up the moonlit path. When breath returned to them, they flung themselves down to the hut to see what had happened to Archer, and almost collided with him in the doorway.

He had been in bed, smoking a last cigarette under the mosquito-net before turning over, when the door-curtain was pushed aside and some big beast came quietly in and lay slowly down on the floor beside the bed.

'One of Miss Bower's dogs,' thought Archer, sitting up. It wasn't quite dark in the hut, but he couldn't see the thing —it was too closely under the side of the bed. Then it occurred to him that Miss Bower's dogs had been sent away to Silchar.

A village dog, then. He peered over the edge of the bed. The mosquito-net obscured the view, and it was very dim in the hut, but whatever it was didn't look quite like a village dog. It seemed a good deal bigger. It didn't look quite like a dog. A slight cold sweat began to break out on him. It was very large indeed; and it was not a dog.

It now seemed that the bed creaked at his every breath. His cigarette was burning shorter. It was almost down to his fingers. He daren't move. There was a piece of fluff in his throat. He couldn't help it. He couldn't control it. He smothered a cough.

The leopard rose up by the side of the bed and sat there like a dog. It gave him the dirtiest look in its repertory and stalked out. It was not seen about the camp again.

CHAPTER XXXII

TAMENGLONG

IN the middle of May we received permission to move forward, permission for which we had been manœuvring for
weeks.

Albright, the instigator of the scheme, had gone by then,
recalled again to H.Q. His last act for us was to make the
final arrangements about our move with local H.Q. at Silchar,
H.Q. 'V' Force, and 14th Army itself. He was relieved by
Bill Tibbetts of 2 V Ops, one of those displaced 'V' Force
officers who were kicking their heels at Manipur Road until
their areas were re-formed. One of them—Betts—curious to
see North Cachar, nearly crossed the 'Tib' off on the signal
so as to go himself, but found that Tibbetts had already seen
it. So Tibbetts came, tall, fair, amiable, and hanging on to
the tail of a ration-convoy mule, and was greeted with howls
of joy by his old comrades the Assam Rifles. Then, in the
second week of May, the coveted signal arrived. The move
was sanctioned.

With six Assam Rifles, fifteen scouts, Ison the signaller
(the best man on the network) and a hundred Zemi porters,
we moved up, preceded by a Mahratta patrol bound for the
Kangpokpi area, and followed, we hoped, by Archer and his
company, who were to sit at Tamenglong with us and harry
any Japs we found for them. We were marching none too
soon. The Rains were almost on us. The Barak, when we
saw it first from the rest-house at Hepoloa, was running thick
and red at the bottom of the valley. Cloud was about us and
it was raining hard.

The North Cachar porters panicked. They were terrified
of the big river. They knew all about the two disasters at
the Falls. In one, a girl eloping with her lover had been
drowned when he, jumping ashore on the home bank,
stumbled and accidentally kicked the raft back into the
current, where, girl and all, it was carried over while the boy

ran helplessly along the bank. Then in the other, a whole
dance-party on their way home had tried to cross while the
river was full and rising. They lost control of the raft and were
swept over, the bucks gathering the girls to them at the last
and hiding from them the sight of death. So the porters
downed loads in the rest-house compound and wouldn't go
on a step. We argued with them, Namkia and I, under the
dripping pines, while the rain stung us and made patterns of
plops in the growing puddles. We got them going at last.
They almost ran down the long, steep, slippery hill—two
miles it must have been—to reach the river while it was still
fordable. But when we came to it, scrambling hand-and-foot
down a newly-cut trace in rank, wet bamboo-jungle, it was
marvellously shallow. Bill and the Assam Rifles leading, we
forded it, the porters hurrying through as though the water
scalded.

On the far bank were an overseer and a gang of workmen.
The old suspension-bridge had been wrecked by a flood, and
at our request the S.D.O. at Tamenglong was having it
reconstructed for our line of communication. But, for reasons
only he knew, the Kabui overseer in charge of the work had
moved it fifty yards upstream, from hard, high ground to a
sandbank, and it looked to me far too low. However, it was
across—there was nothing to be done now; so we turned and
tramped on. The 1938 camp was lost in grass and creepers.
Without the bridge, the river there looked harsher and wilder;
the crags of the far cliff stood out grey and bare. We left the
stream and began the long climb.

Tamenglong had just been strafed in error by the R.A.F.
and we had been warned to duck if we saw fighters, in case
the misunderstanding had not been resolved. None appeared.
Thongkim, one of our leading Kuki scouts—the North
Cachar Kukis were loyal to a man and did sterling service—
met us at the Kabui village with a note from the S.D.O.
Tramping on, we came to the little outpost.

It hadn't changed. The fort was there, and so were the
pines, the streams, the knolls and the perched bungalows.
The R.A.F. had shot the red tin roofs as full of holes as
pepper-castors; that was all. Even a few zinnias survived in

the grass and weeds round the now-ruined summerhouse where we had sat and looked out towards Hangrum, so very remote then. The S.D.O. of that day had told us about the attack and I'd wondered, looking at the saddle and the looming bulk of Hemeolowa, whether I'd ever have the luck to set foot in a place like that.

We settled down in the rest-house and waited for Archer. The clouds thickened; grey masses boiled over us, driving in lower and more and more steadily from the south-west. And still he didn't come.

The S.D.O., we found, had been left there alone since the invasion started. He had done amazingly well with few resources, no orders and no support. He had his own intelligence screen a full three days' march away, and news from it reached him by relay-runner in less than twenty-four hours. In the middle of April, when the Japs were nearest, the Kuki Subedar in charge of the Assam Rifles in the fort had been detected in communication with the enemy. He claimed he was trying to tempt them into an ambush, but his message was ambiguous, to say the least, and, with the Kuki record what it currently was—even Jampi village, west of the Barak, were helping the Japs—it was no time for chances. The S.D.O. arrested him and sent him down for court-martial.

Then as if that weren't enough, there was the matter of Sharp. Sharp, a young Indian Civil Service officer, had served in Imphal and knew the district well. He had been hastily taken into the Army and sent out to organize an intelligence screen in the gap between Watch and Ward and the Imphal-Kohima road. He never reached Tamenglong. The fifty Japs whom we had been expecting turned south along the hills when only a march or so in. Cutting their way through forest, they came out when they were least expected, at Haochong on the Imphal-Tamenglong track, blocking it and turning back the bulk of the Pioneers—so many extra mouths to feed in the box at Imphal. They reached the Haochong rest-house just ahead of Sharp. It was almost certain now that they had captured and killed him. Search continued in the retaken Haochong, but they hadn't yet found his body.

At the end of a week the Mahratta patrol came back.

Archer's Subedar, an old friend, came to us almost in tears because they had had no fighting. They rested a day, and went. Still there was no sign of Archer and his company.

Then things began to go wrong. Something had happened to the arrangements with Imphal. 'V' Force there had been told about our move, but somebody, somewhere, had failed to pass it on—we never found out for certain what happened. Signals flew. And, though we watched the Laisong road like Sister Anne, there wasn't a sign of Archer.

Every day reports of Jap foraging parties came in. There were tales of dumps left unguarded, of mule-convoys laden with rice and escorted by two or three men. We traced their routes on the map, three or four days from us, on their journeys through the villages to levy food. We couldn't get at them. We sat and chafed in the small rest-house. The holes in the roofs leaked; the pine-branches scuffed on the tin; and out between the trees we could see the hills where the Japs were. A mild dysentery broke out, attacking all of us except Ison. Bill Tibbetts, for some reason, had it badly. He was almost incapacitated for the first few days of June.

Then we received a signal that two hundred Japs and a field-gun were approaching Tamenglong and that we must retire at once.

Had it really been so, I don't think we should have minded. But we knew for certain it was a false report, and more than that, nonsense. The heart was out of us. We were tired and sick of all the bungle there'd been. Albright had done so much, had fixed it all, had been to enormous pains to make it all sure; and someone else at a stroke had wrecked the lot. We packed up and turned back. As we had thought, the repaired bridge was too low. The day before we marched the first flood of the year climbed over it. We took the other road, by the south and Joute ferry.

The day we left, Bill's illness lit up again. I was scared, after a while, that he wouldn't make the journey. But he kept going, dosing himself as he went, and never let up or complained. Down in the valley-bottom, where the path turned suddenly into almost virgin jungle along the river, I saw he had vanished abruptly from the line of march. There in front of me was a small ravine. On the far side of it were our leading scouts. Fifty yards behind them should have been Bill, and fifty yards behind him, myself. But there were they and there wasn't a sign of Bill.

If he had fallen out and collapsed in the jungle—which lay, a prickly maze alive with leeches, thick on either side of the small path—he might take days to find, if we found him at all. I had one short, hideous moment of sick panic. Then there was a crash of bamboos in the ravine, and loud profanity. I peered over the lip. Below was a muddy wallow, a bridge in splinters, and Bill, as large as life, thank God, floundering in the ruins.

We stopped that night at the ferry with a hospitable Joute Kuki. Bill was better next day, and we pushed on. At Hepoloa we came on ninety men of the Observer Corps, bound for Tamenglong, right off their route, and in possession of our quarters and transport. The whole show seemed to have gone haywire. We didn't care; we only wanted to get back somewhere where things were sane, as they had been in the old and blessed days under H.Q. We camped in the Naga village, where they were kind to us. Then Impuiloa, a vague blue of soaking wet and exhaustion, of mist and torrential storms and wet firewood; down into the narrow, plunging cleft of the Jiri gorge, up the far side, over the hill, and into the Haijaichak pass by the stragglers' road, to the little look-out and the Mahrattas' trenches, and all the familiar, friendly sights of home.

We found out then what had happened to Archer. He had gone down with dysentery a day or two before he should have started. His Colonel, who was just on the edge of retirement, refused to send another company up, though his British officers were almost mutinous about it, and, if I know the Mahrattas, the men too.

I was due for leave and took it, Bill staying in charge. Down in Calcutta, it was an effort to undress for bed after sleeping so long in my clothes. One felt so unprepared in case of a night alarm, and it was difficult to get used to the idea of security. The second or third night, I woke to find myself groping about on the floor for my Sten gun. When I came back. Bill was recalled to active service, for the war had gone forward again and Watch and Ward was again a back area.

In November, when the war was well down into Burma and there was no more need for us, Watch and Ward was wound up.

Perry, Albright and Scotty came up for the final meeting. All the men came in. Laisong village and the camp were crammed. Magulong, the finest dancers of the Zemi, sent a picked party. Mithan, thanks to inflation, were not obtainable, but Namkia searched the country and found a massive pig.

It was a cool, bright day when we paid them off. A small camp table stood outside the house, the wind flipping the papers and making us grab at them. On three sides of it, in a solid bank, were the gathered scouts; a hollow square of scarlet blankets and jet-black heads, relieved a little here and there by the Kukis' white turbans and tipped on either side by the dull jungle-green of the Assam Rifles.

One by one the scouts were summoned to the table, received their presentations—guns, ivory armlets, knives, certificates or cash—took their discharge-papers and retired. The disbandment over, the kaleidoscope dissolved, those who had been given guns running, their red blankets flapping, to the end of the spur, where Albright was running a shooting competition with flasks of powder for prizes. In the lengthening light the whole camp was a scurry of scarlet, of bordered Kuki cloths, of Magulong in dance-dress, with huge tam-o'-shanters of wound cotton thread, and hornbills' feathers quivering in the stiff breeze. The spectators formed a ring; Magulong began to dance. They danced all night.

Next morning the battered boxes went, the rifles and my old Sten, and Namkia's tommy-gun. The Assam Rifles escort went, and Albright, Perry and Colonel Scott. The long line of porters wound away up the village street and was glimpsed once more, finally, where the road climbs the spur, the point where, long ago, we had first seen Rawdon Wright. Then it was gone. The camp was empty, turned civilian again.

But it was not the same. Too much had happened. The

scouts, scattering to their villages, hugging their treasured guns—they were not the same. They had put their trust in us and we in them, and, when the crisis came, neither had failed. Our varied elements had been welded into such an entity as a year earlier I would not have thought possible. But, most important of all, the glass wall had gone. It had melted, one couldn't say when. What we set out to do had been done.

CHAPTER XXXIII

THE MAN WHO CAME TO CATCH
BUTTERFLIES

THERE was nothing very much in the mail that day except a letter from a Colonel Betts, of 'V' Force, who wanted to come and catch butterflies at Laisong and asked me if I could help him with the arrangements. I wrote him off a line to say I could, and then went on with reading the daily papers.

It was May of 1945. Namkia, I and fifteen ex-scouts had just come back from a jungle training-school, where we had worked as instructors for the last six months. For the first time in years I was at leisure. I'd written to Mr Mills to ask about fresh work. He had suggested the Daflas, up in the northern hills on the other side of the Brahmaputra Valley. There was no use in moving until the Rains were over, so I'd settled down again in the old camp to write up my Zemi notes.

On a soaking wet afternoon a fortnight later, almost the very day that the monsoon broke, Namkia came in to say that a Sahib was arriving.

It was, presumably, this peculiar Colonel. With the monsoon driving in as hard as it was, I hadn't thought he would come. I went rather dubiously out by the back door to have a look.

On the rise before the blank west wall of the house were, silhouetted against a grey and dripping sky, two lonely figures. One was a very long, lean, dampish Colonel, the other a small and sodden Gurkha orderly. They hailed us with relief. When we had brought them in and given them tea, the Colonel in the house, his man in the kitchen, I asked what their future plans might be.

The Colonel said he would like to stay a few days, as Laisong was magnificent butterfly-ground. Only a few weeks earlier, Perry, a keen Aurelian, had seen four rare *Calinaga* on the spur itself, and, what is more, caught two. The camp had been enlarged and there was plenty of room, so I suggested he use the place as a base and let me know when he wanted picnic lunches, and with that, more or less, went back to my notes.

The Colonel, however, seemed curiously slow to start in the mornings. One would have imagined that an ardent collector with only ten days' leave and a field like Laisong would have been out in pursuit of *Calinaga buddha buddha* and *Stichopthalmia Howqa* from the moment the chill was off and his prey moving. But no—ten, eleven o'clock, and the Colonel would still be about. There was something, too, a little unusual in his manner. It wasn't—no, he was a very charming, amiable Colonel; but he did seem reluctant to go and hunt butterflies.

On the fourth day of his stay he came home particularly early. I, who hadn't expected him back before tea-time, was in the kitchen baking a cake when Namkia came in and said the Colonel wanted to see me. Leaving the cake, I dusted as much flour as possible off my trousers and went across to hear what my guest wanted. He was pacing up and down on the far side of the grass as though in some agitation. I wondered if he'd been recalled and had to go back at once.

We fell into step and quarterdecked up and down beside the garden. The Colonel was certainly agitated. He was slightly incoherent. I was listening with only half an ear, most of my mind on the cake, and supposing that we should come to the point some time, when, as we came abreast of the cannas, I found myself receiving a proposal of marriage.

The next few minutes were quite chaotic. At the next lucid interval, we were in the bungalow. We seemed somehow to have become engaged. I was not at all certain it was what I intended—I had, really, been thinking about the cake. But this was hardly the moment to explain. He was so terribly pleased about it all. It wasn't, either, as though he weren't a suitable Colonel. He was a charming man. I couldn't think offhand of one I liked better. Still, it did all seem rather sudden.

Then he kissed me. He was tall and strong. A chair got in the way. The scene resembled a struggle more than an embrace. I was in panic lest Namkia come in. My staff held strong views on that sort of thing, and should he draw the wrong conclusion—he certainly would—the Colonel was in for a mass assault. But the embrace concluded, the crisis passed, and nobody came in.

His baptismal names, it appeared, were Frederick Nicholson, but he was usually known as Tim. His story was the final touch. But I was past the stage of being surprised, the heels of the world were uppermost, we were all mad and a little more insanity couldn't matter.

He had first heard of me by the nickname of the 'Naga Queen' the very first day he joined 'V' Force, eighteen months before. He had even then been intrigued by the idea of a lady guerilla. Then followed the Jap invasion, when he and his camp together were overrun. He had walked out for three weeks right through the Jap Army, arrived at Kohima starving, and been shipped out to hospital just before the siege began. When Bill Tibbetts, one of the subalterns of his detachment, was sent off to my support that summer, his reports, when he returned, roused curiosity still further. But Fate seemed against a meeting. When I went on leave, he missed me by two days at H.Q. in Comilla, and then failed to find me in Calcutta.

A year later, the unit was in Shillong refitting and training. The war was now so far off that there was talk of disbanding 'V' Force altogether. Everything was flat, at a loose end. It suddenly came to him that now was the time to call on the Naga Queen. The war was over, or nearly; if he was ever going to get married, there wasn't much time to waste, and she sounded as if she'd have more in common with him than anyone else he'd met. Anyhow it was famous butterfly-country and he was a keen collector—that gave him an excellent excuse; and if the main objective should prove unsuitable or unwilling—well the time spent wouldn't all have been wasted. He sent a tentative letter off, and, on receiving a fairly mild reply, applied to his Commanding Officer for leave.

The C.O. was loath to grant it and asked for reasons. The reply—that it was for the purpose of reconnoitring the Naga Queen with a possible view to matrimony—knocked the wind clean out of his sails and left him with his mouth open, a thing the Japs had never been able to do. Tim got his leave. What the unit would have thought if they'd known I don't know. My Zemi bodyguard had a reputation.

The journey itself could hardly be called propitious. He missed a train-connection and then missed Perry, and had to sit about waiting for both; the Rains broke as he entered North Cachar. Late on a dark and streaming day he reached the Tolpui pass. Soaking, weary, running with rain, he sat down for a rest. It occurred to him that he was a damned fool.

She might be a frightful, hard-faced, horse-toothed Amazon. She might throw him out on his ear. In a turmoil of indecision, he drew lots. Long straw, she's a harpy. Middle one, she's a peach—but she won't have me. Short one, she's a peach and says yes.

It came out short. He got up, pulled his green beret firmly on his head, and marched off through the rain towards Laisong.

One thing I did insist upon, and that was a six months' engagement. I would not be rushed; I must consider. He went off back again a day or two later, his leave over, and we were to meet again in Shillong in three weeks' time.

When the aged train clanked down off the Hill Section and into Badarpur Junction one afternoon in July, a long, familiar figure was waiting on the platform. He was afraid for a minute I hadn't come, and then Namkia's red waistcoat came bobbing through the crowd, an unmistakable landmark, and we were all together and fighting our way out to the jeep.

As we bowled into the evening along the flat, interminable road which runs westward along the foot of the hills, he dropped the bombshell. He had been posted to Burma in the Military Administration. He wanted the wedding at once.

I said No.

I went on saying No consistently till we reached Shillong. There the Mills family shook my resolution. Tim had been round to call on them and announce his intentions—they were the best friends I had in India—and they were delighted with him. They were all for having the wedding at once.

The next day Tim called for me with the jeep and we argued the matter the length and breadth of Shillong. I said No on the peak; I said No in the Police Bazaar; I said No by the racecourse. At last we found ourselves on the Gauhati road and overlooking the American Remount Depot. Perhaps it was the lengthening afternoon; perhaps it was the sight of several hundred mules. At any rate I said Yes, and the next thing I knew, we were tearing round Shillong on two wheels in search of the padre and a special licence.

When Tim dropped me outside the hotel that evening, the first person I saw was Namkia. I took a deep breath and told him the news.

It was the only time I ever saw him stricken speechless.

Forty-eight hours later, on July 7th, we were married. Cake, wine, wedding-dress, reception—Mrs Mills, by some unfathomed miracle, produced them all. Namkia and Haichangnang stood picturesquely on either side of the church door—Namkia with his well-deserved British Empire Medal just gazetted. There was a guard of honour of Assam Rifles. We came out under an arch of kukries, and the last little rifleman on my side, who was more than usually pint-sized, had to raise his weapon at the last moment to avoid beheading the bride. All things considered, 'V' Force let us down pretty lightly. They delivered the groom at the church in just the proper state of light anæsthesia; and there were only two Army boots and a kerosine can on the back of the bridal car. Then we were in the train and bowling off to Darjeeling and Sikkim, and Tim's orderly, Namkia and Haichangnang, were with us, each one more bewildered than the one before.

There followed sixteen days' trek through Sikkim and Tibet. We went out over the Nathu La and came back by the Jelap La. Half-way to the former a huge Tibetan muleteer at the rear of a mule-train greeted Tim joyously with 'Hello, Joe!' and just beyond Chumbithang we all sat on the roadside for half an hour while Tim, armed with his beret, chased a Camberwell Beauty round a *chorten*. He proved to be quite right, and we had a lot in common, but, as we both seemed to be mad along the same lines, it appeared a very suitable match.

Then he went off to Burma from Calcutta, jolting away up the line with a convoy of trucks, and I and my Naga pair rumbled back up the other line, back through green Bengal, up by the river steamer, into Badarpur at some unearthly hour and up the road from Mahur into the blessed cool. Over the top of the range by the Tolpui pass; and there we were again in the old haven.

The day following our return to Laisong, I saw, in the afternoon, a formal procession composed of all my staff leave the lines and advance towards the house with Namkia moving regally at its head. This was the usual prelude to a petition, and I thought it likely that, in view of my new status as a married woman, they would ask for a rise in pay. They reached the living-room floor and formed up in a line before the table. It was a serried rank of solemn faces. I felt a twinge of alarm. Was this an ultimatum?

Namkia stepped forward and looked me in the eye.

'The Sahib,' he said. 'Is all right.'

The whole lot turned about and trooped out. The tribe had delivered judgement.

I wonder what they'd have done if he was not?

CHAPTER XXXIV

MAGULONG

Except for flying visits, Tim didn't get back till the spring of 1946, when he reappeared finally, demobilized, and trying for a job on the newly-formed North-East Frontier. He found me busy bringing in Magulong to perform in Haflong at the VJ Day celebrations.

The details of that extremely lively expedition are not of importance here. Enough to say that when it ended we found ourselves asked out to stay at the village itself. Magulong was a remarkable settlement, a thing I had come increasingly to realize in the last few years, and its headman Khutuing was not the least remarkable thing about it.

I first came across Magulong on a wettish evening in March of 1940, when a party of them sought shelter in Asalu camp when I was on my very first trip in North Cachar. They were gone in the morning, grey, anonymous shapes of which I cannot now identify one. They reappeared again in the following years as files of salt-traders bound for Mahur market, distinguished from the other bands on the road by the black-and-white striped skirts which the women wore. But, as they lived in Manipur State, outside British India and thirty miles off across forbidding hills, we had no real contact with them till 1944, when, in June, Bill Tibbetts and I recruited scouts from them to watch the Barak crossings. I first remember Khutuing then, when he came to Tamenglong to see us—a stocky, thick-set, short-necked, laconic man in a worn scarlet cloth.

That summer the village had a dysentery outbreak with a heavy death-roll. We sent the 'V' Force doctor there in a hurry and had to provide them with free relief later on. When I passed through the place on one of my last tours, they were still in mourning and could not welcome us as they would have liked to do.

It was when they appeared for the 'V' Force show that

we saw them as they really were. They came down out of the hills like a gale from the past. They were Naga incarnate, tremendous, rip-roaring savages, men who had taken heads but danced like Nijinsky. For drive, for discipline, for skill, for sheer zest, they made our North Cachar Zemi look like a flock of sheep. Oh, they were heady wine, were Magulong, a rich and earthy vintage, splendidly barbarous!

Various things held us up during April and we didn't start till the beginning of May. Eastward we went, down into the narrow Jiri, up over the far hill—it came on to pour at the top, and we climbed into Maovom in sheets of rain, ankle-deep in water running down the path. Before us then stretched a field of great, green hills, shouldering up one after the other in scrub on grass, bamboo on scrub, forest on bamboo, till the high crests cut a sky already cloud-smudged with the nearing monsoon. Down and down we went from Maovom, into the grey-green gulf of the Makru valley. Down, and then up, up; climbing sheer, spirally towards the black-topped forest ridge; up from Saipimual through the dark woods and the elephant-trails, where trees were splintered and scarred and footprints like hip-baths lay water-filled in the soft soil, and through into gentler woods again, to Bungsang.

In the little camp there Khutuing met us.

Seeing him for the first time, short, solid and dwarfed by the taller men with him, you wouldn't have thought him a personality. But as a youth of eighteen he had taken a head during the Kuki rebellion. On great occasions he took from their resting-place among his heirlooms the two long tails of dull black hair cut from his victim's head, and wore them as ear-ornaments, the tresses, faintly wavy, falling far down on his bare shoulders and chest. He was entitled, too, to the great human-hair-tufted shield, the 'ge-ʒe, which only a man who had taken a head might own. Nowhere but in Magulong did one see them now—the young men there used to carry them in sham fights, leaping, bounding, scissoring their legs, and making the war-play till the long black tassels whisked and flew. It was from Khutuing, too, that I learned the headhunter's war-cry, the deep, humming chant of success with which they told the village, and even in the morung it gave me a grue. Khutuing was a headman on the strength of his character, although he was of a founding family, for he was fairly young for the job. You never heard him raise his voice; he hardly ever gave an order; yet, while North Cachar headmen shouted and cuffed and produced no results at all, Magulong functioned like a machine. One word, and the warriors did as he said; a lift of his finger, and the bucks ran to obey.

From Bungsang we passed on down the ridge and sighted Magulong across a grassy valley.

It stood on a spur jutting out from a high, wooded range behind. In the woods we could see cliffs; the hill was high and steep. From the village the ground fell away sheer and smooth, the path zigzagging down it in twists and elbows, past waterfalls, past wild, grey rocks, under crags and into the valley bottom. From our feet a track ran down to meet it, narrow, stepped, tall reed-grass hemming it in on either side. As we halted, a small, drab file among the green immensities, there came floating down to us, faint and sweet, the sound of distant singing.

Tim and I stopped and stared. Still it came; faint, far and haunting. Then, with the field-glasses, we saw. Ranged on a ledge of rock a little below the village, a group of bucks and girls were singing together.

All through the long, hot trek through the grass the distant singing fell to call us on. As we reached and climbed the opposite slope, mounting a narrow ledge which twisted and crept up the fantastic, rugged, Wagnerian hill, the singing came down to us full and clear, the girls' high voices blending with the boys'. At the back of the file our own growing tail of Nagas answered them, and, strophe and antistrophe, verse for verse, we came up the last half-mile to the village gate.

The sound of our party's singing had brought the villagers out. Elders, children and housewives were at the gate. Life dissolved suddenly into a kind of opera, for the people of Magulong were so steeped from childhood in music and dance that they expressed themselves in song just as readily as they did in speech, and slipped from one to the other two

or three times in the course of a conversation. Escorted by
the bucks and girls, still singing, we turned to the gate itself.
The entrance rose steeply, in a narrow flight of steps. Up we
went, through the gap in the cactus hedge; and were at once
in an airy village street, the wide Barak valley lying far
beyond and dark, weathered houses dotting the spur. The
chorus deployed behind us and continued to sing.

Then we took stock of the wide street nearer at hand.
There were the village council, set in a row. There was a
line of forty bottles of rice-beer. There may well have been
many more, we dare not count. There was a small bull-
mithan tied to a post. One of the elders got up and began to
speak.

Namkia and Khutuing explained. Tim and I had been
married, the village knew, by the Sahibs' laws and rites. But,
on behalf of the tribe, there ought to be more. It was right
that I, who was a Zemi, should also be married by tribal
rites as well—the only rites which the Zemi recognized.
Magulong, therefore, proposed to see it done. We consented
faintly. There wasn't much choice.

There were three or four days to wait before everything
was ready for the ceremony. I had heard vague rumours
from the Zemi of a big cave somewhere near Magulong, and,
through Namkia, asked Khutuing if he would take us to see it.
After a moment's weighing of the request—we found out
later why—he said he would; and the next day was fixed for
the expedition.

We started early, most of the headmen, some of the warriors
and several bucks escorting us. Young Namde, the slim,
impetuous, fiery boy who had been Magulong's leading
scout, attached himself to Tim as a gun-bearer and walked
at our heels as impatient as a young leopard of the slow pace.
Up the hill we went, climbing through fields to woods,
higher and higher; up through the untouched forest, far
behind and away, over logs, through underbrush which
thinned as we mounted and trees which grew small with the
height; till at last we were almost at the summit. It rose in
front of us in a dome. On its brow, as we looked at it across
a cleft and between the trunks of the trees, were scrubby

mountain growths and thin bushes; and, splash upon splash of white in the summer sun, were snow-white rhododendrons —huge white blooms, fading a little now with the season old, but caught and hung everywhere about the barrenness of the peak. They came down in a fringe along the slope; and below the roots the ground, with a slash, ended—down went a wall of rock, water-stained, vertical; down out of sight, into space, down to the dull green of the valley below. As we stood waiting for the guides to move on towards the peak, the man leading us turned and slid over what looked like the edge of the gulf itself.

We followed, clawing our way down hand and footholds kicked in a bank of loose earth. They became a ledge, which turned under a rock, and twisting, clinging, we clambered into a cleft. Scrub, gnarled roots, loose scree, scramble and clutch, struggle and hold and pull, round projections and inlets of the mountain-side—goodness knows which way they took us through. A flange of rock stood out from the hill. The path turned left up it, and where it met the edge of the flange there was a small nick over which the guide ahead of me vanished with a vault and a scramble. His head and shoulders reappeared and he gave me a hand over. Right on the edge, in the elbow of the climb, were the remains of a wall; beyond, a rock-shelf led away gently down.

Another twenty yards, and the cliff was jutting above us to form a roof. Abruptly Tim and I stopped, and stood staring.

The cliff on whose ledge we were curved round in an amphitheatre, closing the head of a wild and tree-filled ravine. In that cliff, immediately before us, was an immense rock-arch. Three hundred feet it spanned from side to side and seventy feet from top to bottom slab. Behind was a wide, shallow cave, flat-roofed and sloping-floored, stained with all shades of grey and earthy-brown. Treetops rose to meet it from the depths below and a thin, bright waterfall splashed down over the mouth and into a shallow pool. Here was the secret hold of the village, where in time of war the whole community hid, men, women, children, pigs and poultry; above and below were cliffs, beyond were crags—there was no entrance but the climb over the rib, where one man at a breastwork could hold off an army. Only once before in the history of Magulong had strangers been allowed to see the place; years ago, as a great honour, they had shown it to Gaidiliu.

We reached the cave before the others did, and standing there, saw the long file slipping, with quick and supple gait, down the sloping path. The golden-tawny figures, hard, perfect and Greek, the scarlet cloths and coloured necklaces, the grey-brown background of the weathered rock, were breathless, lovely beauty in the sunlight; blue-green beyond, the forest fell away; and high above, in the last, uplifted cleft of the crags, white rhododendrons tossed against the sky.

We sat for a while in the great, grey, golden-lit shelter, watching the little fall glitter and splash in the black basin of rock. Then someone said:

'There is a spirit here.'

'What spirit?'

'We do not know. But we often hear it call.'

'What sort of call?'

'I can't explain—let's go along and see.'

We left the great half-moon cave by the opposite tip to that by which we came, and scrambled incredibly over rock-ledges thick with serow-droppings—the hill must have been alive with the animals. The ground was broken, full of screes; the slopes were almost too steep to stand. High above us still ran an unbroken cliff. Then, as we struggled through a little wood, there was a noise. The man in front of me stopped.

'There! Did you hear? The spirit.'

We straightened up and stood holding to the mossy branches of the stunted trees; but it did not call again. We were just at the entrance to a shallow bay, stony and walled with cliff, and we scrambled on into it and out of the wood. On the other side of the bay and thirty yards from us was a steep, bare, scree-strewn slope which ran up between crags and ended in crags again. There was a sharp, harsh cry.

'What the devil's that?' said Tim.

One of the men hallooed and the thing squalled back. It seemed to come from the scree, and there were two or three

distinct repetitions of it. It might have been a wild-cat, but
it was no cry that we knew. Tim looked over the slope with
the field-glasses. Though it was close and almost bare of
cover, there was nothing at all to be seen. Then it cried again.
'Could it be a serow?' I asked.

The Zemi laughed. No, it was no serow. It was no beast
that they knew. They had never seen it, but they always
heard the cry here, and only here. Nor could Tim, the
naturalist, give it a name. It was a puzzle to him. The men
shouted to make it answer again, but there was no reply.
The thing, whatever it was, had gone.

Back we went through the arching wonder of the hold, that
superb grey curve framing the greens, the blues, the forests
and the hills away to the last pale mists beyond Tamenglong.
Out by the narrowing ledge we moved and over the rib,
climbing down backwards, carefully, ladderwise. Now not
a trace of the hold remained. Then up the earthy slope,
with struggle and slip and kick, back to the path again; and
down and down through the trees, from mountain forest
out to the open fields, to the evening light, to the Barak's
deep rift, to the village little and small and pale below;
scrambling, running, laughing, hurrying down from an
other-world of beauty and air and light to the sad, unkind,
impermanent land of men.

CHAPTER XXXV

FINALE

IN the next mail came the news that Tim had his appointment in the North-East Frontier service. He had been given the Subansiri Area, the post we hardly dared hope for, the last unexplored tract. Time was short, it was a long way back to the railway; only a day or two more and we must go.

The wedding ceremonies were set in train. First Khutuing adopted me by the name of Katazile, meaning 'Giver of All' —the 'V' Force free relief was the reason for that. It had saved Magulong from famine, and many households still preserved scraps of the salt, part-relics, part-talismans. Tim next presented Khutuing with a spear, the gift of respect, and a hundred rupees as my nominal marriage-price. Khutuing replied with the cloth of betrothal—not a white cloth, as in Asalu and Laisong, but a crimson-bordered *mraipan*, the full-dress cloth of Magulong and its group.

Then came the ceremony proper. A cock was strangled by the village priest and the omens taken from the way it crossed its feet. The flesh was cooked and set in a special dish; and with the shapely cane rice-basket which Khutuing gave me, the symbol of wifely duties—there should have been axe, hoe and spindle too, but there wasn't time to get them—we walked out from Khutuing's house and back to the camp man and wife by Zemi law. The dish of meat was carried by a herculean warrior, Khutuing's lieutenant, and set down in the hut for us to eat, the formal first meal of married life; and that concluded the Zemi ceremony.

Not, however, the celebrations. For a people who sang as much as they spoke and danced as much as they sang an occasion without a party was unthinkable. It began that afternoon at four o'clock, in the great, dark, smoky hall of Khutuing's morung. Vats of rice-beer filled the back of the room. The bucks and warriors of both morungs were there, the elders were there.

A dance in the morung has an atmosphere all its own. The huge hall with its two pillars and fires burning on the floor is part smoky darkness and part yellow light; the dancers pass from one to the other, one moment lit to the last richness of detail, the next lost, a dim movement in the recesses. Behind the fires shadowy figures move and drift and watch, drummers, singers, girls waiting their turn, men bustling with drinks for the swaying choir. Time vanishes, the ages roll back; the stars are the same as they were three centuries ago; the gates are shut against the Angami, and the Zemi dance as their ancestors danced before them—roads, railways, the Government, have rolled away as though they had never been and outside in the night the countryside lies spread under the sky as wild, as beautiful as before the white man came.

We danced, we sang till the sun went down. We danced the moon down, too; all three cockcrows and sunrise, we danced them by; we were dancing still when the housewives woke to the day. At ten o'clock, at our urgent request, the party broke up at last. Chanting, singing, dancing, they saw us home. In the morning sun, the small, hedged compound was filled with feathers and colour. Grouped about the door-way, they sang good-bye. They ended at last with the ho-ho-ing, the *heroa-kai*, that wild, ringing, barbaric chorus which I think would rouse me out of my coffin. They fairly threw the notes out, chord on chord, magnificent, savage, with the clang of bells. Up went a quivering arm. The whole band checked, on one sustained note. A second's pause; then 'HOI!' It was finished.

The next morning we left. Half the bucks of the village wanted to come with us to work. The village suffered from the Barail's disease—shortage of land and chronic poverty. We took down names and told them we'd send back later. Elders, women, warriors, said good-bye. They all addressed us now by proper terms—aunt, uncle, son-in-law, daughter, as the relationship might be. Priests blessed us. Khutuing, carrying a head-taker's shield I had acquired, was to come down with us. At last, at very long last, we left the village gate; rice-beer, gifts, blessings, farewell advice—slowly we cleared them all, and dropped down the long, winding hill to the stream. Far behind us, falling clearly through the empty air, came boys' and girls' voices from the gateway ledge. They were singing the song of farewell to a girl who marries outside the village:

> 'It is as though we lived, and one had died;
> Weeping, we remain.
> O since we weep, return again, ascend!
> O mount the road! O climb the steep again!'

At the bottom, suddenly, between the high walls of reeds, a small boy was discovered to be carrying Tim's shotgun. He was not more than eight, the leader of the pack which had been catching butterflies and locating birds for Tim in the scrub surrounding the camp. It was unauthorized. He was a stowaway. Elders and headmen, in an awful silence, surrounded him.

'What,' said Khutuing, 'are you doing here?'

There was a wet snivel.

'I want to go away and work for the Sahib,' said a small, sad voice. 'He gives you plenty to eat.'

'Have you your father's leave?'

'No.'

'Go home,' said Khutuing.

Mutely the small figure handed over the gun. Heart-broken, bent, it turned round in its tracks and trudged off home. The column resumed the climb to Bungsang.

It was already late in May, an unpredictable month, and as we reached Saipimual the weather broke. Out of leaden skies, sheet upon sheet of water fell upon us. The forest streamed, paths gushed like gutters; and when we reached the Maku bridge next day, we scrambled over a footway just awash. The unbridged Jiri lay between us and home. The rain thinned to a drizzle as we neared Maovom, but the hope was vain. In the small hours we heard a downpour thundering on the palm-leaf thatch and we woke in the morning to steady rain and cloud trailing like smoke-wreaths about the hill. The headman reported early that the Jiri could not be crossed and that he had sent men down to start a bridge. If we went down rather later, about mid-morning, there was a hope that it would be over.

We started as soon as the rain let up a little. In drifting showers and a few rare hints of sun we clambered, by slow and difficult paths, down through fields towards the upper Jiri. We were now at the narrowest part of the river, opposite Thingje, a mile or more upstream from the usual ford. But, as we reached the lower fields and neared the site of the bridge, somebody said that it was not yet ready; so, the rain increasing a little then, we stacked our baggage under the stilts of a field-house and ourselves climbed up to the platform to eat our lunch. Khutuing, meanwhile, put down the hairy shield he had been carrying and, with Namkia, went off down to the stream to give the bridgers a hand.

An hour or so later, tired of waiting, we went down to see. Four or five cold, wet Kukis were sitting about on the bank. There were some stones and a few bamboos; no one and nothing else. Between us and the North Cachar bank the Jiri was coming down as I had never seen it before—rolling, tearing, lashing, whipping; the red water flicking by, flotsam vanishing downstream almost as you saw it. The Kukis said they had started to fell a big tree whose trunk would serve as a bridge. But, as they worked, the river still rose, and as the tree fell the water swelled over it. Two men only managed to dash across, and they had gone to Thingje to fetch help.

It began to rain heavily again. We were all cold. We collected brushwood from under the bushes, where it was fairly dry, dragged up a log or two and lit a big fire. The Kukis squatted round it, shivering. Then, pushing through the wood with a load of bamboos, came Khutuing.

We stood or squatted there by the fire and watched Khutuing, almost single-handed, bridge seventy-five feet of river. He knew how to make a cantilever span, a Zemi type, and the Kukis did not. The Maovom men pushed, hauled, laid stones and cut lashings under his direction. First the upper bamboos went in, well weighted down by stone revetments rammed against the bank; then the footway, four long, stout bamboos thrust home into the soil and lashed to the upper pieces.

They managed to fix one supporting trestle close in to the bank, and after that underpinning was impossible because of the depth and speed of the water.

The rain came still heavier now, beating on us with a greater weight. It drummed down over the fields and forest with a dull roar. We were all soaked. The Kukis' wet, coarse clothes clung damply to them; Khutuing's old kilt—he had shed his cloth—was like wet sacking. He took a long, thin, whippy bamboo rod, cut with a piece of the main stem left to form a hook, and walked out slowly with it on the shaking footway.

The long bamboos which formed this were wet with rain, slippery and untied. They bounced and leaped under him. Carefully, slowly, he reached up with the hooked bamboo till he caught the overhead span. Then he pulled it down till the upper span began to spring, and, still keeping tension on the bamboo rod, sat down and straddled the footway. Locking his legs below it, he passed the straining bamboo rod under, bent it round, held it, and made it fast, and the first support was complete. The Kukis passed him out another hooked rod; still sitting, he fished for the span on the other side, and repeated the process. He moved up two or three feet and began again.

The rain thundered on our backs. Watching the river, we saw it rise. It mounted over the roots, pecked at the bank; the note of the stream deepened, the rocks and boulders grumbled in the bed. The water climbed up over the stone revetment, over the butt-ends of the bridge bamboos, over the end of the footway. Still Khutuing worked. Still the rain came down in a solid wall. It stood like a screen of leaden rods between us and the other bank.

Now Khutuing was out at the extreme end. With every move the unsupported footway quivered and jerked. He was twenty feet out from the bank, the Jiri was running twelve knots, and under him red waves jumped and licked and rolled, rushing down feverishly into a long rapid.

'If he slips, he hasn't a hope in hell,' said Tim.

We went on watching. I don't know what would have happened had he gone in. I think we should both have gone in after him, and I doubt whether any of us would have come out.

The footway was so glassy with rain, so quaking and unstable, that the Kukis would not venture along it. They passed the necessary bamboos out to Khutuing, who could not even turn round lest the footway tilt. With every movement he bounced and swayed a foot or two up or a foot sideways, the bamboos slewing about and giving unequally. The water lapped up another inch or two, covering the first lashing or so at the bank end of the footway.

Then, suddenly, there was a new note in the river, and the Kukis who were at the near end of the bridge broke and ran and fell scrambling outward to the bank, and, branches and limbs looming high over us, a giant tree, the one they had first felled, came rolling down on the flood and right at the bridge and Khutuing.

He didn't run. He'd have fallen off if he had. Quietly, calmly, without the least fuss, he walked back. He didn't even bother to make the bank, but stood above the trestle to watch the tree strike. It hit the bridge squarely. The bamboos creaked and snapped, the structure canted. The tree swung, twisted, veered away and was gone, swirling clear of the bridge and into the rapid below. Khutuing went back to his post, testing the footway, mending broken ties, and sat down to his job as though nothing had happened.

Then on the far bank bare, brown figures appeared. There were shouts. Bamboos were fetched, an opposite span begun. More and more Zemi bobbed there among the trees, scrambled about and dragged bamboos to the spot. His work done, Khutuing came back to the fire. We made some tea and all drank it from the camp mugs. Thingje, over the way, were working like fiends. Out, and out, their side of the bridge grew. Its footway met ours, the upper spans tapped each other. Thingje ran out other bamboos and covered the gap. Up went side-hooks, under went lashings; at four o'clock the bridging was complete.

Khutuing was the first over. He tested the bridge as he went, treading and trying. As he jumped off into the scrub beyond, we and the porters followed. At five o'clock we reached the Thingje camp. It was still raining. Down behind us the Jiri roared.

There was all Laisong camp to pack. While we hammered cases shut, Khutuing, discovering we had no picnic-basket, sat down in a corner and made us one, working the cane as calmly and with the same detachment from confusion round him as he had the bridge. He said he would like to come down to the railway with us and see us on the train—he wanted to shake hands with us when we left. There was a special significance in that gesture. We were not just two white people who called him 'Father' for fun, but were linked to him in a relationship of much greater emotional depth. The handshake was the public expression of this.

At the last moment two Magulong boys joined us. One was young Namde, the other his friend Lungchiwong, the pick of a dozen applicants. Dogs, boys, baggage, we reached the station. The worn and grubby train came clanking in. The boys and servants scrambled for seats, we loaded the luggage. Stepping out, we shook hands soberly with Khutuing.

'Go well, son-in-law. Go well, my daughter. Bring my grandchild to show me if you can.'

'Remain well, my father.'

Namkia, who was going one station up the line, climbed into the train. Khutuing and the porters turned and left. I watched them going down the bazaar path. Khutuing's head was bent. He was crying.

The train pulled out of the station and rumbled away to the north.

GLOSSARY

BASHA	. .	A hut of bamboo and grass, much used in Assam.
CHORTEN	. .	A Tibetan stone monument.
DAO	. .	A large chopping-knife used by the Assam hill-tribes for jungle-cutting, as a weapon, and for every other conceivable purpose.
COMPOUNDER	.	A native medical assistant.
GENNA	.	Commonly used to denote any Naga holy day or religious festival. From the Angami Naga word *kenna*.
GENNA-POST	.	A general term for the wooden posts put up by wealthy Nagas to commemorate individual ceremonial feasts. The type of post varies from tribe to tribe and sometimes from village to village.
JAPPA	. .	A carrying-basket of cane or bamboo, 3 ft. high, closely woven and interlined with leaves. It has four legs or a base of stiff bark, and the basket slopes up from a narrow bottom to a wide circular mouth. The lid is pointed or domed. Used by the Nagas for storing valuables and by travelling Europeans for carrying baggage.
MITHAN	. .	*Bos frontalis*; a domesticated variety of the Indian bison, kept by many of the Assam hill-tribes for sacrificial purposes and as currency.
MORUNG	.	The Bachelors' Hall of a Naga village.
RUPEE	.	The Indian unit of currency. At the time to which this book refers it was worth about 35 cents U.S. or 1/6d.
SEROW	.	*Nemorhœdus rubida*. A goat-like species of antelope living on forested cliffs.

NAGA PATH

MOTOR ROADS ═══════
BRIDLE ROADS AND TRACKS ------

N

Miles 0   10   20   30

TASANGKI
CHATON
KHUANGMUAL
LEIKE
GUILONG
KEPELO
THINGJE
HEGOKULOA
MAOVOM
HAIJAICHAK
SAIPIMUAL
MAGULONG
LAISONG
NENGLO
IMPUILOA
BUNGSANG
TAMMA
IAFLONG
ASALU
TOLPUI
MAHUR
IMPOI
Thumjang Klang 6122
HANGE
Katsingpeo-ki 5706
HANGRUM
NENGTE
PADHEKOTI
SHONGKAI
HEPOLOA
PEISIA
BALADHAN
KHANGNAM
TAMENGLONG

NORTH
CACHAR

THILON
JOUTE

M A N I

AKHIPUR
NUNGBA
LAGAIRONG

He could *dance*!

The unexpected way her body had responded to that first touch of their hands had been disturbing all on its own.

Finding out who was beneath that disguise had been so shocking part of her brain had shut down, and her only thought had been to finish this dance and escape.

Tony Grimshaw! The son of the city's mayor, no less. The rising star of St Pat's cardiothoracic surgical team. Tipped to become the next head of that prestigious department, despite being only in his mid-thirties.

One of life's golden people. Only ever seen to be accompanied by the cream of available women. The wealthiest and most beautiful. Often celebrities, and never encumbered with small dependent children.

But he could dance. *Really* dance. And within moments a forgotten joy was reborn for Kelly.

The spell they were under did odd things to the passage of time. Kelly had no idea how long they danced, and there was no way she was going to suggest a break. The lights became dimmer and the crowd on the dance floor thinned out, but still they danced on.

As if there was no tomorrow.

BILLIONAIRE DOCTORS

*Hot, jet-set docs at the top of their game—
professionally...and personally!*

These desirable doctors are international playboys—
Gorgeous Greeks, sexy sheikhs, irresistible Italians
and Australian tycoons.

Their playground might be the world
of the rich and famous but their
professional reputations are world renowned.

These billionaires dedicate themselves to saving lives
by day—and red-hot seduction by night...

Look out for our next BILLIONAIRE DOCTOR
in:

Secret Sheikh, Secret Baby
by Carol Marinelli
Coming next month from
Mills & Boon® Romance

HOT-SHOT SURGEON, CINDERELLA BRIDE

BY
ALISON ROBERTS

MILLS & BOON

Pure reading pleasure™

First published in Great Britain 2009
Harlequin Mills & Boon Limited,
Eton House, 18-24 Paradise Road, Richmond, Surrey TW9 1SR

© Alison Roberts 2009

ISBN: 978 0 263 20800 9

Set in Times Roman 10½ on 12¾ pt
07-0609-4

Printed and bound in Great Britain
by CPI Antony Rowe, Chippenham, Wiltshire

HOT-SHOT SURGEON, CINDERELLA BRIDE

Alison Roberts lives in Christchurch, New Zealand. She began her working career as a primary school teacher, but now juggles available working hours between writing and active duty as an ambulance officer. Throwing in a large dose of parenting, housework, gardening and pet-minding keeps life busy, and teenage daughter Becky is responsible for an increasing number of days spent on equestrian pursuits. Finding time for everything can be a challenge, but the rewards make the effort more than worthwhile.

Recent titles by the same author:

ONE NIGHT WITH HER BOSS
THE ITALIAN SURGEON'S CHRISTMAS MIRACLE
MARRYING THE MILLIONAIRE DOCTOR*
HER FOUR-YEAR BABY SECRET

*Crocodile Creek

CHAPTER ONE

WHO on earth was that?

The conversation he'd been engrossed in a moment ago became a meaningless blur of sound for Dr Anthony Grimshaw. For just a heartbeat he had caught a glimpse of the most stunning-looking woman he'd ever seen, standing between two pillars on the far side of the ballroom.

Much to the delight of the organising committee, St Patrick's fundraiser had become *the* function of the year, and there was a sea of people moving to the excellent music being provided by a small live orchestra. The dance floor was so well populated it was inevitable that his line of vision was obscured, but Tony still found himself trying to see those pillars again as he tuned back in to the voice beside him. A well respected voice that belonged to a senior colleague: paediatric cardiologist John Clifford.

'…and anyway, didn't I see a photo of you in some gossip rag? Out and about with Morrison's daughter? What's her name?'

'Miranda,' Tony supplied absently.

'Ah, yes! So. As I was saying. The fact that Gilbert's father is on the board should be well cancelled out by you having a prospective father-in-law with the same—if not greater—power to cast a vote in favour of *you* becoming HOD.'

'What?' Tony's attention was recaptured. 'What on earth are you talking about, John?'

'You. And Miranda.'

'There is no me and Miranda.'

'But…'

'We met at some charity do. Not unlike this one but without the fancy dress.' He smiled at the rotund figure of his companion. With his genial expression and fluffy mane of white hair it was no wonder his small patients loved him. Dr Clifford had answered tonight's medieval theme by wearing a king's robe and a crown. 'That outfit suits you, by the way. Very regal. Yes, Miranda and I went out a couple of times, but it's not going anywhere.'

'Why ever not? The girl's beautiful. Wealthy. Probably one of the many that seem to find you irresistible. My word, if I was still your age, I'd—'

The direct look Tony gave his companion was enough to break a flow that would have been extraordinary if they hadn't known each other so well for many years. In his early sixties, John Clifford was a family friend and had been Tony's mentor since he'd joined the staff of St Patrick's as a surgical registrar some years ago now.

'Don't you think it would seem a little blatant to

be dating the daughter of the chairman of St Pat's board of trustees at exactly the same time I'm up for the coveted position of head of the cardiothoracic surgical department?'

John's sigh was resigned. 'But it's the fact that you're young and single that counts against you, Tony. The powers-that-be see you as someone who's going to be distracted by a wife and family in the next few years. Responsibilities that might compromise your ability to lead the department into becoming the cutting-edge facility they've set their hearts on having.'

'I'll be able to assure them that isn't the case,' Tony said with quiet confidence. He tempered any implied criticism with a grin. 'With any luck Miranda will have told Daddy she broke it off with me because she wasn't about to try and compete with my job. That I'm far more interested in research than romance.'

The smile was returned. 'Don't understand it myself. She looked perfect.'

Tony's grin faded to a poignant curl. 'Want to know a secret, John?'

'What is it?'

Tony leaned closer. 'Perfection can be very, very boring.'

His gaze shifted as he straightened. Straight back to where he'd be able to see those pillars if the dancers would just move out of the way. His eyes narrowed as he tried to see past the colourful swirl of ornate costumes, and he only turned away briefly to acknowledge the farewell as John responded to a wave from another group.

What was it about that woman that drew his line of vision so compellingly? He was too far away to recognise her, or even see her features in the soft light from the flames of dozens of gas lamps on the walls of this vast ballroom. Maybe it was something about the way she was standing? Poised. Graceful even without any motion. With an aura that spoke of being alone but not lonely. Independent.

Yes, that was an intriguing enough impression to explain the attraction.

He felt a bit like that himself tonight. Independent. Free.

Part of it could be explained by the costume. Not that Tony had been keen on the idea of being one of the Three Musketeers when the idea had been mooted by one of his registrars, but much to his surprise he was loving it. The soft suede boots, tailored jacket, frilly shirt, and the sword dangling by his side. Even the wig and preposterously wide hat with its ridiculous feather. Not one to do anything by halves, he'd added a mask, moustache and neat goatee beard, which had the unexpected bonus of being a very effective disguise.

The rest of it could probably be attributed to the conversation he'd just been having with John. Or perhaps more to the ending of it. Not that he ever minded talking shop, but he was more than happy to forget the background tension of the career competition he was currently engaged in. He could probably avoid it for the rest of the evening, too, in this disguise. Now that he was alone he could virtually disappear into this incredibly colourful crowd, half of whom *he* wouldn't be able to recognise.

Like that woman between the pillars.

The princess with the dark dress and jewels sparkling in her hair.

He watched the crowd of dancers, enjoying the visual feast of this enormous costume party. The timeframe had been—loosely-adhered to, and the variety was impressive. There were knights and highwaymen, kings and queens and Vikings. Milkmaids and monks and jesters. Crusaders and pirates. More than one Merlin and a good crowd of peasants.

And...*yes*—there she was again!

Dancing, now. With a Robin Hood who was possibly a little merrier than he should be. Not the best dancer, in any case. But the princess...she was on another level entirely. The grace with which she had been holding herself whilst standing still had been a faint reflection of her body in movement.

The way she turned—with that subtle bend, like a leaf in a gentle breeze.

The way her hand traced a shape only she could feel in the air. The shape of the music as it danced in his ears.

There had to be a better position from which to watch the dance floor. One without the frustration of having his view constantly interrupted in this fashion. The best available seemed to be where *she* had been standing. Between those pillars.

Having chosen his desired position, Tony moved with a determination that had the customary effect of people unconsciously moving aside to clear his path.

Who on earth was *that?*

Standing there, at the vantage point she had recently vacated herself.

No—lounging might be a better word, with the padded shoulder of an ornate red jacket shifting his weight onto that pillar. On one foot with the other crossed elegantly at ankle level and just the toe of the boot touching the floor. Kelly almost expected to see him twirl the end of that fake moustache or sweep his hat off as she noticed him watching her.

Was he watching her?

Hard to tell with that mask and the flickering shadows from the atmospheric lighting behind the pillar, but it didn't matter because it *felt* as if he was watching her—and there was something incredibly exciting about the notion. Kelly wanted to be watched. To feel…desirable.

He was tall and lean. In a costume that could only be considered ideal fodder for a romantic fantasy. And that was precisely what Kelly was in the mood for.

This whole night was a fantasy as far as she was concerned. It had been ever since she had become the envied winner of the raffle for one of the astonishingly expensive tickets to St Patrick's annual ball. Not that she'd intended to actually come. That had been Elsie's doing. Her boss. Surrogate mother, almost. It had been Elsie who'd hunted down the costume hire shops and dragged her along after work.

Even then Kelly had been ready to give her ticket away. She'd barely listened to Elsie clucking on about how much she was looking forward to baby-sitting Flipper. Or to the pointed reminders of how much she loved to dance.

'I dance every day,' she'd told Elsie. 'Flipper lives for her music.'

'Not the same as being in the arms of some tall, dark, handsome stranger, though, is it?'

'A man is the last thing I need in my life right now.'

She'd said it with the conviction of utmost sincerity. She'd just been jumping through hoops as she tried to find an acceptable excuse to decline. But then she'd seen the dress in the shop.

Midnight-blue velvet. High-waisted, with a laced bodice over a silver chemise. Sleeves that were shaped with a long, long back to them that would almost touch the ground. Folds of soft material that shimmered when she couldn't resist touching the garment.

It was a dress that could almost dance all by itself, and as her fingers had trailed down the skirt Kelly had known she was lost.

For just one night, she *had* to wear that dress.

And dance like there was no tomorrow.

Robin Hood was an unskilled but enthusiastic

dancer. It was easy to slip from his grasp and put some of her own style into the nondescript pattern they had been locked into. Kelly stepped back, raised her arms to cross them over her head, and, with her hands held like butterfly wings, she spun herself around fast enough to make the full folds of her dress billow. Then she caught the hand of her partner, twirled beneath it, and stepped back into his arms for some more sedate steps.

'Wow!' he said. 'Do it again.'

This time Kelly kept hold of Robin's hand and turned sideways before spinning in to lean on his shoulder. For just a split second before the spin her line of vision had those pillars directly ahead of her, and it was all too easy to imagine that *he* was watching her.

That he *wanted* her.

The orchestra was in no hurry to complete this particular medley, and suddenly neither was Kelly.

Poor Robin Hood was simply an accessory. She was dancing for *him*. The stranger in the shadows. Why him? she wondered fleetingly. There was something about the way he was standing there, she decided. The way he might be watching her, as though he found her attractive. But more, it was a vehicle for unleashing a side of herself that had been neglected for so long it was virtually forgotten.

The sensuous side.

Dancing would have been enough to satisfy her if she'd been with a partner who could have challenged her ability or let her express herself completely.

This fantasy of dancing to attract a total stranger was exciting enough to fill any gap this somewhat stilted movement left. The dress had already made Kelly feel beautiful. Being watched made it real.

She could dance her way into his heart.

Seduce him without touching. Without even seeming to notice him. And then she could melt into the crowd and simply disappear, to leave him wondering who the hell she was. The smile touching Kelly's lips was unconscious. It was a fitting part of this fairytale night. A bit of magic, like a tiny crystal ball she would be able to keep and look into occasionally when she wanted to remember feeling this good.

'Wow,' Robin Hood said again as the music finally faded. 'You're something else! What's your name?'

Kelly laughed. 'Cinderella.'

He grinned. 'Fair enough. Can I get you a glass of champagne, Cinders?'

'No—thank you.'

They both turned at the sound of the decisive negative, and Kelly felt a prickle run down her spine. How had he moved so fast? He must have been waiting for precisely this opportunity.

The musketeer swept a hand up in front of his chest and then moved it sideways in a graceful arc that left his fingers enticingly close to Kelly's.

'*My* dance, I think,' he said.

'Hang on, buddy!' Robin Hood was scowling. 'I was just going to get...'

Kelly could see, no—feel the commanding stare

her recent dance partner was receiving. In normal life that kind of arrogance would have put her back up instantly—but this wasn't normal life, was it? It was a fairytale, and *he* wanted to dance with her.

With a totally uncharacteristic, demure downward glance, Kelly put her hand into his.

The touch of her hand was like…like nothing Tony had ever felt before when his skin had come into contact with that of another person.

Thank goodness she took his hand when she did, because Tony had been experiencing an astonishingly strong desire to say something to Robin Hood that he might regret.

No one, *nothing*, was going to take away his chance to meet this woman. He tightened his grip around that slim hand.

What on earth was happening to him? The Grimshaws never behaved with anything less that the utmost decorum in public. He cast a suspicious glance at the cause of his unusual emotional state, but she was looking at the floor and standing very still in that poised manner she had. If Tony hadn't just spent nearly ten minutes watching her dance and finding his heart rate steadily increasing, his breathing becoming shallow and his tight breeches becoming less comfortable by the second, he might have believed her to be completely innocent.

Robin Hood muttered something unintelligible as he melted into the crowd, and it was only then that the princess raised her gaze. Tony was instantly aware of two things.

That they both knew their behaviour to her last dance partner had been unacceptably rude but also unavoidable. And that something was happening here that was simply meant to be.

Something as unreal as pretending to be part of a medieval gathering.

No. He'd better make that three things.

His awareness of this woman's beauty had been overwhelming even from the distance of the pillars. This close, Tony could believe he was looking at the nearest thing to perfection in a woman he'd ever seen.

Dark, dark blue eyes. Pale skin made all the more dramatic by the fall of that glorious wig. He'd been watching the black ripples that fell to her waist lift and swirl as she danced, and was thankful she hadn't braided it, or bundled it up to wear one of those pointy hats with veils attached at the sides that some women were wearing tonight. Dark stones like teardrops lay against her forehead, and the chain of jewels was the only restraint to her loose, flowing locks.

His hand lifted of its own accord to touch a soft curl.

'Nice,' he murmured. 'It feels almost real.'

'Does it?' A tiny smile pulled up the corners of her mouth and Tony found himself staring. Trying to extinguish what threatened to be an irresistible urge to kiss her.

Right here. Right now. In the middle of a dance floor where people around them had already started to dance to a new bracket of songs. Slightly faster music at the moment. Like his heartbeat.

'Shall we?' He gave a mock bow. Play-acting seemed to be the way forward here, because none of this felt real.

'Please.' The smile had an impish quality. 'But...'

'But?'

'I'm just wondering how safe it is to dance with you.'

Oh, not safe at all, he thought, but he pressed his lips closed on the warning and raised his eyebrows instead.

'Your sword?'

'Oh...' With a slow, deliberate, one-handed movement, Tony unbuckled the big silver clasp and pulled the belt from his waist. He looked up to inform the princess of his plan to drop the accessory out of the way—by the pillars, perhaps, along with his hat.

She looked up at the same instant, from where she had clearly been staring at his hands, and when he saw the tip of her tongue emerge to run across her bottom lip it felt as if some giant vice was squeezing every last molecule of oxygen from his chest.

Yes!

She wanted him. The way he wanted her.

Desire threatened to suffocate him. He could simply walk out of this ballroom and take her somewhere more private, couldn't he? No. It was a long time since he'd been an inexperienced teenager, for whom where lust could obliterate the ability to think clearly. This combination of confidence and anticipation might be heady stuff, but experience had taught him something else as well. It was a thrill that should be savoured for as long as possible.

Somehow he sucked in a breath as he led her to the edge of the floor to get rid of his unwanted accessories. Then he drew her into his arms.

'Did I hear correctly?' he enquired politely. 'Is your name Cindy?'

Those eyes were huge and... Dear Lord, even the way she blinked so slowly was erotic.

'Yes,' she said softly.

'Cindy who?'

'Does it matter?'

'It might.'

He could feel her responsiveness as he manoeuvred them to a clear space on the floor. She felt weightless in his arms, like an extension of his own body rather than a separate partner. God, if she felt like this on a dance floor, what would she be like in *bed?*

He saw the way the soft mounds of her breasts, pushed up by the corset top of her dress, rose even further as she took a deep breath. His mouth went dry.

'Riley,' she said at last. 'My name is Cindy Riley.'

'And you work at the hospital, Cindy Riley?'

'Yes.'

'Whereabouts? Which department?'

'All over.' She was smiling again. 'A bit of everything, really.'

Ah... She must be a pool nurse. Filling in wherever they required assistance. No wonder he hadn't seen her often enough in one place to recognise her. Tony ignored the scoffing sound in the back of his mind. The voice that said he would have only needed to see her once to recognise her again.

'Favourite places?'

'Emergency,' she said without hesitation. He could see the flicker in her eyes that spoke of a real passion for her work. 'And Theatre.'

Tony pulled her a little closer. 'My kind of girl,' he told her. 'And my favourite places as well. I'm Tony Grimshaw, by the way. I'm on the cardiothoracic surgical team.'

'Mmm.' The sound seemed oddly strangled. 'Could we stop talking, please, Tony Grimshaw? And dance?'

By way of response, Tony altered the way he was holding her. He might be rusty, but already the short time of moving with this woman felt natural. He sent Cindy Riley into a brief spin and then caught her, stepping sideways so that she could bend and dip—one arm extending gracefully. Then, the instant she was back on balance, he flipped her into a dip on his other side.

She was laughing as she came upright again, those incredible eyes letting him know that she was happy.

Impressed.

That she wanted more.

CHAPTER TWO

HE COULD *dance*!

The unexpected way her body had responded to that first touch of their hands had been disturbing all on its own.

Finding out who was beneath that disguise had been so shocking part of her brain had shut down, and her only thought had been to finish this dance and escape.

Tony Grimshaw! The son of the city's mayor, no less. The rising star of St Pat's cardiothoracic surgical team. Tipped to become the next head of that prestigious department, despite being only in his mid-thirties.

One of life's golden people. Only ever seen to be accompanied by the cream of available women. The wealthiest and most beautiful. Often celebrities, and never encumbered with small dependent children.

Criteria Kelly could never aspire to attaining. Wouldn't want to, in fact.

But he could dance. *Really* dance. And within moments a forgotten joy was reborn for Kelly.

Like flying. Taking off and swooping and knowing it was perfectly safe because there were strong arms to catch her. A lead that not only provided an impressive variety of moves but one that encouraged independence and gave opportunities to play.

Escape was the last thing she wanted now, and the music fading at the end of the set would have been utterly disappointing except that it went virtually unnoticed. The only change was that Tony slowed down. Held her close and started a tango step. And Kelly could rest her head against his and keep her eyes closed and still think of nothing but the music and the way they moved together so beautifully.

It didn't matter now that she was dancing with the physical embodiment of everything she had run from in her previous life. Or that she had lied about her identity.

It wasn't really a lie, was it?

Cindy Riley was close enough to being Cinderella to be a joke. Part of the pretence. Part of the fairy-tale she was living tonight. And it was…magic.

The spell they were under did odd things to the passage of time. Kelly had no idea how long they danced, and there was no way she was going to suggest a break. That would come all too soon— when the clock struck midnight and she had to flee. The lights became dimmer and the crowd on the dance floor thinned out, but still they danced on.

As if there was no tomorrow.

And maybe the spell was going to last a little longer than midnight.

At some point, drugged by the music and the movement, and barely moving in the slow, slow tango, she heard Tony murmur in her ear.

'I want to be with you,' he said. 'Somewhere else.'

She hadn't expected this. The thought was alarming. 'T-tonight?'

'Oh, yes.' The movement of his hand on her back was subtle. Nobody else would have noticed the way his thumb moved and pressed down along the bumps of her spine. But Kelly could feel the heat spread through her entire body. Into every single cell.

His voice was such a low rumble that Kelly felt rather than heard the two words he added.

'*All* night.'

His lips were right beside her ear. She felt them move like a caress. She felt the tiny coolness of his tongue touching her skin.

Yes!

No!

It was unthinkable! To spend a night with a man she'd just met for the first time? Not even met him honestly, come to that, seeing as he had no idea who she really was.

But maybe that made it less shocking somehow—because it wasn't *her* doing something so risky. So unlike anything she'd ever contemplated doing. She wasn't herself. Wasn't expected to be until around eight tomorrow morning, when she was due to collect Flipper from Elsie's house. Just for tonight— a few more hours—she could continue being part of the fairytale and do things she might never get the chance to do again.

She could believe she was someone that a man like Tony actually wanted.

'Wh—where?' she heard herself whisper.

'The owners of this hotel are family friends. I have a suite upstairs for the night.'

His head was moving as he spoke. His lips brushing her cheek. Any moment now and he might kiss her, and—God help her—Kelly wanted him to. She wanted the touch of his lips more than she had ever wanted anything.

Ever.

It was too easy. Kelly was being led as decisively as he had been leading her in their dancing. Doubts collided in her mind, but wouldn't slow down enough to take shape. Not when he was looking down at her like this and she could see the dark eyes behind the mask.

'Don't worry,' he said softly. 'You're safe. I'll take care of you, Cindy Riley. I promise.'

And that was her undoing.

The thought of being cared for.

Loved.

It wasn't the first time Tony Grimshaw had taken a woman he barely knew to his bed. The only difference between his testosterone-laden teen years and those of most young men had been the playground he'd had available. One where the kind of holidays, clothes, cars and freedom had been a magnet for every pretty girl he'd encountered.

So why did it feel like the first time?

Tony led Cindy through the door of the best suite the Grand Chancellor had to offer, pushed it closed with his foot and pulled her into his arms, dipping his head to claim her lips with his own as part of the same, fluid series of moves.

It was all just another kind of dance, really, wasn't it? And he'd been right. Her responsiveness was… mind-blowing. The way her mouth moved under his and her lips parted. They way her tongue touched and curled against his own. And when he moved his head to deepen the kiss she tilted her own to exactly the angle he needed to explore her delicious mouth a little more thoroughly.

It was some time before he registered what his fingers, rather than his lips and tongue, were aware of.

'Your hair,' he said in amazement. 'It's *real*.'

She laughed. 'Of course it is.'

He smiled back at her. He wanted to make her laugh again because it was such a gorgeous sound. 'Mine isn't.'

It worked. 'I should hope not.' Then her face stilled. 'Take it off,' she whispered. 'I want to feel *you*. Take off the wig. And this—' She touched the moustache that was already half detached after their kisses.

She didn't seem to mind that his own hair was flattened and damp from the wig. Or that his chin felt rough because he hadn't shaved before sticking on that silly beard. Her hands shaped his head, and the pressure brought his lips back to hers for an even more intense kiss.

Tony had to slow things down. He wanted her right now. To pull up the acres of fabric in that dress and take her here, against the wall. But he'd promised to take care of her, hadn't he? And even if he hadn't made that promise, he wouldn't want to rush this. It was too special.

He dragged his mouth from hers, but he couldn't pull right back. He kissed the corner of her mouth. Then her jaw and her neck. She tilted her head back in response to his touch, and the gasp as he trailed his kisses down to the pale flesh rounded over the top of her corset made him utter a sound that was unfamiliar to his own ears.

A primal sound of pure need.

His fingers fumbled with the string at the front of her bodice and then her hands joined his, making deft, sure movements that undid the knot and loosened the lace. And all the time her fingers worked under his, her eyes held his gaze. Tony thought he was going to drown in the deep blue depths. In the desire he could see that so clearly matched his own.

Then the laces were undone and her breasts were free and his hands could hold them and he could bend his head and touch his tongue to nipples as hard as buttons.

And he was lost.

Completely and utterly lost.

Kelly wasn't a virgin, but it had been a very long time since she'd been with a man—and she'd never been with anyone as far out of her league as Tony Grimshaw.

Maybe that was why it felt like a first time.

Or maybe it was because *this* man made her feel different. Every touch made her ache for more, but even the combination of long abstinence on her part and gentleness and strength on his part, overlying the undeniable expertise of his lovemaking, couldn't explain why this felt so different.

He seemed to know her body. Just where to touch her and *how*. With his lips, his tongue, his teeth. His hands and his fingertips. His *eyes*! The way he looked at her body as he uncovered it. The way he held her gaze as he stripped off his own clothing.

And his focus. He'd stopped talking and asking awkward questions when she had wanted to dance, and now there seemed no need for any words at all. With the costumes that represented the first chapters of this fairytale lying puddled on the floor, Tony scooped Kelly into his arms and carried her to the massive bed, softly illuminated by discreet lamps.

He laid her down, took a condom from the drawer in the bedside cabinet and then knelt over her on the bed.

There was no going back now. Even if escape had

been offered, Kelly would have been totally unable to accept. She looked at the beautiful body of the man she was with. The hard lines of muscle. The faint smudges of dark hair. The *size* of him in more ways than the obvious. Because Kelly could sense his generosity of spirit. His ability to care.

That recognition took her breath away.

She was completely lost. She held up her arms to welcome him, but he didn't return her faintly tentative smile. His face was so serious, so *intent*, she experienced a moment of fear that made her heart stop and then thump painfully hard.

He caught her wrists and lowered her arms until he was holding them, crossed over her head. He transferred both wrists easily to one hand and then, as he bent his mouth to hers, his free hand slipped the curtain of her long hair from where it covered her breast. Gentle fingers traced her neck, along her collarbone, and then dipped to come up from beneath her breast and skim her nipple.

The shaft of exquisite sensation made Kelly gasp, and he raised his mouth from hers, releasing her wrists and using both hands to touch her as his lips took over from his fingers on her breast. But only for a heartbeat. His mouth kept moving, his tongue finding her belly button and then leaving a line of fire as it tracked further down.

She left her arms where they were, above her head, and lay still for as long as possible. But with the first sweep of his tongue on that tiny nub of hidden flesh she came—with a shudder and a groan of disbelief. She had to touch him then. To try and give back some of the magic that was dusting this incredible night.

She cried out again later, when he finally entered her and they began a whole new dance. And when she held him after his own shuddering climax she could feel the same kind of wonder emanating from him. And it felt as if she was touching his soul.

It was a night she never wanted to end, but of course it had to.

The magic was fading when Tony finally fell asleep, one arm flung above his head, the other holding Kelly close to his side. But the luxury of falling asleep and then waking to make love yet again was one Kelly couldn't afford. With the first fingers of light reaching into the velvety darkness in the corners of the room, she eased herself from the bed so stealthily that Tony did nothing more than take a deeper breath.

She put the dress back on, but its magic had also evaporated and Kelly could feel reality kicking in. It felt wrong to be dressed like this.

Wrong to have just spent a night having the most astonishingly wonderful sex imaginable?

No.

Kelly took one last, long look at the man sprawled on the bed, deeply asleep.

Something that had felt so right couldn't be wrong.

Softly, she kissed her fingertips and blew the kiss towards the man who still didn't know who she was.

Or anything about the life she was about to step back into.

And that was the way it had to be.

The truth would only tarnish the fairytale, and Kelly wanted to keep it exactly the way it was.

Perfect.

CHAPTER THREE

'YOU'RE in luck, Kelly, love. They're short in ED today.'

'Cool. Thanks, Elsie.' Kelly was still tucking the long coil of her braid under the elastic band of the oversized shower-cap-type hat that was part of her uniform. 'For the whole shift?'

'Yep.' Elsie was giving her a curious look. 'I thought you'd be rapt. Isn't Emergency your favourite place?'

'It is.' Kelly nodded and smiled, but her brain had gone into overdrive.

No wonder Elsie had picked up on something being different. Only last week the prospect of a day in the emergency department would have been a treat.

A poignant treat, mind you—it was like having her face pressed to a shop window that contained something ultimately desirable but equally unaffordable—but still an irresistible one.

'I'm just a bit tired,' she told Elsie, by way of

excusing her lack of excitement. 'I didn't sleep very well.'

'Are you OK?'

'I'm fine.' Kelly's smile was wider this time. Physically, the only thing that had disturbed her rest was the pleasure of experiencing the delicious tingles her body could conjure up with remarkable ease as she remembered the night with her musketeer. 'Maybe I just had too much excitement the night before.'

'Hmm.' Elsie looked unconvinced. 'You haven't said much about that. You did have a good time, then?'

'Magic,' Kelly affirmed.

So fabulous she couldn't begin to try describing it. And she didn't want to, despite sensing that Elsie felt left out and maybe a little hurt.

'I only went because of you,' she added. 'Thank you so much!'

It had been a night of pure magic. One that she intended to treasure for the rest of her life. And that was where the problem now lay. The repercussions that were going to affect a very large part of her life.

Reality couldn't be allowed to intrude, because she knew without a shadow of a doubt that reality would tarnish, if not completely destroy, the joy of that magic. That was why she needed to keep it private, and not diminish its perfection by talking about it. It was also why the dreadful prospect of Tony Grimshaw recognising her at work had made sleep so elusive.

'Is Flipper all right?' Briefly mollified, Elsie was now frowning anxiously. 'I did wonder if she had a bit of a sniffle on Saturday night. I noticed she was breathless going up my stairs.'

'Was she?' Kelly caught her bottom lip between her teeth, her mind whirling in a new direction. 'I'll mention it to Dr Clifford. She's got a check-up scheduled for this week.'

'But she's not sick today?'

'No. She couldn't wait to get to crèche. As usual.'

'What day's her appointment?'

'Wednesday. Sorry, Elsie. I forgot to say I wouldn't be working.'

'Not a problem. That's why I keep you on the casual list and why you get sent all over the show. Speaking of which—' Elsie glanced at her watch '—it's seven-thirty already. They will have finished hand-over.'

'I'm gone.' Kelly stood on one foot and then the other to pull disposable shoe-covers over her old, comfortable trainers.

'Report to the nurse manager when you get there. I'm not sure if they need you out front or in the observation area.'

Kelly took the shortcut of some fire escape stairs, as familiar with the layout of this vast hospital as she was with her own home. It was a world of its own in here, and she loved it despite the fact that her dream had never had her working in quite this capacity.

'Hey, Tom!' Kelly gave a cheerful wave to an orderly pushing an empty wheelchair in the opposite direction. Then she turned abruptly and chose a different direction when she saw the group of doctors coming behind Tom. She could take another route to the emergency department. She could use the service elevator and avoid any risk of recognition.

At least her uniform should be an effective disguise. The shower cap, the shapeless pink smock and the shoe-covers. Almost the same uniform the cleaners and kitchen staff wore—because, as a nurse aide, Kelly was part of the faceless army of people whose ranks stretched from groundsmen to technicians and kept this busy city hospital functioning the way it should. Making up the dark sky that allowed stars like Tony Grimshaw to shine so brightly.

Emergency should be safe enough, Kelly reassured herself as she sped down the final corridor, past the pharmacy and gift shop. It was rare for someone other than a registrar to make an initial assessment of a need for surgery. Being around the cardiology wards or theatre suites might be another matter, however. Kelly would need to stay on guard.

Not that she was likely to forget any time soon. Not when he was still in her head to this degree. When just a flicker of memory made her want to smile. Forgetting it enough to focus on her job might prove to be a problem, but it soon became apparent that her concern—for the moment, at least—was groundless.

The department was busy enough to keep her completely focussed. Fetching and carrying supplies, taking patients to the toilet or supplying bedpans, dealing with vomit containers and spills on the floor. She'd worked here often enough to be familiar with everything she needed to know. Many of the staff recognised her. One nurse looked particularly pleased to see her when she took a fresh linen bag to hang in the main resuscitation area.

'Kelly! Just the person I need. You know where everything is around here, don't you?'

'Pretty much.'

'Help me sort out this mess?' The wave indicated a benchtop littered with supplies that hadn't been put away. 'We've got an MVA victim coming in, and if it's still looking like this when they arrive, my guts will be someone's garters.'

It was fun, working under pressure. Handling syringes and bags of saline and packages containing endotracheal tubes. Things that had once been so familiar. Part of the dream Kelly had been well on her way to attaining.

'Want any sizes smaller than a seven on the tray?' she asked the nurse. 'Do you know what's coming in?'

'Something major.'

More staff were beginning to assemble in the room.

'Where's Radiology?' someone called. 'And the surgical reg—is she on her way?'

'I'd better get out of here,' Kelly said.

'No! Look!'

Kelly looked. Cupboard doors were open below the bench, with supplies spilling into a heap on the floor. They encroached over the red line on the floor that was there to keep unnecessary personnel from the area around a patient. Right at the head of the bed, too, where the person responsible for the patient's airway would be in danger of tripping over them.

Swiftly, Kelly crouched and began to stack the awkward packages back into the cupboards, so focussed on doing it as quickly as possible she barely registered the increasing level of activity behind her.

And then suddenly the double doors were pushed open and controlled chaos ensued.

'Seventeen-year-old, pushbike versus truck,' a paramedic informed the receiving doctor. 'Handlebar of the bike penetrated the left side of his chest. Intubated on scene and decompression attempted for a tension pneumothorax. Oxygen saturation's currently—'

Kelly was rising slowly to her feet, her back to the bench, and she slid sideways to get out of the way, horrified at being somewhere she had no right to be. Her gaze was none the less fixed on the scene so close to her. The transfer of the patient from the ambulance stretcher to the bed.

'On the count of three. One…two…*three*!'

There was a reassessment of all the vital signs, like heart-rate and blood pressure and respiration rate. None of them was looking good. Monitors were being hooked up and requests being called for more equipment and extra personnel. No one had time to notice Kelly, still standing in the corner.

She knew she had to leave. There was no way a nurse's aide could be any use at all in the kind of life-and-death drama about to be played out in here.

Bags of intravenous fluids were being clipped to overhead hooks. The doctor in charge of the airway was bag-masking the teenage boy, his eyes on the monitor screen that was showing him how much oxygen they were getting into his circulation. He didn't look happy with the figures he could see.

'Saturation's dropping. We're below ninety percent. And what the hell's happened to that ECG?'

An electrode had been displaced while moving the boy from the stretcher to the bed. Nursing staff were busy cutting away clothing and hadn't noticed the lead dangling uselessly, tangled up with the curly cord of the blood pressure cuff.

Without thinking, Kelly stepped forward into a gap, untangled the lead, and clipped the end back to the sticky pad attached beneath the patient's right collarbone.

'Thanks.' The doctor hadn't taken his eyes off the monitor, and Kelly could see why. The trace now travelling across the screen was erratic, and the unusual shapes of the spiky complexes suggested that this young boy was in imminent danger of a cardiac arrest.

Another doctor had his stethoscope on the less injured side of the chest. Was it proving too hard for one lung to function well enough to sustain life? Was the heart itself badly injured? Or was this boy simply bleeding too badly from internal injuries to make saving his life an impossibility?

Kelly was back in her corner. Transfixed. She could feel the tension rising with every second that ticked relentlessly past. With every command from the emergency department specialists, who were finding it difficult to gain extra IV access and infuse the blood volume that was so desperately needed, judging by the way the blood pressure was continuing to fall.

'Didn't someone page Cardiothoracic?' a doctor snapped. 'Where the hell are they?'

'Right here,' a calm voice responded. 'What are we dealing with?'

Kelly actually gasped aloud as Tony Grimshaw stepped closer to the bed, pulling on a pair of gloves. Not that there was the slightest danger of being noticed. At the precise moment the surgeon finished speaking, an alarm sounded on a monitor. And then another.

'VF,' someone called.

'No pulse,' another added.

'Start CPR.' The order came from the head of the bed. 'And charge the defibrillator to three-sixty.'

'Wait!' Tony's hands were on the patient's chest, lifting a blood-soaked dressing to examine the wound. 'Have you got a thoracotomy trolley set up?'

'Yes, I'll get it.' An ED registrar leaned closer. 'You're thinking tamponade? What about a needle pericardiocentesis first?'

'Wasting time,' Tony decreed. 'We're either dealing with a cardiac injury or major thoracic blood loss that needs controlling. Can I have some rapid skin preparation, please? We're not going to attempt full asepsis and draping, but I want everyone in here wearing a mask. And let's see if we can get a central line in while I'm scrubbing.'

Masks were tugged from the boxes attached to the wall as trolleys were moved and rapid preparation for the major intervention of opening the boy's chest continued. Kelly grabbed a mask for herself. A perfect disguise—just in case she got noticed when she made her move towards the exit.

Except she couldn't move. A thoracotomy for penetrating chest trauma topped the list for emergency department drama, and staff who had no more reason to be here than she were now finding excuses to slip into the back of the room to observe. House surgeons, registrars and nursing staff were squeezed into the space behind the red lines, and Kelly was trapped at the back. Able to hear everything, and even find a small window between the shoulders of the people directly in front of her, that afforded a good view of the surgeon if not the procedure.

He now had a hat and mask and gown over the Theatre scrubs he had been wearing on arrival. He seemed unconcerned by his audience. Ready to use an incredibly tense situation as a teaching tool, in fact.

'I'll use a "clam shell" approach,' he told the closest doctors. 'The one you guys would be using if I wasn't here.'

'Yeah…right,' someone near Kelly muttered. An over-awed medical student, perhaps?

She saw the flash of a scalpel being lifted from the sterile cover of the trolley.

'Bilateral incisions,' Tony said. 'About four centimetres in length, in the fifth intercostal space, mid-axillary line.'

Blood trickled down the yellow staining of hurriedly applied antiseptic on the boy's chest. Kelly was struck by how frail the young chest suddenly seemed.

'Make sure you breach the intercostal muscles and the parietal pleura. With a bit of luck we might deal with a tension pneumothorax and get some cardiac output at this point.'

They didn't.

Tony took just a moment to watch the screen, however, and his voice was soft. 'What's his name?'

'Michael.'

'And he's seventeen?'

'Yes.'

'Family here?'

'His mother's just arrived. She's in the relatives' room.'

Tony simply nodded, but Kelly was allowing herself to stare at him in the wake of his rapid-fire surprising queries. How had he done that? Made this seem so much more personal? As though he cared more about the patient than demonstrating his obviously not inconsiderable skills? Maybe he wasn't as hung up on his status as rumour had led her to believe.

She held her breath, watching the swift and decisive

actions of this surgeon as he used a fine wire saw to cut though the sternum and then opened the chest with retractors.

'I'm "tenting" the pericardium,' he said moments later. 'Scissors—thanks. Make a long incision like this. If it's too short, it'll prevent access to the heart. Suction...'

What would it be like, Kelly wondered, to have this man as a mentor in a career as a cardiothoracic surgeon? Or just to work alongside him as a nurse? To know him on a personal basis?

Maybe *she* knew him better than anyone else in this room.

A ridiculous thought, given the situation. Given reality. It made her memories of her time with him more dreamlike. Precious, but harder to hang onto. Kelly tucked them protectively into a corner of her mind.

Into that empty space in her heart.

Tony had both hands inside the boy's chest now, massaging Michael's heart. 'Make sure you keep the heart horizontal during massage,' he told the observers. 'Lifting the apex can prevent venous filling. I'm aiming for a rate of eighty per minute here, and I'm looking for any obvious bleeding that we need to control.'

The people in front of Kelly were murmuring in awed tones, and they shifted enough to obscure her line of vision. She heard the request for internal defibrillation, however, and could envisage the tiny paddles that would provide a minimal jolt to the cardiac tissue but hopefully restore a more normal heartbeat.

A collective gasp of amazement rippled around the room seconds later, but she could sense no let-up in control of a difficult situation from the star at the centre of this drama.

'Theatre's on standby. Let's get Michael up there while we've got a perfusing rhythm.'

There was a new flurry of activity as the open chest wound was covered, and the bed, the monitors and numerous necessary staff members all began moving as a connected unit.

Tony stripped off his gloves, dropping them to the floor and reaching for a fresh pair. His gaze scanned the assembled staff as he took a single step to put him within reach of what he needed. Kelly felt the eye contact like something physical. Almost a blow, the way it sent shock waves through her body. Despite the contact being so brief—less than a heartbeat—the connection was so strong she was sure Tony had to feel it, too. He'd glance back—with a frown, maybe. Needing a second glance without having registered why.

But he didn't look back. He barely broke his stride as he pulled fresh gloves from the slot on the box and followed his patient towards Theatre.

Maybe he hadn't seen her. She was unimportant. Invisible.

'Wow,' came a voice beside her. 'I saw it, but I still don't believe it.'

'I don't believe the mess they've left behind. Kelly, would you mind helping clear this up?'

'Better head back to work myself.' The first nurse sighed. 'Guess the excitement's over.'

Kelly tore her gaze away from the open door that had swallowed the figure of Tony Grimshaw.

Yes. The excitement was definitely over.

'Are you sure?'

'I've checked three times since you rang this morning, Mr Grimshaw. I'm sorry, but there's no C. Riley to be found on either the permanent or the casual nursing staff databases.'

'But…'

'Are you sure she's a nurse?' The woman from Personnel was beginning to sound impatient on the other end of the line. 'St Patrick's employs hundreds of people, you know. This Miss Riley you're trying to locate might be a physiotherapist or a dietician or a social worker—or any number of other things.'

'But she said…' Tony paused. She hadn't actually said she was a nurse, had she? She'd said she worked in a lot of different areas and that her favourite places were Emergency and Theatre. He was standing in the theatre suite right now, and there were people everywhere. Nurses, orderlies, technicians. Even a girl polishing the taps on the handbasins.

There were also two registrars waiting for him at a discreet distance from this wall phone. They were running late for a departmental meeting.

'Never mind.' He'd probably started some sort of a rumour by making these enquiries in the first place, but the staff in Personnel weren't to know *why* he was trying to locate the woman. It could be to reprimand her or something. 'Thank you for your help,' he added.

'A pleasure. If I hear anything that might be helpful I'll contact you, shall I?'

Tony could squash any embryonic rumours by saying it really didn't matter.

But it did, didn't it?

Since he'd woken up on Sunday morning to reach out and find his bed empty, he'd been unable to get rid of that sense of…loss.

It should have been easy. He'd thought he had it sorted when anger had kicked in briefly. When he'd started feeling as though he'd been used and discarded. But then the doubts had crept in. Excuses his brain was only too willing to come up with on her behalf.

Maybe she'd had a good reason to leave without saying anything. Mind you, there'd have to be a good reason to justify not wanting to repeat that experience. He knew it had been just as good for her as it had been for him. Nobody could fake that kind of responsiveness. Or sincerity. The princess had been genuine and he wanted to find her.

Maybe she was married?

If that was the case, fine. Tony wasn't about to break up anyone's marriage. It was this not knowing that was frustrating him. That and the peculiar dream-like quality the whole night had taken on.

But it had been real. Utterly different from anything he'd ever experienced before, but there was no denying it *had* happened. Or that the impression it had left made it impossible to forget. Perhaps what was really pushing his buttons was the need to *prove* it had been real. So that he would know what he needed to aim for in his personal life and never allow himself to settle for what had been on offer so far.

Mediocrity. Interest that always became infected with an urge to escape.

'Thank you,' Tony said finally, preparing to hang up the receiver. 'I'd appreciate that.'

His registrar had an armful of paperwork, and there would be a lot more by the end of the usual late Monday afternoon meeting where the cardiologists presented their cases. They would listen to histories, view footage of angiograms showing coronary arteries in various stages of blockage, grade people to score the urgency of intervention and draw up the Theatre list for bypass surgery for the next week.

There would be cases left over from last week who hadn't made it to Theatre because of emergency procedures taking precedence, and there would be debate over issues such as age and lifestyle and circumstances.

A tedious meeting in many ways. Tony was tempted to leave it to his registrar and attend to something more important. Like yet another check on this morning's trauma case. Seventeen-year-old Michael was in the intensive care unit, and he was still a sick lad but he was alive. Tony knew his save was the talk of the hospital, but what concerned him was whether the boy would make it through the next critical day or two. Whether he would recover without sequelae that could ruin his quality of life.

The two men he was leading into the meeting room now had been the other musketeers at the ball. Funny how it seemed such a long time ago already. As they sat down around the long table, Tony impulsively turned his head.

'Josh, you know a lot of the nurses around here, don't you?'

His registrar grinned. 'I'm working on it.'

'Ever come across a Cindy?'

The grin stretched. 'No. No Barbies, either.'

Tony's smile felt strained. This should feel like a joke but it didn't. He nodded at colleagues entering the room, noted that the audiovisual gear wasn't ready yet, and lowered his voice.

'Cindy Riley,' he told Josh. 'Tall. Long, black hair.'

'Not the woman you spent most of Saturday night dancing with? Blue dress with a lacey thing down the front?'

Tony gave a slow nod, hopefully not overdoing the effort to appear casual. It wasn't easy. The memory of that 'lacey thing' almost exploded in his head. The way her fingers had assisted him to undo it. The way her breasts had felt when he'd finally got to touch them…

'Won't be a moment,' one of the cardiologists called. 'We just need another extension cord.'

'She told you her name was Cindy Riley?'

'Yes.'

Josh exchanged a glance with the other registrar. 'And you're trying to find her?'

'Ah…yes.'

Josh grinned. 'Did it occur to you that she might not want to be found?' he ventured.

'What on earth makes you say that?'

Josh didn't respond immediately. Computer print-outs were being passed around, listing the cases up for discussion. Tony took his copy but ignored it. He frowned at Josh.

'It just seems a bit of a coincidence.' Josh shrugged.

'What does?'

'A Cindy Riley. At a ball.'

'Thanks for coming,' the head of the cardiology department said, then cleared his throat. 'We've got a lot to get through today, so let's get started. Case one. Sixty-eight-year-old man with angina occurring with minimal exertion. Investigations so far reveal reduced ventricular function estimated at thirty-eight percent. He has moderate mitral regurgitation. A blocked anterior descending, almost blocked posterior descending, and fifty percent occlusion on his left main.'

The screen flickered into life, and views of dye being injected into coronary arteries were shown from various angles.

Tony was having trouble concentrating. A combination of words had made a loop that went round and round in his head.

Cindy Riley. At a ball.

Again and again the name echoed and merged, and finally morphed into something else.

'Good grief!'

'Problem, Tony?'

His soft exclamation had unintentionally reached the presenting cardiologist.

'Not at all. Ah…could you just rerun that last shot of the left main?'

Josh caught his gaze for a second, the quirk of his lips revealing that he knew exactly why Tony had been surprised.

Cindy Riley.

Cinderella.

No wonder this felt so different. He'd stumbled into a fairytale!

He'd found a princess in disguise.

What would the modern-day equivalent of a dropped slipper be? A mobile phone, perhaps?

Dammit. The only clue he had to go on was that she'd been at the ball alone, and had therefore acquired a ticket by being a member of staff here at St Patrick's.

The woman from Personnel had been fazed by the sheer number of employees. She hadn't been up to the challenge.

Tony straightened in his chair, clearing his throat as he prepared to redirect his focus to where it was supposed to be right now.

For the moment he was satisfied.

He loved a challenge.

CHAPTER FOUR

'I'VE got a bone to pick with you, Kelly Adams!'

'Hey, it's my day off. I can't possibly have done anything wrong.'

'You could have told me.'

'I did tell you. It's Wednesday, remember? Flipper's appointment?'

'Not about that.' Elsie clicked her tongue, but she was peering behind Kelly. 'Where *is* Flipper?'

'Crèche. We've got a two-hour gap until the ultrasound. I asked Flipper if she wanted to come out to lunch with you and me or go and play with her friends, and the friends won, I'm afraid.'

Elsie sniffed. 'I'm far too busy to go anywhere for lunch anyway. I've got rosters to sort.'

'But I really want to take you out for lunch. A nice lunch. To say thank you for babysitting the other night.'

Elsie's sniff sounded even more offended this time. 'Yes,' she said. 'The other night…' She fished in her pocket and pulled out a folded piece of paper.

Kelly watched her open it, her jaw dropping as a slightly fuzzy image appeared.

'Where did you get *that*?'

'Tom was on the hospital website. He thought I might like to see some of the pictures taken at the ball. I got him to print this one off. We both thought you looked like you were having the time of your life, but neither of us could figure out who it is in that musketeer costume.'

Kelly couldn't take her eyes off the image. She was in Tony's arms, laughing up at him. He was bent over her, about to sweep her into a dip, probably, and every line of his body suggested a total focus on the woman in he was holding. It was such a tangible reminder of that night. Kelly could feel her heart rate picking up and a delicious melting sensation deep in her belly.

'Can I...have that?'

'Not unless you tell me who he is.'

Kelly grinned. 'I'll tell you if you let me take you out to lunch. Please, Elsie? I need to stop at the gift shop on the way back, because I've promised Flipper a surprise for being such a wee champion for her blood tests this morning. You can help me choose something she'd really like.'

Elsie refolded the picture and put it back in her pocket. 'I suppose I could escape for half an hour.'

'Let's get our skates on, then. I want to take you across the road to The Waiting Room.'

'You can't afford *their* outrageous prices!'

'Yes, I can. Just for a treat. Go on... Bacon and egg sandwiches. A real cappuccino...'

Elsie might be grumbling, but she was moving pretty quickly for someone in her sixties with more than a touch of arthritis.

The two women made unlikely-looking friends as they walked briskly through the main entrance of the hospital to get to the popular café on the edge of St Patrick's grounds, but there was a close bond between them. One that had been forged by a mutual love for the baby Kelly had been forced to take with her, way back, when she'd applied for the job at St Pat's.

There was a limit to how much Kelly intended to confess to the older woman now, however, which was just as well. Elsie was shocked at simply learning the name of the musketeer.

'Dr Grimshaw? The surgeon?'

Kelly cast an anxious glance around them, but other patrons, many of them in uniform or even scrubs, fortunately seemed intent on enjoying the great food and superb coffee.

'It was just a dance, Elsie.'

'*Was* it?'

Kelly pressed her lips together firmly.

Elsie ate the last bite of her sandwich in silence. Then she looked up. 'You going to see him again?'

Kelly forgot her resolve to stay quiet. 'Of *course* not!'

'What's so "of course not" about it?'

'It's ridiculous, that's why. We come from different planets. It would be like…oh, I don't know…a member of the royal family and a servant.'

Like…a fairytale.

'Imagine if he saw me emptying a bedpan or something?'

'Did you tell him what you do for a living?'

'Hardly. I didn't even tell him my real name. I said it was Cindy Riley.'

Elsie snorted after a moment's thought. 'Very clever.'

'Very temporary.'

'Your planets aren't really so different,' Elsie said as she pushed back her chair. 'You could very easily be standing on his one by now, you know. If it hadn't been for that dreadful accident.'

Kelly picked up her handbag. 'I can't regret any sacrifice I made,' she said quietly. 'Not when it gave me Flipper. She's my family, Elsie. She's all I have that's really mine.'

'I know, love.' Neither woman had risen to her feet yet. 'And I know that you probably don't even admit it to yourself, but there must be times when you're lonely?'

Kelly ignored the gentle query. She couldn't afford to go there. It was something else that would become far too real by talking about it. It would become real and then it would grow. She stood up.

'And that's another reason I won't be seeing him or anyone else again. I'm not going to risk letting someone into my life who might not be prepared to love Flipper the way I do.'

'You'll never know if you don't give someone a chance,' Elsie persisted as she followed Kelly. 'And who said you had to marry him, anyway? Or take him home, even?'

Kelly gasped in mock horror. 'Are you suggesting I engage in an affair that's never going to go anywhere?'

'All I'm saying is maybe you shouldn't be throwing away something that's given you a sparkle I've never seen before.'

It was time to change the subject. Kelly veered towards the gift shop in the hospital foyer and the display stand of toys outside its door.

'Look! Wouldn't she love this pink bear in the tutu? Oh...what about this?' Kelly picked up a large, fluffy green frog. She hugged it, and then laughed as it croaked with a convincing 'rivet rivet' sound.

'Definitely the frog.'

The voice wasn't Elsie's. Kelly's head turned so swiftly she almost lost her balance.

Tony Grimshaw was dressed in scrubs with an unbuttoned white coat over the top. He looked fresh from a stint in Theatre, with his hair rumpled and a pink line across his forehead that must have been left by the edge of a cap. Dark eyes she remembered so well were staring at her intently, and she couldn't miss the sudden gleam of mischief in them.

'Still looking for a prince, Cinderella?' The query was deadpan. 'Try kissing the frog.'

Kelly heard a faint, "Oh, my!" from Elsie's direction, but she couldn't turn her head because that would mean breaking eye contact with Tony.

And she couldn't do that because she was

watching the corners of his eyes crinkle, and she had to see the way the smile spread across his features. She could feel her own face changing. Mirroring his with a smile that seemed to be being pulled from a place she'd never explored. A very joyous place.

'What do you say, Cinderella? Can I buy you lunch and help you decide?'

'No.' Kelly shook her head hurriedly. 'I've had my lunch. But thank you.'

'You're not working today?' His gaze flicked over the civvies—a layered tops and the snug-fitting jeans Kelly had tucked into long boots. 'Or are you doing an afternoon shift?'

'No…I just came in to—' Kelly felt a nudge in the small of her back. Elsie might be pretending to re-arrange the display stand of toys but her elbow carried a very unsubtle message. It also provided inspiration. 'To look at my roster,' she finished.

'You'll have time for a coffee, at least?'

'Oooh.' Kelly would have to tell Elsie how sharp her elbows were. 'I guess a—a coffee wouldn't hurt.'

'And your friend?'

'Sorry?' Was he offering to take *Elsie* for coffee as well?

Tony patted the fluffy frog she was still clutching.

'Rivet-rivet,' the toy said obligingly.

Kelly had to fight the wild desire to giggle like a teenager. She also had to fight the acute awareness of the way his hand had brushed her fingers. This was like a scene from a comedy.

A romantic comedy?

'Here.' Tony took the frog from her hands and turned to Elsie, clearly mistaking her for the woman who ran the gift shop. 'Could you wrap this, please, and charge it to my account? I'm—'

'I know who you are,' Elsie said calmly. 'It will be no trouble at all, sir.'

'Excellent. Cinderella will be in to collect it later.'

'Cinderella?' Elsie managed to inject an amused but questioning note into her voice.

'Private joke,' Tony explained.

The statement gave Kelly a very odd kind of tingle. As though he considered them to be friends. More than friends, even.

'That'll be Miss—?' Tony raised an eyebrow at Kelly. 'It *is* Miss, I presume?'

Oh, Lord…was he asking if she was single? Standing there, in Theatre scrubs, looking just a little rumpled. Holding a fluffy toy with a look on his face that made her think that if they weren't standing in an astonishingly busy thoroughfare of a major hospital he would be kissing her senseless.

And now, thanks to Elsie, he was going to find out who she really was.

He *wanted* to find out.

'Yes,' Kelly managed. 'Miss Adams. Kelly Adams.'

'Excellent,' Tony said again. He gave the frog to Elsie. 'I'd really appreciate it if you could gift wrap this for Miss Adams.'

He led Kelly through the foyer and out of the main door on the same route she had taken with

Elsie not very long ago. 'I'm sure you've made a wise choice,' he said. 'You'll love the frog.'

That brought another smile to Kelly's face. 'It's not for me,' she said. 'I wanted to find a present for a small girl who was very brave this morning, getting some bloods taken.'

'Ah…a patient. How old is she?'

'Three. Nearly four.'

'You must be fond of her. What's her name?'

'Flipper.'

He gave her another one of those intent looks. 'Like the dolphin?'

Kelly laughed. What was it about talking to this man that had her smiling and laughing so easily? Feeling as if…as if that joyous place was just around the next corner.

'Her real name's Philippa,' she said, still smiling. 'She's always called herself Flipper, so now everyone else does.'

'You sound like you know her very well?'

'Yes.'

'One of the special ones?'

'Absolutely.'

Good grief, Tony was leading her into The Waiting Room. A staff member working behind the counter gave Kelly a surprised glance, which made her wonder how many others would notice her being there for the second time in less than an hour.

Tony sensed her hesitation. 'The coffee's so much better in here than it is in the staff café. We could go somewhere else, if you like, but there's not many places I could get away with wearing scrubs. I reckon there's more St Pat's staff in here than members of the general public.'

Yes. A quick glance around while Tony was choosing sandwiches and some fruit confirmed that. In fact wasn't that John Clifford—Flipper's doctor— with a group of other consultants on the far side of the café? Thank goodness he wasn't looking in her direction.

'There's a free table over there,' Kelly pointed out hurriedly as Tony picked up his tray.

'Perfect.'

It was. Tucked into a corner and at least partially screened by a potted palm tree. Tony might know her real name now, but Kelly could still pull a little magic around herself by keeping the rest of reality at bay.

Except that Tony seemed to have other ideas.

'So—tell me about young Flipper,' he invited. 'What's wrong with her?'

'She has…um….congenital heart problems.'

'Oh? What sort?'

It was so tempting to tell him something about her life from the safe perspective of seeming to be discussing someone else. Just to see what his reaction might be.

'It's complicated,' Kelly said cautiously. 'Patent ductus arteriosus with a major atrioventricular septal defect. Some valve abnormalities as well.'

'Poor kid.' Tony paused before taking another large bite of his ham and salad sandwich. 'She's had surgery, I suppose?'

'As a newborn.'

'Hard on the parents.'

'Very.'

'And she's been admitted again?"

'Oh, no!' The thought was horrifying.

'Why the blood tests, then? And the frog?'

'She needs regular check-ups. For all sorts of things.' Maybe it had been a mistake allowing this conversation to continue, but she had—so why stop now? 'She has Down's Syndrome,' Kelly finished matter-of-factly.

Tony couldn't know that his reaction might be under a closer scrutiny than might be expected, but his smile was very sympathetic.

'I take my hat off to parents like that,' he said. 'It's hard enough to cope with sick kids, but the ones with special needs on top of physical problems require an astonishing devotion. From everyone. Family, doctors, nursing staff…' He was smiling at Kelly now, including her in that number. Making her feel as though he understood and approved of any extra effort involved. 'She must be special to warrant a talking frog. What's her surname? I might know her.'

The belated arrival of their coffee was well timed. Kelly had a moment to stop kicking herself for talking about something so personal, however well disguised, and to look for an escape route before she could start clouding any dream with reality and making the mistake of believing it.

'You don't do paediatric surgery, do you?'

'It's an area of interest, but I haven't had the time or opportunity to do anything about it. I did have a seventeen-year-old patient the other day.' His smile had to be the most engaging Kelly had ever seen. 'Is that close enough?'

She dragged her gaze away from his mouth. 'How *is* Michael?'

That diverted him with startling success. 'How on earth do you know his name?'

'I was there,' Kelly confessed, delighted to have a new topic of conversation. 'I saw your thoracotomy.'

'I didn't see you.'

'I wasn't inside the lines. More like part of your audience. It was…amazing.'

'It was lucky, more like it. Good timing. A successful result is dependent on the level of cardiac activity, or on how much time between when it stops and a thoracotomy is performed. I'm not boring you here, am I?'

'Of course not.'

'There've been some big studies done, and I love to keep up with the kind of results of research that relate to what I do. Chances of survival are zero if the victim's arrested at the scene of the accident. Minimal—about four percent—if it happens en route in the ambulance. But you can expect a survival rate of about twenty percent if the arrest happens in the emergency department. Especially if it's isolated trauma to the thoracic cavity, as it was in this case.'

'So he's going to survive?'

'He's out of Intensive Care already. I'm planning to check up on him after lunch.' Tony stilled for a moment, as though struck by a new thought. 'Tell you what,' he said with a smile, 'meet me for dinner tonight and I'll give you an update.'

Kelly shook her head. 'I can't. Sorry.'

'Oh... Not a night shift, is it?'

She pulled a wry face which might easily have suggested the necessity and lack of enjoyment involved in having to work night shift, and Tony simply nodded.

'Not the easiest life, is it?'

'No.'

'But you've had a look at your roster today, yes? I've got mine right here.' A Blackberry emerged from the pocket of his white coat. 'Let's find a night we're both free.'

Kelly said nothing, aware of alarm bells sounding loudly. It was all very well for Elsie to recommend her putting some excitement in her life—and what could be more exciting than a date with the most eligible bachelor on the staff of St Pat's? In the city, even? But Elsie wasn't sitting here, realising just how easy it would be to lose sight of reality completely and make the mistake of falling for a man like this.

As if sex with Tony Grimshaw could *ever* be meaningless.

He glanced up from the electronic device, and must have seen something of what Kelly was thinking in her face because he frowned.

'I'm sorry I didn't see you in Emergency the other day. I hope you didn't think I was being deliberately rude?'

Kelly's breath came out in an amused huff. 'Hardly. Why on earth would you have been looking?'

'Well, maybe I was a little preoccupied at that precise time, but I *have* been looking—believe me.'

'Oh?' Words deserted Kelly.

Tony leaned closer. 'Do you have any idea what sort of idiot I felt like when I realised I'd been pestering the staff in Personnel to track down a Cindy Riley that I'd happened to meet at a ball?'

Kelly bit her lip. 'I never thought...'

'That I'd want to find you? And why not?' He lowered his voice. 'Why did you just leave like that, Kelly? Without even letting me know who you really were?'

'Because...' There had been a flash of something totally unexpected in his eyes. Something like bewilderment. Hurt, even? Did someone like her really have the power to dent the confidence of someone like Tony? He didn't deserve that. 'I didn't want to spoil the magic,' she whispered. 'The whole night had been like a fairytale.'

'Hmm.' The look was assessing now. Probing. She felt as if he could see right into her soul and gauge how honest she was being. But then he smiled. 'Fairytale, huh? I can buy that.'

He reached his hand across the table so that his fingertips touched hers. The tiniest connection in physical terms, but the effect was electrifying.

'It *was* magic, wasn't it?' he said softly. 'I was starting to think I'd dreamt it. Come out with me, Kelly. I'd really like more proof that it *was* real, because…'

The way his words trailed away made Kelly even more conscious of the touch of his skin against hers. It was spreading. Up her arms and into the rest of her body. Making her breasts tingle. Giving her that mind fogging curl deep in her belly.

'Because?' Her prompt came out embarrassingly like a croak.

'It was so different,' Tony said slowly. '*You're* different. I'm not sure why, but I'm a scientist and I can't just put it down to magic.' The smile flashed again. That disarmingly boyish grin. The kind that belonged to a man confident enough not to care about standing in a busy hospital thoroughfare in his scrubs, holding a ridiculous fluffy green toy. 'I think some research is called for here.' He moved his hand to pick up his Blackberry. 'How about Friday?'

'Flipper, have you still got the keys, hon?'

A small hand jangled the set of keys importantly. Three-year-old Philippa Adams was taking her responsibility seriously. She clambered up the steps to the front door of a small terraced house, and then stared at the keys, panting from the exertion of climbing.

'It's the big silver one,' Kelly prompted.

Short fingers fumbled, trying to insert the wrong key into the lock.

'Maybe I should do it this time, sweetheart.'

'No! Flipper do it.'

'I could just help,' Kelly said casually after another attempt, hopefully without making it obvious that this skill was still well above the little girl's abilities. 'It's been a busy day, hasn't it? I think we're both tired.'

'Mummy tired?' A round face appeared as Flipper peered up at Kelly. With its small nose and wide mouth and the almond shaped eyes that disappeared into slits when she grinned, she looked like an adorable pixie. One that was frowning in concern as she considered the possibility that her mother wasn't happy.

The keys were handed over. 'You go, Mummy.'

Kelly ruffled her sparse dark hair. 'Good girl. We'll both do it. You hold the key and I'll hold your hand on top. Like this.'

A moment later they were both walking down the short, narrow hallway of the tiny house. The two front rooms were the bedrooms, and a third door led to the bathroom. At the end of the hallway a single room ran the width of the dwelling—a kitchen-living area that gave an illusion of space, accentuated by French doors that opened onto a compact bricked courtyard.

Kelly peeled the anorak from the small girl, and as soon as she was free from her outdoor clothing Flipper made a series of kangaroo hops to reach the centre of a round rug in front of a small sofa. She held her arms wide and spun herself around in circles.

'Darn!' she called. 'Darn, Mummy!'

'I can't dance just now,' Kelly apologised. 'I need to make our dinner. Want to help?'

'No.' Flipper's bottom lip jutted.

'Hey! You dropped Frog.' Distraction was needed. 'What does Frog say?'

The smile erased the discontented frown instantly. 'Ribby-ribby!' Flipper shouted.

'And why did you get Frog?'

'I was a goo' girl.'

'You sure were.' Kelly stooped to gather Flipper for a quick hug, but Flipper wriggled free of the embrace. She swooped on the toy she had dropped in order to get her jacket taken off, and a moment later she was dancing again, with the fluffy frog clutched in her arms.

The bright green toy even had to sit on the table beside Flipper's plate when they had their dinner.

'No,' Kelly had to say firmly, more than once. 'Frog doesn't eat mashed potato. It goes in *your* mouth.'

As usual, it also went all over her face and through her hair. Flipper's bath was a necessity as well as a time they both enjoyed, but again the new family member created some friction.

'No. You can't have Frog in the bath. He'd get all wet and soggy and then he wouldn't be able to go to bed with you.' Kelly tugged on the toy that was being held with a grip of iron. 'How about we put him on the toilet seat and he can watch while I wash your hair?'

'OK.'

'And we'd better try not to splash too much tonight.'

Soaping the small body after the hair-washing was attended to, Kelly's hands traced the lumpy scar that ran down the front of Flipper's chest.

'We saw your heart today, didn't we? We saw it on the special TV, going lub-dub, lub-dub.'

'Lub-dub-*dub*!' Flipper's hands hit the water with enthusiasm, and Kelly laughed, wiping soapsuds off her own face.

'You should be called Flapper, not Flipper.'

'Dub-dub-*dub*!' And Flipper joined in the laughter with peals of the delicious gurgle that was Kelly's favourite sound in the world.

'He was a nice man who looked at your heart on the TV, wasn't he?'

Flipper reached for a plastic duck.

'I had coffee with another nice man today.' Kelly squeezed a sponge to let water rinse the suds from Flipper's back. 'He wants to go out with me.'

Flipper was pushing the duck beneath the surface of the water and then letting it go so that it bobbed up. Every time seemed to create the same level of surprise and elicited another gurgle of laughter. She didn't appear to be listening to Kelly.

'It's Aunty Elsie's fault,' Kelly murmured. 'She thinks I should go. She reckons I could hire another dress or wear one of hers. She's got all these wonderful retro frocks from the sixties and seventies she's never thrown out, and she wants me to go and try them on and she'll make them fit.'

Flipper threw the duck over the side of the bath.

'Do *you* think I should go?'

A ridiculous question to ask an uninterested child, but Kelly was simply thinking aloud here. Exploring what was, admittedly, a very tempting notion. Elsie thought she should go. She would be only too happy to babysit Flipper again.

'He wants to take me dancing,' Kelly told Flipper.

That got her interest.

'Darn!'

'Mmm.' Kelly touched the sponge to Flipper's nose. 'With the nice man. What do you think?'

'Man?'

'Mmm. A nice man.'

'Man darn?' Flipper was staring up at Kelly now, her eyes as wide as it was possible for them to get.

'Oh, yes,' Kelly smiled. 'The man can dance, all right.'

The stare continued, and then Flipper's face creased into that wonderful smile. Not that she understood what Kelly was really talking about. She was just happy because she thought her mother was happy.

Kelly lifted her from the tub, wrapped her in a fluffy towel and kissed her. 'I love you,' she said.

'Mummy darn,' Flipper said decisively.

Did she mean with her or with the 'nice man'? Could she make her own choice? Kelly kissed her again.

'You know what?' Her smile widened. 'I think I will.'

CHAPTER FIVE

THE exclusive harbourside restaurant was an intimate and discreet haven for those lucky enough to succeed in making a reservation.

It was a favourite haunt for Tony. Usually, the fact that the owner, Pierre, knew him so well and always had 'his' table ready for him was simply taken as a matter of course—by himself and by the sophisticated women who normally accompanied him.

Tonight was different.

It had been ever since he'd pulled up near the nondescript exterior of a terraced house in one of the less desirable inner city streets. One that he'd probably driven through many times with no interest in what lay alongside the road.

The surroundings had been forgotten, however, the moment the door at the top of the steps opened. Kelly had paused for a moment, scanning the limited parking spaces available for his vehicle.

Tony had also hesitated, his hand already on the door handle in preparation for getting out to open the passenger side of his car. It wasn't because of any reluctance on his part, more from being struck by a kind of wonder at the way this woman seemed to pull light around her. Any background would have become dull and insignificant.

She…shone.

Her hair was loose again, and desire kicked in as Tony remembered burying his fingers in those luxuriant waves to draw her close enough to kiss. His breath caught in his chest, allowing no more than a soft, strangled groan as his body decided to relive the exquisite tickle of her hair on his body when he had pulled her on top of him.

Getting out of his car and getting himself on a tight leash had been paramount. Tonight wasn't about the overwhelming lust of the night of the ball. It was about getting to know the reality behind the fantasy. Kelly Adams, not Cinderella. This was a date, and he was an expert in dates.

Except this was so different.

Kelly, with her hair long and loose, and a dress that fitted close on the top but had a billowing skirt with huge blue flowers splashed all over its white background, couldn't have presented a more dramatic contrast to his usual companions with their neat, carefully streaked blonde hairstyles and slinky cocktail dresses.

For the same reason, maybe, it was a little embarrassing to have Pierre greet him personally now, and escort them to "his" table. He didn't want Kelly to think that he came here so often. With so many other women. He wanted her to think she was special. To know that *he* thought she was special.

A trio of musicians was tucked into a corner of the restaurant beside a small dance floor, but even that made Tony vaguely uncomfortable. It was way too soon to ask Kelly if she would like to dance. As much as his body craved the touch of holding her, he couldn't do it while things felt so...different.

Awkward.

Like the way her eyes widened when Pierre brought the customary French champagne to start their evening. He filled their crystal flutes and then stood back, a square of snowy linen draped over his arm, speaking in his perfect English with an accent that made most women sigh, detailing the gastronomic delights the menu had to offer tonight.

It would be easier when they were left alone, Tony decided. They could talk about the food and break the ice.

But Kelly's eyes were shining by the time Pierre had finished speaking. She didn't even open her menu.

'Pâté,' she said decisively. 'And the chicken with truffles. I've never tasted a truffle, and it sounded divine, didn't it?'

'Mmm.' Tony closed his own menu and returned her smile. He needed to find something else to talk about.

Something. Anything that would spark a conversation and give him a reason to watch her. The way those huge eyes took in everything around her, as though it was new and fascinating. The way her face moved to reveal so much of what she was thinking. She was so *alive*.

So real. Unsophisticated, perhaps. Childlike, even. Yet she was the most attractive woman Tony had ever met. And this was…astonishing.

Even more astonishing was the fact that the ice was broken by something that had always been a taboo on any date.

Him—talking about his work.

He wasn't sure how it happened exactly. He made some polite query about her day, and a responding comment about a lengthy meeting he'd been tied up with, and suddenly he was answering questions about his current research with an enthusiasm kindled by the interest he could see in her face.

'It's a drug that can preserve cerebral cellular function in patients undergoing bypass surgery.'

'Oh…' She almost clicked her fingers as she summoned the information she wanted. 'Like—what it's called?—Neuroshield?'

The surprise was a very pleasant jolt. 'That's the parent drug. When I was a registrar I worked in Christchurch under a surgeon, David James, who's married to a cardiologist. Amazing team. They collaborated in the first trials of Neuroshield and it's been in clinical use for years, but now there's a new generation and David wants me to provide an arm of the research project.'

'And you're keen?' Her smile advertised that she knew the question was redundant.

'Research is a dimension to medicine that keeps the fascination alive. The only way to keep us moving forward and improving what we're capable of doing.'

Kelly was nodding, giving every impression of being totally absorbed by the topic. Their entrees arrived, but for once the food didn't become a new focus.

'Neuroshield works by slowing the metabolism, doesn't it? Enough to preserve cellular function when it's being challenged by something like bypass?'

Tony could only nod, his mouth full.

'How do you measure the parameters of something like that?'

It was the kind of conversation he might expect to have with a bright house surgeon or registrar. The kind of junior doctor it was a pleasure to work with. Tony swallowed.

'You need extensive baseline data. Anatomical and functional assessment with a series of neurological tests including CT scans.'

'Sounds expensive.'

'Most research is. The major cost is paying the salaries of the people qualified to do it, but do you know what the real challenge is?'

She simply raised the dark eyebrows that framed those gorgeous blue eyes and it was all the encouragement Tony needed.

'It's finding people who are genuinely interested.'

'But why? I would have thought they'd be lining up to get on board.'

'It's not the most glamorous side of medicine. Not much kudos to be gained from the enormous amount of work it takes to run a project, collate and analyse the data, and then write it up and get the results published. Unless you make a major break-through, of course, and that doesn't usually happen unless you're prepared to devote years and years to it.'

'But you are?'

'I… Yes, of course.' Where had that hesitation come from? Inexplicable, but apparently significant. Enough for him to see a reflection of it in the way Kelly's eyebrows flickered into a tiny questioning frown.

'I've been heading towards this for years. Ever since David got me excited about the possibilities. It's a huge goal, but it's getting closer a lot faster than I'd anticipated. It all hinges on whether or not I get the head of department position.'

'I heard that was coming up.' Her glance was shy—as though she was so impressed she wasn't sure what to say. 'It's a big step up, isn't it?'

'Huge. And I know I'm young to be considered, but it's an opportunity I can't afford to pass up, Kelly. Imagine the influence I could have. I could make research a priority for the department. Attract funding. Employ the kind of people who will help it grow and succeed.'

She was watching him carefully, her food forgot-ten. 'But you'll miss being so involved in the clinical side of things? Theatre, for instance?'

Tony stared at her. He'd dismissed that as being a major issue in the interview he'd had with the board of directors earlier today. He'd believed himself. Who in their right mind would miss an overload of the pressure and tension that came with too many hours spent in an operating theatre? But could Kelly see something he might not have given enough thought to?

It was time to stop talking about this. If anyone had told him he could go on a date and have a thought-provoking conversation about his research and his career, he would have snorted incredulously. She couldn't possibly be as interested as she seemed. Or have any insight he didn't have himself. Tony pushed his plate aside.

'Enough shop talk,' he decreed. 'It's time we had a dance.'

It was still there.

The fantasy.

The feel of a man's arms holding her and his body moving in perfect unison with hers as they gave their own interpretation to a superbly played medley of slow, romantic songs.

Not just any man, though. This was Tony.

Kelly glanced up, and another sense kicked in to add to her pleasure as her eyes drank in the angular lines of his face and the shadow of his jaw that the soft lighting accentuated. She could see the enviable length of his black eyelashes and she caught a whiff of rainforest from his aftershave. His formal white shirt was crisp beneath her fingers, and she could almost taste the kisses she knew would come later tonight. Every sense was heightened by movement.

Such intense pleasure. So much more than the first time they had danced together, because there was intimacy as an undercurrent now. They were playing with the physical fire they knew could be ignited between them. That they were in public again was intoxicating. Touching within proscribed limits, but the slide of his hand on the bare skin of her shoulders and arms sparking erotic images that had the memory of reality to inflame them.

His face was so close. She only needed to raise her face a little to be close enough to touch it with her lips and feel the roughness of that shadow. Touch it with her tongue, even, and taste the musky warmth that was uniquely his.

And then Tony looked down and caught her gaze. Held it for a long, long moment as he slowed their dance and drew her closer. So close she could feel his heart beating against her own. And then he smiled, still holding her gaze, and the moment was so perfect Kelly could feel herself being sucked into the fairytale.

The wedding bells.

The happy-ever-after.

Pure fantasy, of course. But what was the harm of indulging for the limited time they would be on the dance floor? The food for their main course would arrive at their table at any moment and they would have to return. To sit still and, to outward appearances at least, be in touch with reality.

But that held a new appeal for Kelly now. A kind of fantasy all of its own. She couldn't have the career in medicine she'd always dreamed of, but talking about it—wrapping herself in the edges of someone else's passion—was curiously satisfying. Intellectually stimulating. Balm to an area of her soul that had been closed off and left to wither.

Tony's ambition was palpable, but it came with an ethos that Kelly could understand and admire. He wasn't doing this for personal kudos or wealth. She had the impression that wealth meant very little, because it had always been part of his life. The desire to excel in his career was there because he cared about what he did for a living. He wanted to do his job to the best of his ability and he cared enough to want to keep raising the bar for the standard he delivered.

It was impressive.

He wasn't the golden boy she had assumed from a distance. A rich playboy who was in this profession for the status. If he was, he certainly wouldn't be planning to dedicate his career to research. Or to take on the demanding position of HOD and all the extra hours it would entail to further his dream. He certainly wouldn't be prepared to sacrifice the amount of time doing something he really loved— the hands-on battle to improve or save a life.

His research was fascinating.

He was fascinating.

Disappointingly, Tony was clearly determined not to talk shop any more this evening, having led Kelly back to their table. Wines were chosen and plates of gorgeously arranged and delicious food arrived. Kelly sipped her wine and then tasted her truffle-infused chicken, and she had to close her eyes for a moment to savour this new sensation.

She opened her eyes to find Tony watching her. Smiling.

'Nice?'

'Heaven.'

His nod was an agreement. 'I don't think I've ever had a bad meal here. You?'

'I've never been here before.'

'Really? But Pierre's has been an institution for decades now. Are you not a local girl?'

'Yes, but this isn't the kind of place my family could ever afford to go.' It was another facet of the fantasy. The snowy linen and sparkling silverware. Champagne and music and food to die for. 'And I...don't eat out much.'

His glance was curious, but they ate in silence for a minute. Then Tony reached for his wine glass.

'So where did you go to celebrate special occasions when you were growing up?'

'We had our celebrations at home. You couldn't beat Mum's roast lamb and her melt-in-your-mouth pavlova.'

'Mmm. Lucky you. I don't think I've ever seen my mother cook.'

Kelly blinked. 'Not even toast?'

'We had a housekeeper. Betty. She was a kind of second mother to us.'

'Us? You have siblings?' It was intriguing to

imagine Tony as a little boy. But a wistful desire to see photographs seemed an odd thing to experience on a first date.

And it was a first date, wasn't it? Even though Tony knew things about her that no man had ever learned before. You couldn't count the night of the ball as a first date. Fate had thrown them together, and for Kelly, at least, it hadn't felt as though she was accepting an invitation to spend time with Tony. More as if she was being carried away on a current she had no chance of successfully resisting.

And coffee? Again, that meeting had been at the hands of fate. This time, though, Tony had asked her to be with him, and she had accepted—so, yes, this had to be seen as their first date.

'I'm the baby,' Tony was telling her with a smile, as her thoughts wandered. 'I've got an older brother and a sister. You?'

'One sister,' Kelly said, hesitating only for a heart-beat. 'Four years older.'

'Your family still lives in town?'

'N-no.'

He got it, even before she'd finished uttering the single word. His fork paused in mid-air and he stilled. Waiting. There was a softening of his features that felt like a safety net. He was a step ahead of Kelly, but how on earth could he possibly know?

Could being honest destroy this fantasy? Make the romantic setting and the wonderful food and the prospect of dancing again insignificant? The reality was harsh, but how could Kelly be less than honest when he was looking at her like this? A look that felt like a touch of sympathy.

'There was an accident. Nearly four years ago.' She tried to sound matter-of-fact. 'A terrible car crash. My parents, my sister and her husband were all in the car.' A tiny quiver crept into her voice. 'There were no survivors.'

'Oh, my God,' Tony breathed. 'You lost your whole family?'

Kelly had to look away from the gentleness in his face. To press her lips together as she nodded. She felt her fingers grasped from across the table.

'Kelly, I'm *so* sorry.'

He was. The words rocked her with their sincerity. It was a gift of caring that she suddenly felt afraid to accept. She managed a nod, but then drew in a determined breath as she pulled her hand free and reached for her glass of iced water.

'Tell me about *your* family,' she said, changing the subject. 'I know who your father is, of course, but what about your brother? And sister?'

'My brother has a gift for languages. He's fluent in at least six, and did a PhD that explored similarities between some languages. Did you know that Japanese and Maori have some astonishing similarities? The same words for some things, even.'

'No.' Kelly was more than happy to be diverted. 'It sounds fascinating. What does he do now?'

'He started his career as an interpreter, and he's now living in Geneva and has an important position with the United Nations.'

'Wow. And your sister?'

'Meg did a PhD in physics. Of the nuclear variety. She lives in the States and works for NASA.'

Kelly's jaw dropped. 'Your sister's a rocket scientist?'

'Yeah. Pretty impressive, isn't it?'

'No more than what you and your brother do. Heavens, what a high-achieving family. You're all doctors! Your parents must be very proud of you all.'

'Satisfied might be a better word.'

'Oh?' Something in his tone made Kelly want to touch *his* hand. To offer sympathy.

'Failure was never an option in my family.' Tony was smiling, but there was a hint of something far less flippant in his eyes. 'My mother's a very successful lawyer with her own firm. Dad made millions with his construction company and then got bored. Local politics gave him a challenge, but I suspect he's looking for something new again now. His philosophy is that if you get a prize you don't stop. You just look around until you can spot a bigger prize.' Tony was turning his attention back to his cooling dinner. 'He's got a mayoral reception happening tonight, and I think he might be planning to announce a decision not to run for a third term in office.'

'A reception? What happens at those?'

Tony swallowed his mouthful. 'A lot of overdressed people stand around, eating fancy bits of finger food and drinking a little too much wine. They seem very interested in everybody else, but what they're really doing is networking with people who might be useful in furthering their own interests. They're astonishingly boring affairs and I was delighted to have an excuse not to attend.'

Kelly's food went down her throat somewhat faster than she had intended. 'You were expected to be there?'

'My parents are quite used to the demands of my career. It's not often I *am* available to wave the family flag.'

'But…you *could* have been there tonight.'

'I chose to be with you.'

The look Tony gave her and the tone of his voice held so much promise. Too much. Any moment now and Kelly would actually start believing in this fantasy.

'I feel guilty.'

'For stealing me away from my filial civic duty?' Tony grinned. 'If it would ease your conscience, we could always skip dessert and drop in on the way home. It's not far from my apartment.'

He was planning to take her home to his apartment? A step further into his personal life?

This felt huge.

'I…um…'

'You might like to see firsthand what a mayoral reception is like. You could meet my parents.'

Kelly simply stared. Being invited to his home was huge in itself. Being introduced to his parents was even bigger. Reality was crowding in on the fantasy. Merging. Making those dreams on the dance floor a possibility instead of just indulgence.

This was dangerous. Exciting. Way too much to get her head around when this was moving so fast. Too fast. A romantic ride in a runaway train. One that was highly likely to crash. But there was no way off at this precise moment as far as Kelly could see.

She was caught by this man. He already had a hold on her body and her mind...and her heart.

There was no question about whether or not she could fall in love with him. She was in freefall. Was there something she could catch hold of to save herself? Did she really need or want to? This sensation was so compelling that for this moment in time it seemed worth the risk of whatever might break when the crash happened.

She could handle this. As long as Flipper wasn't involved, and it was only herself in danger of being hurt, then it didn't matter. Not in the big scheme of things.

The sensible part of Kelly was reminding her that she had responsibilities. That risk-taking should not be on the agenda. Her spirit was rebelling. Nothing ventured, nothing gained, it put forward. What if she took the safe option and spent the rest of her life wondering "what if"?

What if there was some magic out there and this *did* have a chance of working?

What if she stepped into his world and found there was a place for her?

What if he was feeling the same way about her as she was about him?

What if she said no and never saw him again?

Skipping dessert wasn't an issue. Kelly's appetite had fled and her mouth was too dry to swallow anything.

Her smile felt curiously shy. 'I'd love to,' she said.

CHAPTER SIX

It WAS a palace.

Never mind that Kelly sat in a low-slung, luxury sports car instead of a converted pumpkin coach as she rode through ornate iron gates and up a long driveway lined with majestic trees. She was definitely back in the fairytale, and arriving at the modern-day equivalent of a palace.

Framed by manicured flood-lit gardens that featured two vast ponds with fountain centrepieces and blankets of flowering water lilies, was the biggest house Kelly had ever seen. The brickwork had been softened over time by ivy that crept up to the second storey, but there wasn't enough time to count all the windows before Tony eased his car into place with all the other sleek European vehicles accommodated in and around what must have once been a stable block.

There was enough time to do some counting as they walked towards the Georgian pillars that supported a roof designed to provide shelter whilst waiting for the massive front door to open, but Kelly was too distracted to think of it.

The lower floor of the enormous house was lit up like a Christmas tree, and heavy drapes on each side of the windows had been left tied up. Huge chandeliers hung from intricately moulded ceilings, and the light made the scenes within the frame of the windows as bright as movie clips for anyone approaching in the dark.

Someone was playing a grand piano, and Kelly could hear the muted background of classical favourites. A kind of steady foundation for the rise and fall of animated conversation and the occasional tinkle of feminine laughter.

Waiters carried silver trays of champagne flutes that caught shards of light from the chandeliers.

And there were people. So many people. Men looking glamorous in evening suits—a dark foil for the glitz of the women in their beautiful dresses.

Kelly had to fight the urge to turn and run. What on earth did she think she was doing? She didn't belong here. She would be spotted as an impostor the moment she walked through the door, and Tony would realise he'd made a terrible mistake.

He must have sensed her trepidation, because he caught her hand. But he didn't use the contact to encourage her to keep going forward. Instead, he paused, pulling Kelly close and then looking down at her without saying a word.

A second ticked past and then another. Kelly waited, holding her breath. Had he, too, realised that this wasn't a place she ought to be? Was he searching for a polite way to make an excuse and take her away?

Just the hint of a smile touched his lips, and he bent his head very slowly and deliberately to place a feather-light kiss on Kelly's lips.

'We won't stay long,' he murmured. 'I don't think I can wait much longer to take you home.'

It was the only encouragement Kelly needed. She belonged here because this was part of Tony's world and he wanted her by his side. That was enough.

Or was it?

Fifteen minutes was more than long enough for Kelly to change her mind completely. To have alarm bells ringing so loudly she was fighting embarrassment, disappointment, and something close to panic.

It started with the way people stared as she came into the first of the crowded reception rooms. Conversations trailed into silence, and Kelly could actually *feel* the touch of eyes running from her head to her feet. The men smiled at her, but the women exchanged glances and smiled at each other.

Knowing smiles that said: *Whoever the hell she is, she has no idea of fashion or style. What on earth does Tony Grimshaw think he's doing?*

Then there were the photographers. Why hadn't she expected that, when it was some kind of civil function and the local newspapers would be duty-bound to provide not only an account but plenty of fodder for the social pages? As a mystery woman accompanying the mayor's son, of course she would be the most interesting tidbit they had discovered so far. Lightbulbs flashed. Questions were asked.

'What's your name, love?'

'How long have you known Dr Grimshaw?'

'Is it serious between you two?'

Tony steered her through the reporters with the ease of someone who found being treated like a movie star commonplace.

'Take no notice,' he said to Kelly, even while flashing an easy smile in the direction of the cameras. 'And you don't have to tell them anything.'

He turned his head, must have interpreted her stunned expression correctly, squeezed her hand and grinned.

'Tell them your name's Cinderella,' he whispered.

That made her smile. It was enough to shut out the knowing looks and the flashes from the cameras. For just a moment it shut out the whole world around them. Here they were, the centre of attention because of who Tony was, and he was thinking of *her*. Making her feel as if she still belonged by his side by using a private joke.

Their joke.

The moment passed all too soon, however, and Kelly found herself being introduced to Tony's parents.

His father was wearing his mayoral robes, and had a heavy gold chain with a huge medallion around his neck. Bernard Grimshaw was as tall as his son but more solid, and had waves of iron-grey hair. The thought that Tony would look this good when he was in his sixties gave Kelly an odd tingle. Maybe it was the knowledge that she could spend decades with him and still find him attractive? It was more than good-looks. Bernard also had a presence that was a more mature version of Tony's charisma. One that made Kelly instinctively want to trust him.

No wonder he had done so well in politics. Kelly had her hand gripped, firmly but briefly, in a welcoming version of a handshake.

'Delighted to meet you, Kelly,' he said.

The sincerity might have been enough to chase away the horrible feeling of being a fish out of water—except all Kelly could think of as he gripped her hand was the astonished stare she was receiving from the woman who stood beside Bernard.

Tony's mother had to be the most sophisticated woman Kelly had ever seen in real life instead of in the pages of a glossy magazine. Blonde hair drawn back into an elegant chignon, with not a single hair escaping to mar its perfection. A black sheath of a dress that hid nothing of a slender body as perfect as the hairstyle.

In her billowing skirt, with its big, bright flowers, Kelly felt as if she had dressed in old curtains. Her long, loose hair felt about as appropriate as showing up to work totally naked.

'So you're a nurse,' Louise Grimshaw said after the introductions. 'How nice!'

Kelly got the distinct impression that she would have used exactly the same tone if Tony had told her that she was a cleaner. Or a fish factory worker. Or… or an employee of an escort agency.

She didn't belong here. With these people.

A waiter offered her champagne, but Kelly shook her head. The effects of any alcohol she'd had at the restaurant had worn off enough for her to realise that a clear head might be her only hope here. She needed to keep her wits about her if she was going to deflect the kind of verbal barbs Louise and her contemporaries could fire so expertly. A glass of champagne might undermine her control, and she would feel compelled to defend herself.

However sweetly she might be able to send the barbs flying back, it might embarrass Tony—and he didn't deserve that. He had brought her here in good faith. And he had promised they wouldn't stay long. Kelly could cope with whatever was coming her way. All she had to do was hang on until escape became possible.

Kelly was hating this.

Tony could sense her discomfort in the way she was holding herself. Taller. Straighter. Her smile was different because it didn't reach her eyes. Part of him was admiring the way she was dealing with something she didn't like. A bigger part was administering an inward kick for putting her in such a situation.

He should have known.

Any woman from his past would have been revelling in this experience. A chance to meet the movers and shakers in the city. A taste of being a celebrity, thanks to the attention of the press.

For some stupid reason he'd lost sight of how different Kelly was. Maybe that was because of the time they'd just spent together in the restaurant? The way it had felt to hold her in his arms again and dance with her. The spell had been reactivated. The one that made the rest of the world so distant and unreal. There had been a new dimension added, as well, finding out that Kelly had lost her whole family so tragically.

It explained so much. Like the strength he could sense in her. You had to be strong to survive something like that.

And no wonder she gave the impression of being independent. The need to stand alone had been cruelly forced upon her.

But she was an orphan and, no matter the outward appearance, she had to feel lonely. She needed comfort whether she was aware of the need or not.

Tony watched uneasily as his mother edged Kelly away from his side.

She needed protection.

His protection.

But his father had stepped between them now, and Kelly was being moved further away. Towards a group that seemed to be eagerly anticipating introductions.

'So...' Bernard eyed his son. 'Can I find you a drink?'

Tony shook his head. 'I've had my limit for tonight.'

Bernard nodded. 'Admirable restraint—but you're not on call, are you?'

'No, but I never have more than could wear off in an hour or two. You never know when there's going to be some kind of emergency.'

'Can't argue with that kind of devotion to your career, lad. Now, tell me about this Kelly…'

'Mmm?'

'Serious?'

Tony quirked an eyebrow. An effective 'neither confirm nor deny' gesture he had learned from his father.

Bernard grinned. 'Fair enough. None of my business. But—'

'But what?' Tony's words were quiet.

Both men turned by tacit agreement to look in the direction Louise had taken Kelly. She now stood on the far side of the enormous room, with a group that included a very pregnant young woman.

'She's…different,' Bernard said. His tone was a curious mix of appreciation and puzzlement. 'It's not just the dress. She's…'

'Yes,' Tony said. A corner of his mouth lifted and he was aware of something like pride warming him. 'She is.' He turned back to his father. 'So—are the rumours true? Are you planning to announce that you're not running for another term?'

Politics was a safe topic. A guaranteed distraction. Tony didn't want his father to talk about Kelly any more. To imply, however discreetly, that she didn't fit in here.

Bernard tapped the side of his nose and smiled. 'Wait and see, son. What's this I hear about *you*, more importantly? Sounds like you made a very good impression on the board of trustees this morning.'

'Who have you been talking to?'

'CEO of St Pat's. Have you forgotten that Colin Jamieson is a golf buddy of mine?'

'What did he have to say?'

'Said he thought you were a chip off the old block. That he'd never come across a young man so devoted to his career. Did you really tell them you have no intention of any family commitments distracting you from your professional goals?'

'I did.' And he'd said it sincerely. He'd believed it. So why did it strike a strangely discordant note to hear it said back to him now?

His father gave a single, satisfied nod. 'So it's not serious, then. I thought not.'

Tony opened his mouth. He was about to say something along the lines of being capable of choosing any goals he wished, and making sure he succeeded, and if that included having a family he would make it work—but he didn't get the opportunity.

A shriek came from the side of the room where Kelly was.

And then there was a contagious, horrified silence that spread rapidly outwards.

Tony turned to see Kelly standing beside the pregnant woman, her hand gripping the woman's arm. Supporting her?

Yes. The woman was leaning forward, looking on

the point of collapse. A man grabbed her other arm, an expression of deep concern on his face.

'Paige? Are you OK?'

'Good grief,' Bernard said. 'That's Nigel Finch— my deputy.'

People were stepping back. A woman lifted the hem of her long dress, gazing down in distress at an obvious stain on the cream carpet.

'Oh, my God, Paige! You're not going to have the baby *here*, are you?'

'No!' the pregnant woman wailed. 'I can't. It's not due for more than three weeks. Nigel! *Do* something!'

Tony was moving forward as others stepped back, but it was Kelly who took control.

'I can help,' she told Paige.

'Yes.' Louise was backing away quickly now. 'She's a nurse. She'll help.'

'Could you call an ambulance, please, Mrs Grimshaw? And you.' Kelly turned her attention to a couple beside her. 'Can you please get the table-cloths from over there? You could hold them up to make a screen and give Paige some privacy.' She was easing the woman to the floor. 'We need to see what's happening,' she told Paige. 'Are you OK with that?'

'Let Tony Grimshaw through,' someone called. 'He's a *doctor*.'

A cardiothoracic surgeon, Tony was tempted to remind these people. One who'd done a minimum amount of obstetric training, a very long time ago.

Screens were being held up in the form of long

white linen cloths that had been ripped off tables, scattering platters of canapés. The men holding them up had turned their backs. They opened the barrier to admit Tony.

Paige was sitting on the floor, peering forward as Kelly lifted her dress.

'Oh, my God! What's *that*?'

'The umbilical cord,' Kelly said calmly.

'Good grief.' The man kneeling beside Paige was as pale as the linen tablecloths. 'That's not supposed to come first, is it?'

'No. It's not ideal.'

Tony had to admire the calm in Kelly's voice. He might belong to a completely different specialty, but he knew damned well a prolapsed umbilical cord could be a medical emergency. And he knew what it took to stay calm in the face of an emergency. Confidence. Skill. A belief in yourself.

'We have to see how close you are to delivering the baby,' Kelly was telling Paige. 'What I need you to do is turn onto your knees, put your head down on your forearms and your bottom as high in the air as you can. Nigel, is it?' She looked towards the pale man gripping his wife's hand.

'Y-yes. I'm Paige's husband. The baby's—'

Kelly was helping Paige move.

'Why do I need to do this?' Paige was sobbing now. 'It hurts. I...I feel like pushing, and I can't do that if I'm upside down.'

'This takes the weight of the baby off the cord,' Kelly told her. 'I'm going to see whether the baby is coming and how far your cervix is dilated. If it's close, then I'm going to get you to push as hard as you can. Otherwise, you'll need to stay exactly like this until we can get you to the hospital.'

'Nigel!' Paige wailed.

'I'm here, honey. You'll be fine. This lady sounds like she knows what she's doing.'

She did indeed. Tony stripped off his jacket, flicked the studs from his cuffs and rolled his sleeves up. 'Can I help?'

'Don't suppose you've got some gloves in your pocket?'

'No, sorry.'

Tony's admiration for the way Kelly was handling this went up a notch. How often had they had personal safety drummed into them in their profession? Protection at all costs from the blood and other bodily fluids of a patient. And here Kelly was, kneeling in blood-stained amniotic fluid, oblivious to her dress being ruined, and about to give this woman an intimate physical examination.

It didn't take long.

'She's fully dilated,' Kelly reported seconds later. 'And the baby's head's engaged. Want to take over?'

'No. You're doing fine.' In the distance, Tony could hear the wail of approaching sirens. 'The cavalry's on its way.'

Just as well. With the cord emerging first, and the baby's head now engaged, its blood supply was cut off. They were only minutes away from tragedy.

'Right. We're going to lie you down again, Paige.

The safest thing for the baby is for it to be born as quickly as possible. Do you think you can push as hard as you can with the next contraction?'

'Y-yes.'

'Good girl.'

'You can do it, honey,' Nigel encouraged, but Tony could see the fear in his eyes. And the way he kept his gaze glued on Kelly as he gripped his wife's hand and waited for instructions.

'Pant for now,' Kelly told her. 'As soon as the next contraction starts, take an extra deep breath, hold it, and then push for all you're worth.'

Paige's knees were bent and Kelly was between them, her hands poised to assist a delivery that had to be fast if this baby was going to survive.

The siren got louder and then stopped. Tyres crunched in the gravel of the driveway just outside the windows. A door banged.

'They're in here,' someone was yelling in the foyer. 'Hurry!'

But Paige was pushing now.

'Keep it going,' Kelly urged. 'Harder! Push *harder*, Paige. Take another breath, grab hold of your knees and push again.'

'*Push*, honey!' Nigel's voice was strained. 'You can do this.'

Kelly's hands were hidden—presumably trying to get a grip on the baby's head and help it out quickly.

Tony heard an agonised groan from Paige, saw a rush of blood and more fluid, and then there was Kelly, holding the limp form of a tiny baby.

Paramedics appeared behind him with a stretcher laden with gear.

'Whoa!' one of them said. 'Looks like we've missed the party.'

'The cord's still pulsing,' Kelly informed them. 'But he's…' She stopped, focussed on the baby who was starting to move. Screwing up a bright red face.

The mouth opened and then shut. Tiny fists moved and the mouth opened again. This time a warbling cry emerged. The shocked and silent crowd around them gave a collective gasp and then an audible sigh of relief.

Paige burst into tears. So did Nigel.

Kelly handed the baby to the paramedics. The cord was clamped and cut, the baby wrapped in a soft towel and then handed to Paige.

'Let's get you to hospital,' they said.

'Hang on,' Kelly warned. 'The placenta's coming.'

Bernard Grimshaw was now close enough to see what was happening. Louise stood beside him. She stared in horrified fascination and then went very pale.

'What's *that*?' Her appalled whisper was loud enough for Tony and probably Kelly to hear.

'The placenta,' he told his mother. 'It's perfectly normal. You delivered one yourself three times.'

'I don't want to even *think* about that,' Louise said. 'Bernie?' Her whisper became urgent. 'Can the caterers cope with cleaning this up, do you think?'

'Shh. It can wait. It's a baby, Lou. Born in our lounge. How 'bout that?'

It was a baby, all right. A healthy-looking boy, now in the arms of his mother, who was being comfortably settled on the stretcher. A proud father reached for Kelly and gripped her hands.

'Thank you' was all he could manage, before emotion removed his power of speech.

One of the paramedics dropped a blanket around Kelly's shoulders. 'You're a bit damp,' he said. 'You'll get cold any minute. Just drop it back to the emergency department at St Pat's some time.'

Nigel turned back for another attempt at expressing his appreciation as he began to follow the stretcher.

'I... You... We're...' He gave up. 'Thank you.'

The thanks were well deserved. Would Tony have remembered the position a mother needed to be in to keep her baby safe in a case of prolapsed cord? Probably. Would he have been able to assist in a delivery fraught with potential disaster in such a calm and efficient manner?

Thank goodness he hadn't had to find out.

'You're a star,' he told Kelly. 'The heroine of the hour.'

'Hardly.' But she was glowing, and her eyes sparkled with unshed tears as she watched the stretcher disappear through the doors.

'You've had obstetric training, obviously.'

'A long time ago,' Kelly answered. 'And it was fairly limited.'

'It was enough.' Tony tucked the blanket more securely around her shoulders. 'You saved that baby.'

Kelly shook her head. She looked down at the front of her ruined dress and then scanned the room around them. It was only then that she seemed to remember where she was.

If she'd been noticed on her arrival, it was nothing to the attention she was getting now. Bulbs flashed again—and where on earth had that television camera crew materialised from?

'I have to get out of here,' Kelly whispered in horror.

'No problem.' Tony put his arm around her shoulders. 'My coach is waiting, Princess.'

Somebody started clapping as Kelly fled. Others followed suit. Then a cheer began, and the wave of sound could still be heard after the front door closed behind them. Kelly pulled the blanket more securely around herself as she climbed into Tony's car and fastened her seat belt.

'I really need a shower,' she said, as Tony started the car and headed down the driveway.

She sounded apologetic, but the mental picture of Kelly in a shower was anything but unappealing for Tony.

'That can be arranged,' he assured her.

'I'm sorry.'

'What on earth for?'

'I... Well, I need to go home and...'

For a moment they drove in silence. Tony didn't understand. Changing gear made something more than mechanical slip into place, however. He'd seen how modest the exterior of Kelly's house was. She'd just been exposed to the opulence of his parents' home. She was very wrong if she thought that a contrast in their circumstances would make any difference to him, but he had no desire to make her uncomfortable.

'I have a shower,' he said. 'It's great. Hot water and everything.'

The chuckle was encouraging.

'It's big enough for two,' he added.

She ducked her head as he sent a grin in her direction, but it was too dark to tell if his impression that she was blushing was correct.

'But… I don't have any clean clothes to put on.'

Now it was a mental picture of Kelly forced to remain naked for a length of time that was threatening to distract Tony from his driving. His words were a contented rumble.

'No problem.'

CHAPTER SEVEN

TONY'S apartment wasn't far from St Patrick's hospital. It was within the same inner city circle as Kelly's rented house, but it was a world away in every respect other than location.

The eighteenth-century, slate-roofed stone buildings had once been a boys' school, but had been converted in recent years to luxury apartments. One end of the complex included a turret, and Tony's spacious living space incorporated the upper portion of this turret as the main bedroom. It was the *en-suite* bathroom attached to this round room that Kelly was led into.

'Help yourself to towels and shampoo and anything else you need,' Tony invited. 'If you give me your dress, I'll rinse it out and put it in the dryer. If it's OK to do that?'

Kelly simply nodded. She hadn't uttered a word since entering Tony's apartment.

This was all so unreal.

Stunning.

The surroundings were a statement of wealth, but rather than being ostentatious they gave an impression that the man who lived here was dignified and intelligent.

Floor-to-ceiling bookshelves were full, but only the bottom shelves were stocked with medical tomes. Kelly could see at a glance that Tony read incredibly widely, and enjoyed novels as well as non-fiction. A beautiful antique globe caught her eye, and it took a moment to register that it was of the night sky and stars rather than the earth and its land masses. A powerful-looking telescope stood nearby, and a glance upwards revealed a purpose built skylight.

Gorgeous Persian rugs were scattered over a richly polished wooden floor dotted with leather couches. The deepset gothic arched windows looked as if they belonged in a church rather than someone's living quarters, but, while the room was quintessentially masculine and exquisitely decorated, it had the warmth of being a home and not just a living space.

A very special home.

The round, uncovered stone walls of the master bedroom were breathtaking, and the adjoining bathroom had somehow been designed to look as if it belonged, with its slipper bath and polished brass fittings.

What was even more stunning than the apartment, however, was the fact that she was here.

That Tony had brought her into his home.

Further into his life.

Still wordless, Kelly turned, holding up her hair

so that Tony could unfasten the zip on the back of her dress.

'Wouldn't want you to have to go home in a bathrobe later,' Tony said as he complied with the unspoken request.

Having undone the zip, he slipped the shoestring straps from her shoulders. The dress fell away, but Tony's hands lingered.

And then Kelly felt the brush of his lips on the bare skin where the straps had rested.

'Much later,' he murmured.

With a visible effort at self-control, Tony moved to turn on the shower. He picked up the dress.

'I'll be right back,' he promised.

Kelly was standing amongst the multiple jets in a shower that was almost the size of her entire bathroom by the time Tony returned. Her heart tripped and sped up as she saw him start to unbutton his shirt. He really did intend to share this enormous shower.

Would they make love in here? It would be a new experience for Kelly if they did, and it was just a little scary. Would it work? Could it possibly be as good as the first time they had been together?

Tony stepped into the steamy space. He picked up the soap and moved to stand behind Kelly as he lathered his hands. She could feel the whole length of his body behind her. His chest on her shoulder-blades. His thighs against the back of her legs. The hard length of his erection nestled against her buttocks.

Then his hands, slippery with soap, came around her shoulders and smoothed themselves over her breasts, bringing her nipples to life with sensation so sharp it was painfully delicious. His hands travelled to her belly, but didn't linger on their downward journey, and Kelly leaned back, tipping her head so the warm rain fell on her closed eyes and open lips.

No. This wasn't going to be as good as the first time.

It was going to be even better.

Wet.

Wild.

Incredibly arousing and intensely exciting.

And just when it seemed their time together couldn't get any better, Tony wrapped her in fluffy towels and scooped her up, carried her to his bed and made love to her all over again. This time so slowly and tenderly Kelly thought her heart might break as she lay in his arms, the beat of their hearts almost audible in the quiet moments that followed her final cry of ecstasy.

She must have slept then, at least for a little while, because awareness that Tony had moved and was watching her came slowly in the wake of a gentle touch that smoothed strands of tumbled hair from her forehead.

'You're amazing.' In the soft light of the moon through the arched windows it seemed that Tony's gaze was as tender as his touch had been. Then it shifted, to follow his hand as he slowly traced the outline of her body.

Down her cheek, over her jawbone and down her neck. Kelly could feel the pulse at the side of her throat meeting his fingertips. He followed her collarbone to her shoulder and then, so softly, shaped the curve of her breast. The movements paused as he reached her belly, his touch making a tiny circle around her belly button.

A flicker of new desire sprang to life and Kelly closed her eyes, waiting for his touch to go further. To where the desire would be fanned, yet again, into overwhelming heat.

But the circle was repeated. Slighter bigger this time.

'So flat,' Tony murmured. 'So perfect.'

'It just looks flat because you saw an eight months pregnant woman not very long ago.'

The pressure of his fingers changed. As if Tony was imagining what it would be like to be touching a pregnant woman this way. Kelly's breath caught in her throat. *She* could imagine it. Just the soft bulge of early pregnancy. Knowing that there was a new life growing within her belly.

A baby.

Tony's baby.

He would touch her just like this, wouldn't he? Soft, slow strokes. And when he spoke he would have that kind of wonder in his voice—the way he had just a minute ago when he'd told her she was amazing.

'What would it be like, do you think?' Tony asked quietly. 'To have a baby in there?'

He was thinking about the same thing. Did he also feel that poignant curl deep inside that could so easily become longing?

'If it was the baby of someone you loved, it would be the most magical thing ever,' Kelly responded.

Tony was silent for a moment. His hand flattened and became heavier.

'Do you want to have babies, Kelly?'

Another silence. Lulled by the feeling of safety that being in Tony's arms gave her and by the lingering intimacy of the lovemaking they had just shared, it would have been easy to ignore any alarm bells the loaded question might have set off. Caution came simply because Kelly feared she might jinx a dream by talking about it out loud.

'One day,' she said slowly, 'I would love to have my own baby. To be pregnant by someone who loves me the same way I love him. To make a family.'

Tony was silent longer this time. Long enough to make Kelly feel just a little uneasy.

But when he spoke his voice was sympathetic. Understanding. 'You miss your family—don't you, Princess?'

'Of course.'

'And you love children?'

The prickle of unease grew. 'You don't like children?'

'They're an alien species.' Tony was smiling. 'I've had as little as possible to do with them.'

'You don't have any nephews or nieces?'

'No. I don't think my brother or sister have even

considered the possibility. I guess families don't really go with high-flying careers.'

Tony had a high-flying career. Was he trying to tell her he never intended having children? Or a family? In the watch of her expressing the ultimate goal for her own life? A tiny shiver came from nowhere and rippled through Kelly's body.

'You're cold.' Tony reached out to pull the duvet over them both.

'You were lucky, you know,' he said a few moments later. 'You had a loving family and a happy childhood.'

'Yours wasn't happy?' Kelly had had that impression earlier tonight, during dinner, when he'd said that his parents were satisfied with rather than proud of their children's achievements. Asking such a personal question would have been unthinkable until now, but this had been a remarkable 'first date'. She felt closer to Tony than she had ever felt to any man before.

'It was privileged,' Tony replied thoughtfully. 'We wanted for nothing.'

'Except your parents' time?'

'We competed for their attention. Maybe that's why we've all been successful in our own fields? But…yes. Looking back, I think we all felt a certain lack. Maybe that's why none of us have had families of our own. Maybe we don't want to do that to another generation.'

'No pressure for any grandchildren from your parents, then?'

'Good grief, no!' Tony chuckled. 'My mother would have to start admitting her age if she became a grandma.'

Kelly made a sound that could be interpreted as sharing his amusement, but his words were a warning she couldn't ignore.

She'd seen his mother's horror at the mess of her carpet after the delivery of Paige's baby tonight. She'd been aware of the aura of perfection that Louise Grimshaw exuded from the first moment she'd met her.

To imagine her in the same room as Flipper, never mind accepting her, was a real source of humour. Kelly could just see Flipper whirling in circles as she 'danced'. Sending some priceless ornament flying to its doom. Her daughter had a lot to learn before her eating habits became less than messy, and she would take longer than most children to accomplish that skill. And, no matter how deeply Kelly loved her little girl, there was no getting away from the fact that, in the eyes of the world, Flipper was not 'perfect'.

It was a no-brainer. Kelly and her daughter would never fit into the kind of world Tony came from. It wasn't just his background. As a famous surgeon and head of a prestigious department, he would always have that kind of social life. And he didn't want a family anyway, so the writing couldn't be clearer on that mental wall.

This relationship was going nowhere.

But did that matter when Kelly had never felt

happier than she did at this moment, cradled in the arms of the most amazing man she'd ever met? It was too late not to fall in love with him. Why couldn't she just take it as it came and enjoy their time together for what it was, without ringing a death knell because it had no future?

'I'd be hopeless with a baby.' Tony's words broke into the whirl of Kelly's thoughts. 'Couldn't get away from Obstetrics fast enough, to tell you the truth. Messy business.'

'Worth it,' Kelly said softly. 'You must have felt that magic when Paige's baby started moving. Like it was coming to life in front of our eyes.'

'It *was*, thank God.' Tony's sigh was an echo of the relief they had both experienced at the time. 'I'm just glad you knew what you were doing.'

'But I didn't,' Kelly confessed. 'If anything had gone really wrong I would have been in deep trouble. I only did a short run in O&G.'

'Run?' Tony moved so that he was looking at Kelly's face. 'I'd only expect a medical student or junior doctor to use a term like that. Not a nurse.'

Kelly could see curiosity in his face. She could also see softness. And something else. An expectation that she could do more to impress him than she already had tonight?

Kelly wanted to impress him.

She also wanted to trust him. And he had just made it possible to take another step in that direction without compromising the safety of what was most important in her life.

'I *was* a med student,' she told him.

She could *feel* him absorbing what had to be startling information. Analysing the implications. Adjusting his opinion of her? He pulled her closer again, resting his chin on the top of her head.

'Somehow,' he said at last, 'that doesn't surprise me. You acted like a doctor tonight, Kelly. Calm and capable. How far did you get with your training?'

'To the end of my fourth year.'

'So you were ready to get right into the clinical side of things?'

'Yes.'

'You were doing well?' His tone suggested he expected nothing less.

'Top of my class.' Kelly's pride was something she hadn't felt for a very long time.

She could feel his nod. 'How long ago did you leave?'

'About three and a half years.'

'Did it have something to do with the accident that took your family?'

It was Kelly's turn to nod. 'It had everything to do with the accident. I...simply couldn't afford to continue.'

They were getting onto dangerous territory here. Kelly wasn't ready to tell him about Flipper. She could feel herself shrinking away from revealing that much, but at the same time she had to resist the pull to tell him everything.

To trust him with everything.

No. That way lay the potential for hurt that might

never go away. She could take it for herself, but she wasn't going to let Flipper be rejected by anyone. Not by Tony's mother or, worse, Tony himself.

With a bit of luck Tony would interpret her statement as meaning she had had financial problems. If he was as connected to her thoughts as he seemed to be he would also realise she didn't want to talk about it any more. It was a reasonable denial. Traumatic events were downbeat, and why would either of them want to spoil this time together?

If he respected her, he wouldn't push.

The silence grew.

Tony didn't want to break it. He lay there, holding Kelly in his arms. In his own bedroom but in a place he'd never been before. With this astonishing woman who made him feel…

Tony sighed, pressing his lips against her hair as he expelled the air slowly from his lungs. He didn't know *how* she made him feel.

He just knew that being with her changed things. That she was beautiful and clever. That she had a strength of character that blew him away. That she had so much to give and that right now he was lucky enough to be a recipient.

He wasn't going to embarrass her by asking questions about the financial difficulties she must have faced in the wake of losing her family that had enforced her dropping out of medical school.

Neither was he going to dwell on any aspects of their time together that undermined his intention of spending more time with this woman. In fact, when he thought about it, the way people had been cheering when they'd left his parents' house earlier could be seen as a stamp of approval. Of acceptance that pointed to the possibility of overcoming any antipathy to her being there that had come from both Kelly and the reception attendees.

So they came from very different backgrounds.

So what?

The things they had in common mattered a lot more. Like a shared passion for medicine. *That* was why he was able to talk about his work with Kelly and not feel he was breaking unspoken rules or, worse, boring her senseless. If her circumstances were different she might return to medical school, even, and join him as a colleague. An equal.

A love of dancing was something else they had in common. They were like two halves of a single unit on a dance floor. Lifted by music and so light they could fly.

And that was part of their physical connection that could be public. The private part was like nothing Tony had ever experienced before. Her response. Her generosity. Her…

What *was* the extraordinary sensation that came at the climax of making love with her? A feeling that they almost merged. That she became an extension of his own body. A part that he didn't want to live without.

A dangerous line of thought. Ridiculously fanciful. Totally unscientific and probably no more than hormones in overdrive.

Distraction was needed here.

Or possibly further research.

Tony's lips curved. He traced Kelly's face until he reached her chin, and then he lifted her face so he could kiss her lips. He wanted to touch her again. To taste her. To lose himself inside her.

With a groan of renewed desire, Tony drew back the duvet. There was no place for any kind of barrier right now. He felt Kelly's arms come around him and then the touch of the tip of her tongue invited him to deepen their kiss.

There was no hesitation in his response.

He was lost...again.

CHAPTER EIGHT

IF FLIPPER hadn't dropped her fluffy toy frog at precisely the point they had stepped through the automatic doors at a side entrance to St Pat's that led to the outpatient department, Kelly wouldn't have spotted it.

'Ribby!' Flipper wailed in distress. Still hanging onto Kelly's hand, she planted her feet and dropped her weight to act like an anchor. The manoeuvre was successful.

'What is it this time?' Kelly noted the downturned bottom lip with dismay. 'We're going to be late to see Dr Clifford at the rate we're going.'

'Ribby,' Flipper sniffled.

Kelly looked behind them and sighed. She let go of Flipper's hand and stepped back to swoop on the toy whose novelty had yet to wear off. The thought of getting through a doctor's appointment with the beloved object missing didn't bear thinking about.

Straightening, Kelly flicked her gaze over the big metal box that contained copies of the city's major daily newspaper, and suddenly any anxiety about the appointment or even reaching it in time faded into insignificance. Stunned, she handed the frog to Flipper and fished for the wallet in her handbag.

'Wait,' she instructed Flipper, a little more tersely than she had intended. 'I—have to buy a paper.'

It was difficult to feed coins into the slot that released a copy of the paper for purchase because her fingers were shaking.

Small bright eyes were watching. 'Flipper do it!'

'No, hon. Not this time.' But the coin slipped and rolled to the floor, and the frog was dropped again, on purpose this time, as Flipper pounced on the coin with delight. It was too hard for her to pick the coin up from the shiny linoleum, however. Kelly picked it up. She saw the hopeful look on Flipper's face and sighed again—but this time it came with a smile.

'OK—you do it.'

She stared at the visible portion of the front page of the paper as Flipper, her tongue poking out as she concentrated, did her utmost to slot the fifty cent piece into the box.

The photograph must have been taken without a flash. Otherwise she surely would have noticed a photographer getting that close. The moment captured had been just after Paige's baby had been born. Kelly was looking down, holding the baby in her hands, and it must have been just after she'd realised it was going to be fine, because even in profile her expression was clearly one of amazement. Relief. And joy.

'Yay!' Flipper had succeeded in her task and jumped up and down with pleasure as Kelly pulled the paper free.

The main picture on the front page was much larger. A smiling Nigel standing beside a hospital bed, his arm around Paige, who was resting back against the pillows, her newborn son cradled in her arms.

'Unexpected Delivery' was the banner headline.

'Baby Arrives to Reception for Mayor' read the print a size down.

Kelly took another glance at the second photograph on the front page. The one of *her*. A renewed wave of shock kept her feet rooted to the spot. The last time she had had a personal connection to a front-page story had been the dreadful photographs of the aftermath of the accident that had wiped out her whole family.

By a strange quirk of fate here she was again, but this time the article was about the joy of a new family being created instead of the tragedy of one being lost.

Kelly ignored the tug on her skirt, her eyes running swiftly over the lines of print.

Deputy Mayor Nigel Finch's firstborn son arrived during a reception held in honour of visiting dignitaries at the home of Mayor Bernard Grimshaw on Friday evening just after ten.

'Mummy?'

'In a sec, sweetie.' Kelly tried to read faster.

'It was totally unexpected,' Nigel was quoted as saying. 'And it happened so fast. No warning at all. I don't mind admitting I was alarmed, to say the least, but all's well that ends well.'

Kelly's gaze flicked back to the main photograph and its caption: 'William James Finch, weighing in at almost six pounds, safe in St Patrick's Maternity Unit after his dramatic entrance to the world.'

She tried to find the place she'd left in the article.

'I want to express my heartfelt gratitude,' Nigel said, 'to the nurse who assisted Paige. To the ambulance crew and to the staff here at St Patrick's Hospital. They are all a credit to our wonderful city.'

But she wasn't a nurse! Kelly bit her lip, taking another look at the photograph of herself. At its caption. 'Kelly Adams' it said in tiny print. 'A member of St Patrick's nursing staff'.

'Mummy!'

'Yes. Right.' Kelly folded the paper hurriedly, glancing around as if she half expected someone to point. To say she was the fraud she suddenly felt herself to be. Except she'd never *said* she was a nurse, had she? And an aide could be considered part of the nursing staff, surely? Papers were always getting things wrong.

Her picture was in profile and her head was bent, partly screened by her hair. Would anyone recognise her? Tony would know, of course, but that didn't matter because he didn't know what her actual position on the staff of St Patrick's was. It was those who did that could make this a problem. The people who could tell him before she found the right moment to correct his assumption that she was a qualified nurse.

If only she'd said something right at the start— but how could she have? And why? The reality of bedpans and mops was on another planet from the fairytale she'd stepped into at the ball. Irrelevant. And now he was so impressed that she'd been a top student at medical school. She'd been too proud to admit the spot at the lower end of the medical spectrum that she now occupied.

The sinking sensation in the pit of Kelly's stomach suggested that she knew the fall was coming. There was just a very slim hope that she could avoid the worst of it.

'Look.' She crouched beside Flipper for a moment, showing her the picture still visible on one of the folds. 'Who's that?'

Flipper looked. She beamed. 'Bubba!'

'It *is* a baby. A really tiny one. Who's holding the baby?'

Flipper squinted. 'Bubba,' she repeated, and then turned away, any interest forgotten.

Maybe it was premature, but the fact that Flipper hadn't recognised her own mother in the picture was a comfort.

St Patrick's employed hundreds and hundreds of people. Most of the staff Kelly worked alongside only knew her by her first name because that was the only name on her badge. Most would never have seen her with her hair loose. Thanks to the horrible shower cap, most would have no idea what colour her hair was, even.

Kelly Adams? She could imagine an exchange in a nurses' locker room. *You know her?*

Never heard of her. You?

No. Doesn't work on our ward.

And then it would be forgotten. By tomorrow it would be yesterday's news and nobody would care.

Kelly hurried into the outpatient department, pausing to stuff the newspaper into a rubbish bin. If she could put this aside, who else was really going to be bothered by it?

John Clifford, that was who.

'You're a bit of a star, Kelly' was the first thing he said when she took Flipper into the consulting room a few minutes later. 'Nice photo.'

'I…um…just happened to be there.'

'Oh?' The way his eyebrows rose made Kelly flush.

'I saw you last week,' John said with a smile. 'At The Waiting Room.'

With Tony. Kelly sat down a little heavily on the padded chair. 'Oh…'

The connection wouldn't have been hard to make. Why else could Kelly possibly have gained admittance to a mayoral reception? Everybody knew who Tony was. Who his father was.

Kelly was a nobody.

Was that why she could detect something like concern in Dr Clifford's expression? Disapproval, even?

That stung. John Clifford had been Flipper's doctor for years now. Both Kelly and Flipper thought he was wonderful. A father figure, almost, for Kelly. A source of wisdom. A rock in times of need. One of the few people who had shared the joy of the milestones Flipper was reaching. Someone who cared.

But he didn't think Kelly was good enough for Tony.

He couldn't see her in the role of partner to a renowned surgeon.

Or was it that he didn't see Flipper as being part of an acceptable ready-made family?

He couldn't be thinking anything that Kelly hadn't already thought herself, but somehow, coming from him, it was…embarrassing. Humiliating.

Kelly didn't know what to say.

Flipper, bless her, saved her from having to say anything at all.

She trotted towards Dr Clifford and held up her frog. 'Ribby, ribby,' she said, and then grinned.

Kelly watched the transformation of the cardiologist's expression. He feigned astonishment, and then crouched to put himself more on the level of the tiny girl. He returned her smile.

'What have you got there, young Philippa?'

Flipper hugged the frog and made it croak again. Her grin stretched from ear, to ear and was so happy Kelly could feel a squeeze on her own heart.

John Clifford grinned back. 'Goodness me,' he chuckled. 'Whatever next?'

Flipper gurgled with laughter and squeezed the frog again. The doctor ruffled her hair, a smile still on his face as he moved to sit at his desk. He took another glance at Flipper before reaching for the thick set of patient case notes. The warmth in that look was unmistakable. Flipper had touched his heart the way she did everybody who knew her.

It wasn't beyond the realms of possibility that Tony could be charmed in exactly the same way. If Kelly let him into her life—trusted him enough to meet Flipper—it *could* happen. Couldn't it?

Flipper came back to Kelly and stood beside the chair, leaning on her.

Dr Clifford was frowning as he flipped open the notes, as if he knew that what was in there was a matter of concern.

A trickle of apprehension ran the length of Kelly's spine.

'Why don't you show Frog to the other toys while I talk to Dr Clifford?' she suggested to Flipper, making an effort to keep her voice light. 'Remember what's in the box over there? I'll bet Barbie would like to meet Frog.'

Flipper obligingly moved to the corner of the room and upended the plastic container of toys. She sat down and pulled her frog onto her lap before reaching for a doll.

Kelly watched the doctor flip through the notes, presumably to find the results of last week's investigations. When he looked up, however, he seemed to be thinking of something else. His stare was curious and went on just a shade too long. Then he cleared his throat.

'How *are* things for you at the moment, Kelly?'

It seemed an odd question.

'Fine,' she answered. 'We're doing really well.'

Oh, help. Would he interpret that as *Kelly* doing really well by snagging the interest of someone like Tony Grimshaw?

'Flipper's happy,' she added hurriedly. 'She loves going to crèche and she fits in so well. She's starting to learn her colours and her numbers, and her vocabulary is increasing every day. I think she'll be able to attend a normal school without any problems.'

'And physically? You haven't noticed any changes since her last check-up?'

He sounded as though he expected she would have. Kelly frowned, searching for evidence of anything she might have forgotten to mention last week.

'We're very careful,' she answered. 'Our GP's wonderful. She knows to get Flipper onto antibiotics at the first hint of an infection. It's been over a year since she was admitted with that pneumonia.'

Dr Clifford nodded. 'I'm thinking more of day-to-day stuff,' he said. 'Is she active?'

Kelly smiled. 'It's hard to keep her sitting still for long.'

'She still loves her music? The dancing?'

Flipper looked up. 'Darn!' She held the Barbie

doll by its head and bounced the legs on the floor. 'Dolly darn!'

Kelly's smile widened, but then faded. 'She does get a bit out of breath when she's dancing, and I noticed she was puffing when she got to the top of our steps last week. Elsie mentioned it, too.'

'Elsie?'

'My boss. She's a good friend. She babysits occasionally when I…go out.' Kelly dropped her gaze, catching her bottom lip between her teeth.

Elsie had babysat so she could go to the ball and stay out all night. And again so she could go out and end up at the Mayor's house, delivering a baby and getting her photograph on the front page of the paper.

But Dr Clifford seemed to have forgotten the publicity.

'The tests we ran last week have shown a significant deterioration in Philippa's condition,' he said gently. 'It looks as though more surgery will be likely rather than just possible.'

Kelly's indrawn breath was a gasp. 'No,' she whispered. 'Oh, please…*no!*'

Her gaze flew to her daughter, who had given up trying to make Barbie dance and now seemed to be getting her to try and kiss the frog. Intent on her task for the moment. Happy. She didn't need more surgery, surely? With its horrible risks and the pain and…

And she really ought to be listening more carefully to what Dr Clifford was saying.

Yes, she'd always been aware of the possible need

for further surgery as Flipper grew, but it had always been in the future. A cloud that had almost vanished over the horizon after so many weeks and months of doing so well.

The cardiologist was talking about test results that showed that the valves in Flipper's heart were not coping now that she was older and more active. That she was already in a degree of heart failure that was going to need management with medication, and that the possibility of complications was of grave concern.

'If she had another bout of pneumonia it could tip her over the edge,' Dr Clifford continued. 'It might put her into an episode of failure that we wouldn't be able to treat effectively.'

Was he saying that Flipper could *die*?

Oh, *God*!

'And surgery would be the answer?'

'It's the only way we can achieve anything like normal cardiac function for her. The procedure's a common one. There's every chance that the result would be what we'd hope for.'

'But she's *had* surgery.' With the degree of medical knowledge Kelly had acquired she knew it was a pathetic thing to say, but this was Kelly as a mother talking. A mother who wanted to spare her child the ordeal of open heart surgery.

'I know.' John Clifford's tone was sympathetic. 'I'm sorry, Kelly. I wish I had better news. I'm going to refer you back to the paediatric cardiac surgical team. Brian Grieves is the best in the field. I'll make sure you get an urgent consult.'

'It's *urgent*?' Kelly felt a wave of panic. She wanted to scoop Flipper into her arms and take her somewhere else. Somewhere she'd be safe. But she couldn't protect her from this, could she? She had to trust this doctor. And the surgeons.

She closed her eyes for a moment, fighting panic. This was *so* hard. But they'd been here before and they'd come though. She had to do whatever was necessary to look after Flipper.

'Kelly?'

She opened her eyes.

'Are you all right?'

She nodded. 'Is it OK for Flipper to go to crèche today? I'm supposed to be working after this appointment.'

Dr Clifford nodded. 'In the meantime there's no reason not to carry on as usual. We'll keep a closer eye on her, and I want you to bring her into hospital if you have any concerns. If she gets particularly out of breath, for instance.'

Kelly nodded again.

'I'd like to listen to her chest again now. We'll talk about the medication I want you to start after that.'

Kelly was running on autopilot as she helped undress Flipper. Smiling a lot because she didn't want to communicate any of her fear to her child. She even managed to laugh, along with Flipper, when Dr Clifford made a show of listening to Frog's chest before he put the disc of the stethoscope on Flipper's chest. She felt dangerously close to tears, seeing how large the stethoscope looked against the tiny ribs, unable to stop herself imagining them being spread apart to give a surgeon access to her heart.

There was a prescription to take as well, and an appointment card to see the surgeons. It was all overwhelming, and Kelly felt dazed. It was a huge relief to be able to leave, but John Clifford had something else he wanted to say. He walked to the door with Kelly.

'I know this is none of my business,' he said quietly, 'but I'm a family friend of the Grimshaws and I've known Tony for a very long time.'

Kelly stared at him. She couldn't think of anything other than what lay in the near future for Flipper right now. It was actually an effort to remember the beginning of this interview, when the photograph had been mentioned.

'You know he's in the running to become Head of Department for cardiothoracic surgery?"

Kelly said nothing.

'He has an astonishingly bright future ahead of him but he's very young to be considered for a position like this.'

Kelly continued to stare. What on earth could this possibly have to do with *her*?

Dr Clifford shook his head. 'Forget I said anything, Kelly. Most unprofessional of me. I…just think you have enough to cope with without…complications.'

It wasn't until Kelly had dropped Flipper at

crèche, changed into her uniform and gone to find where she was being sent for the day that she understood what John Clifford hadn't put into words.

Being associated with Kelly could undermine Tony's chances of getting the position he wanted. She was unsuitable. If Tony found out about Flipper he would end their relationship and she would be hurt, and she didn't need that on top of everything else she had to deal with at the moment.

Or maybe Tony wouldn't, but what if it made a difference to his success? He was passionate about his work. His research. What if he fell in love with her and it wasn't until later that he realised the damage it had done to his career?

Kelly had always known she had no basis other than dreams to imagine a future for this relationship. And didn't the magic of a fairytale depend on someone being given something they wanted more than anything else? Taking something away or even risking it was certainly not part of any happy ending. Now was the ideal time to call a halt. When she had far more important things to think about than her love life. John Clifford had hit the nail squarely on its head. She couldn't afford complications.

Flipper's heart was in more danger than her own.

Elsie thought she should take the day off. 'You can't work when you're so worried about the little one.'

'It's the best thing I *can* do,' Kelly said. 'Put me somewhere really busy, Elsie. Like Emergency. I have to work if I'm going to pay the bills, and if I'm busy I won't be able to worry so much.'

'They do need someone in Emergency. If you're sure?'

'I'm sure.'

'What's the blood pressure?' Tony was frowning, seconds after picking up the phone on the surgical ward's office desk.

'One-oh-five on sixty. And falling.'

'Jugular venous pressure?'

'Elevated.'

Damn. 'Have you ordered an echocardiogram?'

'Tech's on her way.'

'So am I. Check out the availability of a theatre, would you, please, Josh? We may need to take him back upstairs.'

So much for catching up with long overdue discharge summaries in his already late lunchbreak. The Dictaphone and patient notes were left strewn on the desk as Tony headed for the post-surgical intensive care unit.

He took the stairs rather than waiting for an elevator, but he still arrived after the requested diagnostic equipment, which was now set up beside the unconscious man, still on a ventilator after his extensive heart surgery that morning.

He watched the young technician as she angled the transducer, searching for any evidence that might confirm Tony's suspicion that this elderly patient was bleeding post-operatively around his heart.

'There!' she said. 'Collection of fluid in the peri-cardial sac. I'd estimate about fifteen mils.'

'Enough to compromise cardiac function.' Easy enough to remove, but if the bleeding continued his patient was in trouble.

'We'll do a pericardiocentesis, ' he told his regis-trar. 'If there's any evidence of further bleeding we'll have to head back to Theatre. You want to do this, Josh?'

'I've got ED paging me. Chest trauma.'

'You go, then.' Tony nodded. 'I'll deal with this.'

It was clearly going to be one of those days. Like yesterday had been. He wouldn't miss being on call for acutes when—*if*—he became HOD. He would find out some time this week whether his bid for the position had been successful, so it wasn't surprising it was in his thoughts a lot.

He put it aside easily enough as he started the pro-cedure to insert a needle into his patient's chest and remove the blood that was creating pressure and preventing it beating efficiently. The beeping of his pager was an irritating interruption.

'Can you answer that, for me, please?' he asked the nurse assisting him. 'Take a message.'

She returned just as he was removing the blood-filled syringe.

'That was Colin Jamieson's secretary,' the nurse informed him, a note of awe in her voice. 'He wants you to call him as soon as possible.'

Tony simply nodded, his gaze glued to the monitors which were showing an improvement in his patient's condition. Cardiac output was improving, and the blood pressure was creeping up towards normal limits.

The only reason he could think of why the CEO of St Pat's would be wanting to talk to him was about the HOD position. Maybe there was a new contract, waiting for him to sign?

The readings on the monitors steadied, remained that way for several minutes, but then slowly, inexorably, started dropping again.

'He's still bleeding,' Tony said grimly. 'We're going to have to open him up and find where it's coming from.'

His day had now gone from busy to impossible, but Tony knew they would all simply have to cope. As they always did. He left the ICU staff to organise the transfer of his patient and walked towards Theatre, unclipping his mobile phone from his belt as he moved. Getting some good news in the few minutes he had available right now might be just the lift his day needed.

The first words from Colin Jamieson were not quite what he was expecting, however. 'Have you seen today's paper?'

'No. Haven't had a chance to see anything yet.'

'There's a picture of Nigel Finch and his new baby on the front page. The baby that was born at your father's house on Friday night.'

'It was fairly dramatic.'

'I've got the press hounding Personnel right now. Trying to find this nurse that delivered the baby.

Apparently Nigel is keen to thank her, and get some more publicity at the same time.'

Colin Jamison sounded irritated.

'She deserves the thanks.' Tony kept the phone to his ear as he pushed open the fire stop doors to gain access to the stairway. 'She did a great job. But—' He went down several steps in silence, caught by an image of Kelly. The way she hadn't been able to escape fast enough after that drama. There was a modesty about her. She wouldn't like publicity. In fact, Tony was quite certain she would hate it.

The need to protect her was an irresistible urge.

'But what?' Colin Jamieson snapped.

'I doubt that she'd be keen to co-operate.'

'I spoke to your father about this. It was Bernie who told me this woman was at the house as a guest of *yours*.'

'That's correct.'

'Then perhaps you can tell me why Personnel has never heard of a Kelly Adams.'

Tony could sympathise with the CEO's obvious frustration. He knew what it was like to have Personnel unable to track someone down. But surely trying to find Kelly Adams would be a doddle compared to looking for a fantasy character by the name of Cindy Riley?

'I have no idea,' he told Colin Jamieson. 'Maybe the data base is inaccurate?'

'I intend to find that out, I can assure you. In the meantime, will you be seeing this woman again?'

Several responses sprang to the tip of Tony's tongue.

That's absolutely none of your business, wasn't quite the thing to say to Colin Jamieson.

As often as possible for as long as possible, didn't seem advisable either, given the assurance he'd made recently in front of this man that he was a single, dedicated professional who intended to stay that way, and therefore his young age was no deterrent to his taking on the demanding position of HOD.

'Not immediately,' he said cautiously. But only because he was on call today and tomorrow.

'Do you have a telephone number for her?'

'No. I don't.' His response was a little curt. Why *had* Kelly been reluctant to give him her number? He'd had to work quite hard to get her to agree to have lunch with him, and he had to wait until Wednesday for that. Was she playing hard to get? No. As confidently as he knew she would hate publicity, Tony knew that Kelly was not into game-playing.

'Ah…' There was a satisfied note in the sound. Much the same as there had been in his father's voice when he'd decided that Tony wasn't seriously interested in Kelly.

It rankled.

Tony made his own choices, dammit. If he wanted to get serious about Kelly Adams then that was exactly what he would do.

'I've got to go,' he told the CEO. 'I'm due in Theatre.'

'No problem.' The voice was happier now. In control. 'I'll deal with this. You can forget about her.'

Really?

Tony entered the locker room to find a fresh set of scrubs. Even if he never saw Kelly again, he was hardly likely to forget about her.

Not that he was intending to get serious about any woman, but the way she'd made him feel the other night... Holding her in his arms. Feeling she was a part of him that he wouldn't want to live without.

Funny how that feeling wouldn't quite go away. It was just there, all the time. A kind of awareness that didn't interfere with anything he needed to do but was very pleasant to tap into.

Comforting?

Tony snorted, pulling a clean tunic over his head. He was a high-flyer. His career was taking off and he enjoyed the thrill of riding a wave of success.

Comfort was the last thing he needed in his life.

Bumping open the doors that led to the scrub room, he pushed the awareness aside yet again. Right now, he needed to save a life.

CHAPTER NINE

IT WAS just as well nobody's life depended on how well Kelly could do *her* job that day.

Simple tasks like changing bedlinen and helping patients undress, or moving unobtrusively through a busy department fetching supplies or removing bedpans and vomit containers were about all Kelly was capable of managing right now.

For once it was a relief to be following orders and not having to think for herself. She could do this automatically and feel as if she had a tiny bit of control in a life that had just been derailed.

Again.

She'd worked so hard, and just when she was coping so well—when there was the new excitement of a possible future to dream about—fate had blindsided her and left her feeling helpless, in the control of forces she had no way of fighting. She had to go with the flow and try to cope with one thing at a time to the best of her ability.

Just as she had when the accident had happened.

When her dreams of becoming a doctor had been torn away from her and she'd found herself a single mother instead. She had coped then—somehow. And she had ended up with something so precious in her life that she couldn't imagine being without it now. Something precious under threat. That was all Kelly could think about. She hated being apart from Flipper, but it was another of those things she had no choice about.

Or did she? There was a mother sitting in the emergency department with her child near the bed Kelly was changing. The small boy had fallen off the couch at home and he was waiting for an X-ray to confirm a broken collarbone. He sat on his mother's knee, giving the that impression that he was used to having her with him all the time. They were playing 'I Spy'. Kelly envied the way they presented a solid unit to face the world.

Part of her mind at present was dealing with the necessity of being away from Flipper *more* in the short term. Picking up some extra shifts so that she could afford the time off when her little girl had surgery and a recovery period, whenever that might be. Her budget was too tight to cope with unforeseen events, and careful planning was needed.

'The lady in cubicle four needs a pan, Kelly,' a nurse said as she dashed past. 'And could you find a disposable nappy for the baby in two?'

'Sure.' Kelly finished stuffing the pillow on the bed she was making into its clean case and headed for the sluice room.

'Starts with "C",' the mother was saying to the small boy. 'Like "cat".'

'Car?'

'No. Good try, though, darling. Have another look. Over by the doors. It's something someone needs to walk with when they have a very sore leg.'

How wonderful would it be to spend so much time with her own child? To practise letter sounds or colours or numbers through games, accelerate her learning by having fun?

Kelly ducked into the sluice room and collected a bedpan, still warm from the steriliser. She slipped a paper cover over it and tucked it under one arm while she reached for a disposable nappy with her other hand. It was an instant reminder of caring for her own baby when the memory was in no way distant.

Had she made the wrong choices back then? To go back to work when Flipper was less than twelve months old and put her baby into a crèche?

Two medical students on an intensive emergency department run had paused just outside the sluice room door, and Kelly hesitated, not wanting to push her way between them laden with toilet necessities. And, as she often did, she eavesdropped shamelessly on their professional discussion.

'He had cardiac catheterisation four years ago, which showed mild aortic regurgitation. No symptoms until about three months ago, when he noticed blood in his urine.'

'Any investigations done?'

'Yes. He underwent cystoscopy as an outpatient and the results were normal.'

'Is he on any medication?'

'No.'

'How old is he?'

'Thirty-two. He's a vet.'

'So what's brought him into the department?'

'He's feeling very unwell. Pale and clammy, and has a fever of 38.6. Pulse is one ten and regular and BP is one forty on sixty.'

'Abdo?'

'Clear.'

'Heart sounds?'

'Diastolic murmur. Lung bases have widespread crepitations. Oh, yeah—he's got splinter haemorrhages under his fingernails as well. Quite marked.'

Kelly couldn't resist any longer. She stepped through the door and smiled at the students.

'Make sure he has some blood cultures taken,' she said. 'My guess is bacterial endocarditis.'

The students stared at Kelly, their jaws dropping.

'It's a classic combination,' she added. 'Infection, underlying valvular heart disease and splinter haemorrhages.'

She walked away, leaving the students still gaping, and for the first time since she'd left Dr Clifford's office that morning Kelly was smiling.

For just a moment she'd forgotten about her personal life and the forthcoming stress and misery. Just for a blink of time—but it had achieved even more than a lift to her spirits. It had reminded Kelly why there was no point in revisiting the latest worry her mind had chosen to gnaw at.

Kelly knew she had chosen the life that was best for both herself and Flipper when she had taken this job. Flipper was in a place where she had a peer group. Trained teachers who loved her and resources Kelly would never be able to provide if she was at home on some kind of social welfare benefit. The isolation of being a stay-at-home single mother would have been detrimental to Flipper's development and hard on Kelly as well. She knew she was a better mother through the stimulation she got from being with other adults, being at least on the periphery of the world of medicine she loved. It was a real pleasure to remember snatches of her training and to keep learning through observation.

And sometimes there were moments, like the one she'd just had with those students, where Kelly gained a deep sense of personal satisfaction from who she was and what she knew. Never mind that she had to go and deal with the more menial tasks that working with patients demanded.

Except that she couldn't get back into the department. A stretcher was blocking the doors, and a highly distressed patient was trying to climb off it, fighting with the paramedic who was trying to hold a bulky dressing onto his wrist.

'Call Security,' the paramedic called to his colleague.

'My hand!' the patient was yelling. 'Let go! You're hurting me.'

'Arterial bleed,' the paramedic warned the triage nurse who was approaching. 'Industrial accident. Partial amputation. It's been difficult to try and keep any pressure on.'

Kelly could see the evidence of that struggle. The paramedic's white shirt was heavily bloodstained. So was the sheet on the stretcher. So was—

'Look out!'

With a wild swing the patient rolled clear of his restraint moments before two burly security guards appeared. He ripped at the dressings on his arm but then stopped, staring in horror at his hand only loosely attached to his arm. The spurt of arterial blood fanned out across the floor. And then the accident victim crumpled into a heap as he fainted. The paramedics grabbed dressings and applied pressure to the wound, and the security guards hovered.

'Get him into Resus One,' the triage nurse directed. 'I'll call the trauma team.' She took a look over her shoulder at the astonishing area the blood had managed to cover. 'Kelly—clean this up, please? As fast as you can.'

This was more urgent than bedpans or nappies. Kelly raced back to the sluice room and donned a heavy plastic apron. She made sure her hair was completely tucked under her cap and donned some bright green rubber gloves as her stainless steel bucket was filling with near boiling water. She took a large bottle of the bleach-based disinfectant needed to deal with a spill of potentially infectious body fluids, and also an armful of small bright orange plastic cones which would demarcate the area and keep people clear. She'd have to come back for the "Caution Wet Floor" sign.

Armed with all her gear, Kelly set to work. She mopped, rinsed the mop, squeezed it through the roller mechanism on top of the bucket, squirted liberal doses of disinfectant around and mopped again. The urgency of the task was helpful, because it stopped her thoughts reverting to her worry about Flipper, so she concentrated hard on finding every drop of blood and eradicating its threat.

'Kelly? Kelly Adams?'

The voice was loud enough to be startling. About to insert the mop into the steaming bucket once more, Kelly froze, turned and looked up.

A flash went off.

'What the—?' Kelly stared at the photographer. 'What the hell do you think you're *doing*?'

'You *are* Kelly Adams?'

Why was this man taking her picture? Why now, when she looked…? Oh, God! Kelly was clutching a mop, wearing an oversized apron, rubber gloves and her shower cap hat.

'You're a cleaner?' the man queried.

'No, she's a nurse aide.' Another staff member was approaching. 'Who are you and what are you doing in here?'

'I'm covering a story about St Pat's ED and its staff. Didn't anyone tell you?'

'No,' the nurse said coldly. 'Where's your security clearance?'

'Damn…must have forgotten it.' The stranger
didn't sound overly concerned, however. He was
checking the image he had scored on his digital
camera. 'Great photo. Wanna see it, Kelly?'

'No.'

'Get out,' the nurse commanded. 'If you're not out
of here in thirty seconds I'm calling Security.' She
looked away from the photographer's rapidly retreat-
ing figure to raise her eyebrows at Kelly. 'What was
that about?'

Kelly tried to damp down a nameless fear. She
shook her head. 'I have no idea.'

'Neither do I, but let's hope that's the end of it.
Let me know if he comes back.'

The photographer didn't come back. Kelly was
left alone to get through what seemed an interminable
shift when all she wanted was to get home with
Flipper. To spend her evening with cuddles and
stories and music and dancing and forget about the
day.

Oh, God! Was it still safe to let Flipper dance?
How could she know how well her heart might be
coping with the stress of activity like that? What
would happen if it wasn't? Kelly wished she hadn't
been so dazed at the end of that appointment with Dr
Clifford. She had so many questions she wanted to
ask now. Would Flipper simply become more breathless with any exacerbation of her heart failure? Could
she faint? Have a cardiac arrest and need CPR? The
fear was going to be crippling, wasn't it?

'Kelly?' The nurse who had dealt with the photographer earlier that afternoon was staring at her with such a strange expression Kelly wondered if she had been talking out loud to herself.

'Mmm?'

'I've just had the weirdest call. From Colin Jamieson's secretary.'

'Who's Colin Jamieson?'

'The CEO of St Pat's. He wants to see you. In his office.'

'What?' Kelly blinked. 'What on earth for?'

'She didn't say. She just said it was urgent.'

Kelly could feel the blood draining from her face. Something had happened to Flipper. Something terrible. If the CEO was involved it must be bad enough for it to have potential consequences for St Patrick's.

'Are you all right, Kelly?'

'Just tell me...where do I find his office?'

Tony rapped on the door.

'Enter.'

It wasn't the first time he'd gone into the luxurious top-floor office suite that belonged to St Pat's CEO, and he wasn't about to waste time enjoying the view or the décor.

'Ah...Tony. Glad you could make it.'

'It sounded urgent. I haven't got much time, though. I'm sorry, Colin. I'm a bit tied up in ICU with a post-op case.'

'I shouldn't need to keep you long. Come in—don't stand by the door.'

Tony took a step or two into the office, feeling somewhat out of place in here wearing his scrubs. Two wing-backed leather chairs were positioned in front of the massive mahogany desk that Colin Jamieson was ensconced behind, and it wasn't until Tony had moved forward that he realised one of the chairs was occupied.

'*Kelly*! What on earth are you doing in here?'

She looked dreadful. As white as a sheet. Her hair was bundled into a theatre-style cap, but she wasn't wearing scrubs as he was. She had a smock on like the cleaners wore and… Good grief—was that a pair of rubber gloves she had clutched in one hand?

'Take a look at this,' Colin Jamieson commanded. He tapped a sheet of paper on the desk in front of him. 'The editor-in-chief of the *Chronicle* gave me the courtesy of advance warning on the article that's been written to accompany this picture.'

It was a picture of Kelly. Looking startled. Holding a mop and standing beside a bucket. Wearing the kind of gloves she now had in her hands. Looking, for all the world, like a…*hospital cleaner*?

'I don't understand,' Tony said.

'No,' Colin snapped. 'I don't suppose you would, having told me today that you had no idea why Miss Adams' name couldn't be found on the database of nursing staff at St Patrick's.'

Tony was staring at Kelly. She met his gaze, but only for a heartbeat. She looked terrified. Of *him*?

'Miss Adams is a member of the domestic staff here,' the CEO informed him. 'She is a nurse aide.

A casual staff member. It was quite a task to track her down.'

Tony was trying to catch Kelly's gaze again. What on earth was going on here? Whatever it was, she didn't have to be so frightened, surely? He didn't believe she had done anything so terribly wrong.

'Just how long have you been masquerading as a qualified nurse, Miss Adams?'

Her chin lifted. Her voice sounded a lot stronger than Tony might have expected. 'I…I haven't.'

'Dr Grimshaw believed you were a nurse.'

'I never *said* I was a nurse.'

She hadn't, had she? 'I met Kelly at the hospital ball,' Tony told Colin Jamieson. 'I knew she was on the staff. I made an assumption about her level of qualification.'

'Which wasn't corrected?'

'I…no, I suppose not. We haven't spent much time together since then.'

And the time they *had* spent together they'd had far more important things to talk about. Like his work. His research. His family. Good grief, how much did he really know about this woman?

'You've spent enough time together for you to have taken her to your father's house as your… companion.'

Tony frowned. He didn't like whatever implication the CEO was making with that tone.

'Enough time to allow her to fraudulently practise medicine in public.'

'Excuse me?' Tony looked from Kelly back to Colin. 'What on *earth* are you talking about?'

'Obstetrics,' Colin snapped. 'Delivering a baby. One presenting with complications that could have been serious, according to the specialists I've spoken with today. The specialists that some journalist from the *Chronicle* has also been having a conversation with, I might add.'

'Kelly knew what she doing. She dealt competently with a situation that occurred well away from any hospital. She was administering first aid.'

'From what I've discovered, Miss Adams does not even hold a certificate in first aid. She has no medical qualifications whatsoever!'

'She attended medical school,' Tony snapped back. The shock of seeing Kelly dressed in a uniform that marked her as being on the lower ranks of hospital employment was wearing off. He could understand why she hadn't told him because, to his own consternation, he knew it might have influenced his decision to keep seeing her. Now he knew her well enough to know it didn't matter. 'Her marks were excellent. Isn't that right, Kelly?'

She was avoiding his gaze again. 'Yes.'

'You dropped out of medical school, didn't you, Miss Adams?'

The response was quieter this time. 'Yes.'

'So as far as the general public is concerned this baby was delivered by someone who had no right to be involved. Our city's deputy mayor is horrified. So is your father, I might add, Tony. If this actually hits the papers, St Patrick's is going to have one hell of a lot of damage control to do.'

Tony eyed the picture on his desk. '*If* it hits the papers?'

'The editor-in-chief happens to owe me a favour. I've managed to put a lid on the story for the moment. If I can deal with it to the satisfaction of all the public figures involved, it's possible we can bury this whole sorry mess. And I *am* dealing with it. Miss Adams—your employment, casual or otherwise, with St Patrick's is herewith terminated. Please collect your belongings, hand in your uniform and anything else you have which is hospital property, and be off the premises within thirty minutes.'

'Hang on!' Tony was as shocked as he knew Kelly must be. 'You can't do that.'

'It's all right, Tony.' Kelly was standing up. The stained smock, the horrible hat, even those ridiculous rubber gloves seemed to fade into the background. The fierce glow of a dignity that it must have required enormous strength to summon made her physical appearance irrelevant. 'Mr Jamieson is simply doing what he has to do. I have no intention of making trouble for St Patrick's, and I apologise for the inconvenience I've already caused.'

She cast a fleeting look at Tony as she left the room. One that conveyed a misery that gave him a stab of discomfort in his gut. It was full of apology as well. To him.

He tried to send a silent message back. One that said this would be all right. That it was *his* fault she was in trouble and that he would do something about it.

The way Kelly continued smoothly to the door

and then let herself out of the office made him feel he had failed.

He got to his feet, intending to follow her, but the clipped voice of the CEO made him pause.

'I wouldn't do that if I were you, Tony,' Colin Jamieson said coolly. 'The way I see it, this sorry business has now been dealt with.'

'I'm not so sure about that.'

'Well, be sure about this.' Colin reached for the printout of the photograph and tapped it. 'If you continue your association with Miss Adams, you can kiss goodbye to any aspirations you have to head the cardiothoracic surgical department here at St Patrick's.'

CHAPTER TEN

HER life hadn't simply been derailed.

It was travelling at alarming speed into a chasm that appeared terrifyingly bottomless.

Kelly had to push the buttons for the elevator more than once because her tears were blinding her. It took an agonisingly long time for the elevator to arrive and for the doors to open, and just when those doors were closing again and she thought she was safe a hand broke the beam and made them open again.

Tony Grimshaw stepped into the small space.

'Hey!' He was peering at her with deep concern written on his features as the doors slid closed behind him. 'Are you OK?'

A strange sound halfway between a strangled sob and laughter escaped Kelly's throat.

Tony groaned. 'Stupid question! Come here.'

He pulled her into his arms. He tugged off her cap and took the gloves from her hand and threw them into the corner of the elevator. And then he wrapped her even more closely against the solid wall of his chest.

Had he pushed the button for the ground floor? Unlike her desperate wait for the elevator to arrive, it would be no time at all before it descended. Precious seconds to feel the comfort of Tony's arms holding her.

'It'll be all right,' Tony was saying, his lips against her hair. 'You'll see. I'll talk to my father. To Nigel Finch. I'll sort this out and make sure you get your job back.'

'No.' Kelly shook her head. 'You can't.'

'Of course I can. I *want* to. This is my fault, Kelly. I took you to that reception. I stood back and let you deliver that baby. This is crazy.' She could hear an edge of anger in his voice now. 'Just because you haven't got a piece of paper to say you're qualified it doesn't mean you didn't save that baby's life.'

'No.' With a huge effort Kelly pushed away from the wonderful warmth and solidity of Tony's chest. The doors of the elevator slid open and she stepped back, breaking all physical contact.

Feeling as if her heart was breaking at the same time, Kelly took a deep breath. 'You can't involve yourself with this, Tony.'

'Why the hell not?'

'Because it will cause more trouble. You...' Kelly dragged in another breath. She had to find out if there was any truth in that unspoken warning John Clifford had been trying to give her. Lord, was it only this morning? 'It would mean you didn't get the job as HOD.'

Tony's eyes narrowed. 'What did Jamieson say to you?' His huff of breath was incredulous. 'Never mind. I can guess. Don't let him intimidate you, Kelly. I'm certainly not going to. He's not the only voice on that board of trustees.'

So it *was* true. But Tony was prepared to risk a job he wanted very badly for her sake.

God, she loved this man. Heart and soul.

Too much to let him risk ruining his career for her sake. He was angry himself, now. Outraged. He needed time to think about this. To realise how much damage defending her might bring.

A chance to decide if being with her was worth the fallout.

And if he did? What would that give them? An opportunity to continue a passionate affair that was going nowhere? Tony didn't see a family in his future, and family was the driving force of Kelly's life—wasn't it?

Family.

Flipper.

Kelly had no more choice here than she'd had years ago, when she had chosen to forsake her own career. From now on she had to focus on the most important person in her life. The vulnerable one who had only her to depend on.

Her daughter.

'It's over, Tony,' she heard herself saying in a strangely tight voice that didn't sound anything like herself. 'We can't see each other again. There's no point.' She glanced over her shoulder to check that no one in the foyer was listening to this exchange. 'There never was.'

The flicker of shock in his eyes sent a shaft of pain through Kelly.

'Because of this mess? I can sort it out. I promise.'

'I don't want you to.' Kelly stood up straighter. 'I can look after myself. I...I don't need you, Tony.'

'And you don't want me, either? Is that what you're saying?' Shock had given way to disbelief.

Was he thinking of their intimate moments together and wondering how anything in their right mind could *not* want that?

Flipper.

The name echoed in Kelly's mind. This had to be about Flipper. Forget about herself. Forget about Tony. Forget any of those dreams of what might have been.

This was agony, but it had to be done.

'Yes,' Kelly said, her tone wooden. 'That's exactly what I'm saying.'

'Oh, my dear! You look terrible!'

'Gee, thanks, Elsie.' Kelly's smile was wry. If her looks reflected the state her life was in right now, she must look a fright indeed. She had a sick child, no current means of supporting herself and that child, and she had just pushed the man she would probably love more than any other in her lifetime firmly out of her life. With a sigh, Kelly pulled her front door open wider. 'Come on in, Elsie.'

'I don't want to interrupt your day, dear.'

Kelly's laugh sounded hollow. 'Are you kidding?

We've almost run out of things to do and it's only lunchtime.' She found a more convincing smile for her former boss. 'Please come in. Flipper will be delighted to see your face. Would you like a cup of tea?'

'I'd love one.' Elsie followed her down the hallway.

'Don't trip on these toys,' Kelly warned. 'The place is a bit of a mess. I'm sorry.'

More toys and a big-piece jigsaw puzzle of a clown that was half finished lay on the rug in the living area. Flipper was also lying on the rug, chewing on the lower legs of the clown. Her own lower legs were in the air, waving in time to the song a group of enthusiastic young people were singing on the television.

Kelly shoved paper and crayons to one side of the table. 'Sit down,' she invited Elsie. 'I'll put the kettle on.'

Flipper spotted their visitor. She rolled over, tried to get up too fast, fell over and then tried again. This time she managed to launch herself towards their visitor.

'Hug!' she demanded.

Elsie complied willingly.

'Darn!' Flipper tugged on the older woman's hand.

'Let me catch my breath first, pumpkin,' Elsie begged. 'I had to walk very fast to get here in my lunchbreak.'

'Oh...you're not missing your lunch, are you?' Kelly opened the cupboard over one end of the kitchen bench but it was distressingly bare. A week of not working and buying nothing but the essentials Flipper needed was already making a huge impact. A scary one. 'Can I make you some toast?' she offered apologetically. 'With some baked beans?'

Elsie's face was creased with sympathy. She understood. Kelly was dismayed to find herself suddenly very close to tears. After a week of being so strong, too. Coping. Or was she?

'I brought some sandwiches from the cafeteria,' Elsie said. 'It's nothing exciting, but I couldn't land on your doorstep at lunchtime with nothing in my bag.' She reached into the supermarket carry bag she had placed beside her chair. 'I've got some cake, too. You like cake, don't you, Flipper?'

Flipper stopped turning in circles. 'Cake!' She threw the piece of clown puzzle aside and it hit the screen of the television. Reaching up with her short arms, she tugged at another chair.

'Pick up your toys first,' Kelly instructed. 'And turn off the TV so we can hear ourselves think.'

Flipper ignored her mother. With a frown of determination she tugged harder at the chair and it tipped over backwards, knocking the small girl to the floor and landing on top of her. A frightened wail ensued.

'Oh, no!' Kelly moved swiftly from the kitchen sink. 'Are you hurt?'

'She's fine,' Elsie said. 'It was just a little bump.' *Don't make too much of a fuss*, her tone warned. *You'll only blow it all out of proportion and make Flipper think she's hurt herself.*

Kelly froze. She wouldn't normally be rushing to her child like this, would she? She *was* overreacting. Elsie was helping Flipper to her feet and onto her knee, but Flipper was still crying and the sound cut through Kelly like a knife. She'd be crying a whole lot more after she had her surgery, wouldn't she? This was nothing compared to—

'The kettle's overflowing,' Elsie warned.

'Oh, God!' Kelly had forgotten to turn the tap off. Water was pouring over the top of the electric jug and running over the bench to trickle down the cupboard doors and puddle on the floor.

It took a few minutes to sort the mess out. By then Flipper had completely forgotten the bump from the chair. She climbed off Elsie's lap and stood in front of the television, singing loudly and tunelessly along with the song.

Kelly put a mug of tea in front of Elsie and sat down with another sigh.

'Sorry.'

'What about, love?'

'This…' Kelly's hand made a gesture that was intended to cover the mess, the noise of the television and the small upset with Flipper, but she felt as if she was pointing to her entire life. 'I…I thought I was actually coping, you know?'

'You are, love. You have every right to feel stressed. You're worried. How *is* Flipper?'

'I'm watching her too carefully. Reading too much into small things. It's driving us both nuts, I think.'

'It would do you both good to have some time

away from each other. There must be a crèche nearby? Or a playcentre?'

'They cost. And I'm going to have to be really careful until I find a new job.'

'I've written a reference for you. It was one of the reasons I came today.' Elsie's eyes looked suspiciously bright. 'I just wish there was more I could do.'

'Thank you, Elsie. You're a good friend. But you can't fix this. Nobody can.'

'I'll bet your Dr Grimshaw could. It's because of *him* that you got into all this trouble.'

'He's not *my* Dr Grimshaw, Elsie. And he's not going to do anything to try and help.'

Elsie looked offended. 'Why not?'

'Because I told him not to. I said I didn't need him. That I didn't want anything more to do with him.'

Elsie was silent for a moment, searching Kelly's face. 'Oh, my dear! It's not true, is it?'

'Yes. No…' The tears that had been kept at bay successfully for a week now were gathering strength. A single drop escaped and trickled down the side of Kelly's nose. 'It's impossible, Elsie. It could never work.'

'Love can find a way of making all sorts of things work. Oh, love, you *are* in a misery, aren't you?' Elsie put her hand on top of Kelly's and gave it a squeeze.

There were thumping sounds behind Kelly. Flipper was whirling round and round to the music on the children's programme.

Kelly scrubbed at her face and sniffed. 'Things

will get better. I'll make them better. I'll get another job and find a new crèche for Flipper. I've got all the paperwork to apply for benefit until then. I just haven't got round to filling it in. And your reference will be a help, I'm sure. I—'

Elsie wasn't listening. She had turned her head to watch Flipper.

Kelly turned as well.

Just in time to see her daughter's strangely blank expression, and the way her eyes rolled back as she crumpled and fell to the floor with a dreadful thump. She just lay there. A tiny and very still shape in the middle of the rug.

Another chair tipped over backwards as Kelly made a dive towards Flipper, but it went unnoticed. Kelly turned the little girl gently onto her back. She tilted her head to open her airway and then bent over her, her cheek beside Flipper's nose and mouth and one hand resting on her chest to feel for air movement. Her other hand was on a chubby neck, searching for a carotid pulse.

'She's not breathing,' she whispered in horror, seconds later. 'There's no pulse! Oh, my God... Elsie—call an ambulance, please. *Hurry!*'

Kelly bent her head to breathe into Flipper's mouth and nose. She put her hand in the middle of the tiny chest and began compressions.

The huge whiteboard in the main corridor of St Patrick's operating theatre suite was a series of boxes.

Theatre numbers were listed on the left hand side.

The scheduled start time for surgery in that theatre came in the next column, then the names of the surgeons, the procedure being done, and the name and age of the patient. Special details like allergies or MRSA status that could affect protocols could go in the last column.

Tony rubbed at the ache in his neck as he paused to check the start time for his third case of the day. Two p.m. He looked at his watch. Was thirty-five minutes time to snatch a drink and a bite to eat? Check on the latest lab results on that woman on the ward that Josh was concerned about, and check his e-mail to see if there was any word on an announcement regarding the HOD position? Colin Jamieson had put the matter on hold until there was no further threat of any adverse publicity for St Patrick's, but it had been days now. Long, challenging days.

Being this busy was the way he wanted things, however, wasn't it? It was the best way in the world to stop him thinking about anything other than his work.

Mind you, the hurt was wearing off. Had he really been prepared to lose his chance of being HOD for the sake of a relationship? Given the way Kelly had dumped him with such apparent ease, it was just as well he hadn't travelled any further down *that* road.

Yes. There was a good smear of relief at the silver lining of that particular cloud. He was getting good at simply burying such errant thoughts, in any case. An extra glance at his watch did the trick. Sent him straight back to thinking about the afternoon workload. He probably had a little longer than the scheduled time. He would get beeped when the theatre was free of its current case and being set up for the next, and that would give him at least thirty minutes' grace to get back, change into fresh scrubs and scrub up.

The case in Theatre 3 looked complicated, so it could well run over time. The writing in the box for the procedure was tiny to fit it all in. Valve replacements and a heap of other work on a three-year-old girl. Good grief! The name leapt out at him. Philippa Adams.

Flipper?

His gaze flicked to the end column on the right. Yes. Down's Syndrome was recorded as a special detail.

Adams? The child was related to Kelly?

God! It was so easy for his mind to skip. Like a damaged disc or something. It would catch on a memory and replay it until he made the effort to jolt it forward—or, preferably, switch it off.

This time it took him straight back to the night when the things that would send their relationship pear-shaped had been put into place by fate. When the Finch baby had been born.

He remembered the conversation. He could actually *hear* Kelly's voice in his head. Soft and clear and...warm. Saying that one day she would love to have her own baby. To make a family.

And then Tony had to close his eyes for a moment, as another, far more powerful memory superimposed itself. The way he had touched her belly, marvelling at its flat perfection. He could feel her skin now. His fingers actually prickled at the memory of how electric that touch had been.

Jolting his mind forward took a huge effort this time. The glance at his watch was automatic. He was wasting time he couldn't afford to lose. Turning away from the board, Tony strode decisively away. He pushed open the fire stop door, walked a little further, and then stopped dead in his tracks. He was right beside the relatives' waiting area.

The unanswered question was not going to leave him alone, was it? If Kelly was related to that child she would be in there, wouldn't she? Two steps took him to the door of the area. And there, curled into an armchair near a window, staring out with no apparent focus, sat Kelly.

She looked so…so small, curled up like that. Frightened. And alone. Completely alone. There weren't even any other relatives waiting for their cases to finish, to share the space and tension with her. He couldn't leave her like that. She might tell him to go away. He might have to hear once more that she didn't need him or want him. But there was no way he could keep going with the image of her sitting like that on his mind.

He walked quietly into the room. Kelly was obviously waiting for news, because she sensed his approach and turned. The fear in her eyes hit Tony like a physical blow.

'Tony!' Kelly's chest heaved as she drew in a shuddering breath. She licked dry-looking lips. 'I thought it was... *You* haven't come to tell me about Flipper, have you?'

'No. I'm sorry, I don't know how the case is going. Would you like me to go and find out?'

'Yes, please. No!' The catch in her voice made Tony turn back instantly. 'I...'

'Want some company?' Tony held her gaze. He couldn't have looked away, no matter how much he might have wanted to. And he didn't want to. It didn't matter what Kelly had said to him. Her need to have him here with her right now was in her eyes. She needed him, and that was all that mattered.

He sat down beside her. Took hold of her hand.

'What's going on?' he asked gently. 'Do you want to talk about it?'

'How did you know I was here?'

'I saw Flipper's name on the whiteboard.'

'But...' Confusion was added to the mix of fear and misery in her eyes.

Such a deep, dark blue at the moment. And there were deep furrows in her brow that Tony wanted to smooth with his thumb.

'But how did you *know*?' Kelly asked. 'About...'

Nobody could look as Kelly did at that moment unless they cared passionately about the outcome of a life-threatening operation. He'd seen this kind of fear before. In the eyes of parents. It wasn't much of a guess.

'About Flipper being your daughter?'

'Y-yes.'

'I didn't. Oh, Kel. Why didn't you tell me?'

'I...couldn't.'

'But why not?' Tony didn't understand. 'You told me about your family. About the accident. Was that really why you had to leave medical school? Didn't Flipper have more to do with it?'

'It was the same thing.'

Tony didn't jump in with another question. He could sense that Kelly wanted to tell him now. She needed time to collect herself.

Which she did. She took a deep breath and then let it out in a long sigh. She didn't look at Tony, but she did grip his hand tightly.

'My sister Karen was pregnant at the time of the accident. Close to full term. The reason they were all in the car together was because Mum and Dad were taking them shopping. To buy baby stuff, like a really nice pram.' Kelly swallowed audibly. 'Karen was the only one in the car who didn't die at the scene. She arrested in the emergency department, though, and...they couldn't get her back. She was just too badly injured.'

She was holding his hand so tightly Tony's fingers were going numb. He didn't move.

'They did a post-mortem Caesarean. Right there in the department. It was...just terrible.'

'My God, you were *there*?'

Kelly simply nodded. 'I'd been in a tutorial in the orthopaedic department. Just down the corridor.' Her voice wobbled precariously and she struggled for control. 'They gave me Flipper to hold as soon as they'd checked her breathing. I think they already knew there was something wrong, but I was allowed to hold her for a few minutes. While I...while I said goodbye to Karen.'

Not only to Karen. She'd had to say farewell to her entire family.

'That tiny scrap of a baby was all I had left of my family,' Kelly continued in a voice that was no more than a whisper. 'And then I found out that she had major heart problems and would need surgery when she was no more than a few days old.'

Kelly had had to organise and attend multiple funerals. She'd had to add the stress of a baby needing open heart surgery to the horrendous grief she must have been suffering.

God. No wonder he had sensed the enormous strength of this woman.

'I gave up medical school because there was no way I could do justice to raising my niece other-wise.' Kelly looked up and met Tony's gaze steadily. 'I don't regret my choice. I'd do it again in a heart-beat. She's my little girl and I love her to bits. I'd do anything for her. Even—'

Even what? Sacrifice a relationship?

Tony frowned. 'Even what?'

She looked away from him. 'Even if other people see her as being...um...less than perfect.'

'What does it matter what other people think?' His frown deepened. 'Did you think it would make a difference to me? To how I saw you? *Us?*'

'Of course.' Kelly gave her head a tiny shake, as if the question was ridiculous.

And Tony knew that he had his answer. Nothing was as important to Kelly as her child. Her next words confirmed that.

'You have no interest in children, Tony. You're the same as your brother and sister. You have a high-flying career that doesn't leave space in your life for a family. Let alone a family that includes a child with special needs.'

'And that's why you said there was no point? That there never had been?'

Something cold inside Tony was melting. She hadn't told him the truth when she'd said she didn't need him. That she didn't want him.

His career! How many of his relationships had foundered already because of his wonderful career? All of them. But he'd thought things were different with Kelly. The way he could talk to her about his work. Share his passion. And it hadn't really mattered in the past. This was different.

Kelly was different.

'It's not just your career, Tony,' Kelly said quietly, as if she could guess where his thoughts were leading. That he could change something in his life to make it possible to include a family. 'Your family only accepts success. Perfection, preferably. Can you imagine your mother's reaction if she knew you were having a relationship with a woman who had a Down's Syndrome child?'

He could. All too well. The only times Tony had ever felt loved as a child had been when he'd been able to produce evidence of distinction. A prize or a certificate or a silver cup. Kelly was right. His mother would never accept such a child.

But why did that have to be so important? Tony was an adult. The opinions of his parents shouldn't actually matter. Or the opinion of his peers. It was the combination of his background and his career that had been too much for this unexpected diversion his life had taken. The Grimshaw world was one where Kelly and her daughter would never fit. He wouldn't want them to. Because that would make them the same as everybody he'd ever known, and what he loved most about Kelly was how different she was.

No wonder she'd hated being at that reception so much.

No wonder she hadn't told him about Flipper. Her precious daughter.

He tightened the grip on her hand. 'Are you sure you don't want me to go and find out how thing's are going?'

He could feel Kelly flinch. Could feel her gathering new strength. Then she nodded. 'Yes, please.'

'Will you be all right? On your own?'

The faint smile was all the answer he needed. She'd been on her own before, through the worst times in her life. She would be all right.

Tony pulled a mask from the box on the wall outside Theatre 3. He went inside, just far enough to see how things were going. Judging by the atmosphere in here, the lengthy and complicated surgery had gone very well. Tony would have easily picked up the smallest signals from the body language of the paediatric surgeons, and there was no hint of tension.

Parameters being measured, like arterial blood gas and acid-base balance and urine output, were all satisfactory, but he'd arrived at the moment of truth. They were preparing to take Flipper off the bypass machine.

The surgeon was using a syringe to remove all the air that had entered the small heart.

'Clamp can come off,' he said. 'How's her temperature?'

'Coming up nicely.'

Now there was tension in the room. Everybody was waiting to see if defibrillation would be needed to coax the heart to start beating again. Whether the end of this life-threatening procedure would be smooth sailing and the result what they had all spent the last several hours working towards.

'VF', the anaesthetist said quietly, for the benefit of those not leaning over the table with the heart in direct vision. Those people would actually be able to see the uncoordinated movement of the heart. A helpless wriggling that would be fatal if it couldn't be changed.

The anaesthetist's gaze was glued to the monitor. Tony moved a little closer so he could watch the trace. A blip appeared through the squiggle. And then another.

'Here we go,' the anaesthetist said finally, satisfaction in his tone. 'She's in sinus rhythm.'

Within a few minutes Tony was able to leave the

theatre. He ripped off his mask and walked so quickly towards the exit that a nurse gave him a startled glance.

'Is something wrong, Dr Grimshaw?'

'Not at all,' he said, without breaking his stride. 'Quite the opposite.'

Kelly jumped to her feet as though she'd been shot as he entered the waiting area.

'It's almost over,' he said as he walked towards her. 'It's gone really well. She'll be on her way to Recovery very soon and then you'll be able to go and sit with her.'

Tony thought that Kelly might be about to faint. He closed the final distance between them and caught her in his arms. She clung to him, silent sobs racking her body, and all Tony could do was hold her.

And feel…responsible.

Thanks to him, she'd lost her job and her means of supporting a child she'd already sacrificed so much for.

Including him. She did need him, whether she was prepared to admit it or not. She wanted to be with him the same way he wanted to be with her.

Maybe there was no way they could be together again, but it wasn't good enough to leave things like this. Tony had come into her life and had made it harder, and Kelly *so* didn't deserve that.

Somehow he had to try and fix this.

CHAPTER ELEVEN

THE worst was over.

It had to be.

Kelly was far too exhausted to consider any of the potential complications Flipper might still be facing.

She had wrapped herself in the reassurance Tony had given her, and the words from the surgeon a little later had been a ribbon to tie up the most precious gift ever.

'It all went superbly well, Kelly,' he'd told her. 'She's a tough little thing, your daughter. I'm confident she'll bounce right back, and the future's looking very much brighter.'

The time in Recovery had morphed seamlessly into this new vigil that the paediatric intensive care unit represented. Kelly was in a glass-walled cubicle, not far from the main central desk, as much a part of the setting as the bank of monitors and the spaghetti junction of tubing and wires surrounding Flipper's bed.

A nurse brought a figure, gowned and masked, to the door of the cubicle.

'I'm only allowed to stay for a minute or two,' Elsie whispered, clearly overawed by her surroundings. 'I told them I was family.'

Kelly looked up from where she was sitting, holding Flipper's hand, and smiled. 'You *are* family, Elsie.' She kept her voice low as well. Not that it was going to disturb Flipper, but there were other parents nearby keeping watch on their critically ill children. 'I couldn't have got through the last few days without you.'

Elsie made a snuffling noise behind the mask, but she didn't step any closer. 'I've brought your clean undies. And those DVDs for Flipper. But I still can't find that frog toy.'

'Oh...' Kelly's heart sank.

It had been three days now since Elsie had come for lunch and ended up being part of that dreadful emergency with Flipper. Elsie had been back to the house several times since, to get whatever Kelly needed so that she didn't have to leave Flipper's bedside, and every time she had conducted a search for Ribby the frog. Flipper had been tearfully begging for the toy ever since that miraculous moment when she'd started breathing for herself again, and had opened her eyes and recognised her mother.

'Did you check at the bottom of her bed? Under the sheets?'

'Yes. And under the couch cushions and in the cupboards. He's vanished. I'm sorry, Kelly.'

'Don't be. You've been a rock. I'll be able to slip home myself before too long. In a day or two, I should think. Maybe a fresh pair of eyes will spot something.'

For a moment both women were silent. The sound of the monitors beeping and the rhythmic hiss of Flipper's breathing, currently controlled by a ventilator, filled the small space.

'Poor wee mite,' Elsie murmured, her voice catching.

'She's doing really well.' Kelly stroked a few strands of hair from Flipper's forehead with her free hand. Her other hand still hadn't moved from where it was curled gently over Flipper's. 'Her cardiac output's better than it's ever been and her blood pressure's normal. Kidney function is good, and her oxygen levels are perfect.'

Elsie's frown showed the medical terminology meant little. 'Has she woken up yet?'

'She's still sedated. They'll lighten it tomorrow, and if she keeps this up she'll be back on the ward in a day or two. It's amazing the way kids can get over this sort of thing.'

'That's good to hear,' Elsie nodded. 'I'd better go, love. That nurse is staring at me. Unless you'd like me to sit with Flipper for a while, so you can get some sleep?'

Kelly shook her head. 'I'm good.'

'You look done in.'

'I am, but I'm still good. There's no way I'm leaving her, Elsie. Not yet.'

When Elsie had gone, and many more quiet minutes had ticked past, Kelly stroked Flipper's forehead again. And again. A feather-light touch. A movement that spoke of exhaustion and relief. Of a mind-numbing state that didn't allow for conscious direction of thought.

Instead, Kelly found herself thinking in snatches of the rollercoaster her life had been over the last few weeks.

When had she stepped onto that wild ride?

When she'd purchased the raffle ticket for entrance to the ball?

Or had it been the ball itself? That moment when she'd seen Tony watching her from between the pillars and she'd been dancing. For *him*.

That had certainly been the start of the upward sweep.

Rediscovering the joy of dancing. Learning for the first time what it was like to really fall in love.

There had been smaller dips. Like meeting Tony's parents and knowing that she could never fit into his kind of world. That conversation about babies and realising that a family didn't fit into Tony's future. The results of Flipper's tests and the worry that had come in their wake.

Losing her job had to have been the stomach curdling moment when she'd known the downward rush was just about to begin.

Then rock bottom. When Flipper had collapsed and Kelly had thought she'd lost her.

And now?

Now it felt like an upward roll again. One that had begun when Tony had been holding her as she sobbed out the relief of hearing that Flipper's surgery had been a success.

And here she was, touching her little girl. Feeling her warmth. Watching the rise and fall of her small chest with every breath. Hearing the reassuring soft beeps of the monitors.

It was all she could ask for right now.

All she wanted.

It was late.

The longest day in the longest week of Tony Grimshaw's life, but he couldn't go home just yet.

He went to the paediatric intensive care unit instead.

To the central desk, to find which of the dimly lit cubicles Kelly and Flipper would be in. He'd spoken to the surgeon not so long ago, so he knew how well Flipper was doing. It wasn't enough to hear that Kelly was also coping well. He needed to see for himself.

The nursing staff were quietly occupied elsewhere, but Tony didn't need to ask or even check the list he knew would be on the desk somewhere. As soon as he reached the central area he could see her, straight ahead of him.

His forward movement ceased and Tony simply stood there for a minute, his gaze riveted on the scene in that cubicle.

Kelly was sitting beside the bed but her body was tilted inwards, almost curling over the tiny girl to offer protection. He could see her brushing back Flipper's hair. Again and again.

So softly.

A gentle touch he knew so well he could feel it himself as he watched.

But what really transfixed him, brought a lump to his throat and actually threatened to bring tears to his eyes for the first time in living memory, was the expression on Kelly's face.

Fierce, pure love.

The kind that would let nothing and no one harm the beloved if it was within human power to offer protection.

The kind that Tony hadn't really believed existed outside a fairytale. Not like this. Not when someone had chosen to bestow it, despite obstacles that would have turned many people away.

It was partly the physical problems Flipper had, partly that she was a special needs child, but mostly Tony could relate to the fact that Kelly had sacrificed her career to bestow this love.

He knew so well the passion and dedication it took to become a doctor. His parents had both had careers. Would his mother have considered *him* more important as a baby than her law practice? Would his father have given up his political aspirations?

No. Tony had never been loved like this.

Flipper had to be the luckiest little girl in existence. Even with everything she had been through and was going through now, she had experienced that kind of love. The best that life could offer anyone. Celebrations in her life would be with home-cooked food prepared with love. Not in a fancy restaurant where no more effort was required than making a choice from a menu. Where someone else dealt with the mess. Tony knew what was real. He knew what he would have chosen for the child that had been himself.

And it was too late.

Or was it?

It beggared belief that Kelly could love her daughter this much and still have the same kind of love to offer someone else, but he knew she did. He could hear her voice again, softly expressing her wish for a family. To have a baby with someone who loved her as much as she loved him.

Someone who would be the luckiest man in the world. Someone who hadn't been programmed to think that what mattered in life was success. Public accolade.

It took a moment or two to recognise the ugly feeling that the thought of that person generated.

Someone other than himself being loved by Kelly.

Making love to her.

Making a baby.

Jealousy. That was what it was.

The idea was so abhorrent. It was unacceptable. It couldn't happen. Tony wasn't going to allow it to happen.

Somehow he would have to convince Kelly that they could make it work. But not right now. He couldn't disturb her. The bond with her daughter was too tight at the moment. And too important.

The rest of his life was at stake here. Being patient for a day or two was a small price to pay if it was going to improve the odds.

'You've just missed her, I'm afraid.' The nurse's badge was a bright flower, with "Jo" written in the centre.

'When will she be back?'

'Not for a little while. She's gone home to find a toy that Flipper's been begging for.'

'Ribby!' said the small girl in the cot.

Tony smiled. 'Ribby?'

He was rewarded with the grin of a pixie.

'Ribby's the name of the toy,' Jo explained. 'I believe it's a frog, and it's been lost for a few days.'

Tony nodded, but he was still looking at the small face. The way this little girl was standing up and hanging onto the top rail of the cot with such a determined grip. It was only three days since her surgery. 'She's doing well, isn't she?'

'She's fabulous.' Jo leaned over and ruffled Flipper's hair. 'Aren't you, tuppence?'

'Darn!' Flipper held up both arms.

Jo laughed. 'You'll be dancing again soon enough, pet.'

Tony found himself stepping closer. 'You like to dance, Flipper? Your mummy likes to dance too, doesn't she?'

Flipper was holding his eye contact. Smiling so hard her face was a mass of crinkles. She nodded, and moved along the cot like a crab, holding on with only one hand. The other hand was stretching towards Tony.

'Darn!' she commanded.

'You can't run around yet,' Jo reminded her. 'How about I put on one of your DVDs? Or read you a story?'

Flipper shook her head. Her grin was fading rapidly and her bottom lip quivered.

'Is she allowed to be picked up?'

The nurse gave him an astonished look.

'I like dancing myself,' Tony said with a grin. 'Maybe…'

Jo sucked in a breath. 'It's OK to pick her up, and if anyone knows what they're doing I'm sure you do, Dr Grimshaw. But—'

'I'll be gentle,' Tony promised. 'And quick. We don't want tears, do we?'

Without giving the nurse time to argue, Tony leaned over the cot and found two chubby arms wound trustingly around his neck. He held the child with one arm, and with the other he kept the IV pole close. He stepped back, then forward, then turned in a small circle.

'See?' He smiled at Jo. 'Dancing!'

'Faster!' Flipper said. She thumped Tony on his back.

There was a new spring in Kelly's step today.

It was only a week since Flipper's surgery, and she was doing so well they were talking about letting her come home.

And Kelly had a new job. Flipper's nurse, Jo, had thought of it. She had a friend who worked in an old people's home that happened to have a crèche right next door. It was quite a long way from where they lived, but they could catch the bus every day and it might even be fun.

Jo had been so excited when she'd arrived at the hospital this morning. She'd seen her friend the night before, and apparently they were looking for a new staff member at the home. So Kelly had dashed out this afternoon and gone for an interview and they'd loved her. She didn't have to start right away. Not until Flipper was ready to go to the crèche. It was perfect.

A short detour into a corner shop was made, so that Kelly could buy some of the jelly snakes that were Flipper's favourite treat. Having made the purchase, she found a sense of urgency in getting back to the hospital and picked up the speed of her walk. Not that Flipper would be missing her unduly. She was having a ball on the ward. Other children were drawn to her friendly grin, and the staff could never resist the freely given cuddles. Every day her condition had improved noticeably—to the point where it was getting hard to keep her anywhere near her bed. Both the surgeon and Dr Clifford had laughed about it this morning.

'Time to think about sending her home, I think,' the surgeon had said. 'Are you happy with that, Kelly?'

Happy? She couldn't get any happier.

With the little bag of jelly snakes clutched in her hand, Kelly sped through the hospital corridors towards the paediatric ward. Flipper's room was near the entrance to the ward, but she wasn't a bit surprised to find it empty. Flipper would be down in the playroom, probably, with the other children. She turned to go in that direction, down the wide corridor.

It was late in the afternoon now. Sunshine poured in through this side of the building at this time of day, so the figure down at the end of the corridor was a dark shape. An oddly lumpy shape, that was moving in a very peculiar fashion.

Stepping forwards and backwards rapidly. Spinning. *Dancing!*

The peal of childish laughter was instantly recognisable. Someone was whirling around with Flipper in their arms. Spinning and—dear Lord—dipping now. Holding her precious little girl sideways, with her head almost touching the floor.

Kelly's heart missed a beat, and then kicked in at a ferocious speed. Her feet picked up the same rhythm as she hurtled down the corridor to rescue her daughter. But then the speed ebbed as fast as she'd turned it on. Her jaw dropped and she came to a complete halt.

The person dancing with Flipper was *Tony!*

And he wasn't just dancing the way you might with a small child, with token moves and a lot of laughter. He was seriously dancing with her. As though he was enjoying it. As though it *mattered*.

Kelly knew what it was like to be held like that. To have Tony so focussed on holding her. To feel the sweep of movement and the beat of his heart. Not that there was any music happening here.

So why was her heart singing?

Why did this, more than any of the joy of watching Flipper's rapid recovery over the last week or so, make her throat close up and tears sting the back of her eyes.

'Mummy!'

Flipper had spotted her. Tony stopped the dance abruptly and bent to let the small, wriggling person escape his hold. She ran to Kelly and wrapped her arms around her mother's knees.

'Darn, Mummy!'

'You *were* dancing, darling. I saw you.'

But Kelly wasn't looking down at Flipper as she spoke. Her gaze was caught by the man in front of her. By the expression in his eyes. He looked...hopeful? Was he expecting her to be angry at the level of physical activity he had been encouraging? Or the fact that he was dancing with her daughter?

Kelly had to clear her throat. She rested her hand on the top of Flipper's head. 'It was beautiful dancing,' she said softly.

'Wasn't it just?' Jo appeared from the shadows further down the corridor. 'She's come along a treat in her dance lessons in the last few days.'

'Few days?' Kelly's eyebrows shot up. 'You've been doing this for *days*?'

'We're dance partners,' Tony admitted. There was a faint upward tilt to the corners of his mouth. 'Only because you weren't here.'

Kelly was really confused now. 'You came here to *dance* with me?'

Flipper had bent her head backwards so she could stare up at Kelly without letting go of her legs. 'Darn, Mummy?'

'I came here to *talk* to you,' Tony said. 'But you weren't here. You'd gone home to get Ribby. He was lost, wasn't he? Where did you find him?'

This was so weird. Hearing Tony say that ridiculous name as though it was perfectly ordinary. The man who had no interest in children. In families. Talking about a fluffy toy as though it was important.

'He was in the washing machine,' Kelly said cautiously. 'I think Flipper thought Ribby needed a bath—didn't you, sweetie?'

'Ribby!' Flipper repeated happily. She let go of Kelly's legs. 'Wanna play with Ribby.'

She trotted off and disappeared into her room.

Kelly stared at Tony, a curious bubbling sensation happening deep inside. 'You wanted to talk to me?'

He nodded. 'I kept coming back. I always seemed to miss you.' His gaze held hers as it softened. 'I *do* miss you, Kelly. Too much.'

Jo's jaw dropped. 'I'd better go and see what Flipper's up to,' she said hurriedly. 'And the dinner trolley's going to be arriving any minute.'

'I miss you, too,' Kelly said softly. 'I've been hoping I'd see you.'

'You have?'

'Mmm. I wanted to thank you for being with me the day of the surgery. It was a…a very special thing to do.'

'I wanted to be there,' Tony said. 'I want to be with you, Kelly.'

'But…'

She didn't get time to articulate why it wasn't a good idea. Why they'd both end up getting hurt if they tried something that had no hope of working out. Flipper was back. Ribby the frog dangled from one hand. She stopped and looked up at Tony. Then she looked up at Kelly.

'Darn?' she asked hopefully. Her mouth widened in a confident smile that brought the prickle of tears back to Kelly's eyes. Thank God she was this happy. This healthy now.

'Sure.' Kelly reached down. 'I'll dance with you.'

'No.' Flipper pushed Kelly away. '*You* darn.'

She grinned up at Tony. When neither of the adults moved, she marched forward, took hold of Tony's thumb and dragged him towards Kelly. She dropped Ribby so she could also take hold of Kelly's hand, and then she pulled both the much larger hands together.

'Darn,' she commanded, clearly satisfied that she had sorted the matter.

'Your daughter wants us to dance,' Tony murmured. 'With each other.'

'Mmm.' Kelly's fingers were curled loosely inside Tony's palm. She could feel his fingers moving.

Taking hold of hers. She could feel that grip tighten around her heart as much as her hand.

'Shall we?'

Kelly turned by way of response. So that she was facing Tony and they were only inches apart. She lifted her free hand and put it on his shoulder. He stepped in so that their bodies were touching.

And then he started moving. Leading her in a dance. A slow kind of tango, where their heads stayed close enough for a quiet conversation to continue.

Now was the time to say something. Before she was sucked into this feeling of completeness so deeply it would be impossible to say anything to end it.

'It could never work, Tony. Everybody knows that I was a nurse aide. Pretty much the same thing as being a cleaner. You'd never live it down.'

Tony dipped her. He leaned over her with his face just above hers. 'And you think that what you do is what really matters?'

Flipper hooted with glee. 'More!' she shouted.

'It's who you are that's important to me,' Tony said as he lifted her upright again. 'The woman I love is strong and independent and loving. She's the most amazing woman I've ever met. Or ever will.'

He *loved* her?

The wave of sensation was so intense it made Kelly's head spin, so she rested it on Tony's shoulder. It didn't matter that they had no music to dance to. They could still keep a perfect rhythm.

Flipper was holding Ribby by his fluffy front legs. She was dancing beside them and singing tunelessly. Dancing with her toy in her own little happy world.

A world that couldn't be allowed to be tarnished.

'Can you imagine Flipper living in your home?' she asked Tony quietly. 'Singing and dancing like this when you've got some kind of reception you have to hold as Head of Department?'

'I'm not the head of department. I never will be. Well, maybe in twenty or thirty years, when I don't have more important things to keep me busy.'

'What?' Kelly lifted her head. 'But—'

Tony grinned, swirling her in a circle. 'I pulled out of contention,' he told her. 'I realised where I'd gone wrong. *You* made me realise.'

He gave her a series of swirls that made Flipper laugh in delight, but Kelly was feeling alarmed. He'd given up wanting to be HOD because of *her*?

'My life has been one long series of ambitions,' Tony said, pulling her close again and slowing the dance. Moving her to one side of the corridor to let the dinner trolley get past. 'One goal after another. I've chased them and I've caught them, but they've never been enough—and do you know why?'

'No,' Kelly whispered.

'They've been the wrong goals. I never knew what the most important goal of all was until I met you. Until I saw you with Flipper.'

Some more children had joined Flipper.

'What are they doing?' one of them asked.

'Darn—sing,' Flipper enunciated proudly.

'Cool.' The children lined up to watch.

'What's Flipper got to do with *us*?' Kelly asked in wonder.

'Everything.'

That was the right answer. Kelly could feel her smile starting. Growing.

'She's the luckiest little girl in the world, being loved so much.' Tony sent her out, made her spin around, then drew her back so fast she landed against his body with a soft thump. 'More particularly because she's loved by *you*.'

Kelly caught her breath. Tony could be too, if that was what he wanted.

He *looked* as though that was what he wanted.

She wanted to tell him. She wanted to stop moving just for a moment, so she could find the right words to tell him how much she loved him. But there was movement everywhere. All the children who had been watching were dancing now as well. Even a boy on crutches was hopping in small circles.

'Dinnertime!' Jo's cheerful call cut into Kelly's whirling thoughts. 'Or are you lot planning to dance all night?'

'I wish,' Tony muttered. But he let Kelly go. 'Flipper needs you.'

So do you, Kelly wanted to say. *We need each other. All of us.*

But Tony was turning to leave. Then he turned again. To wave at Flipper and smile at Kelly.

'I'll be back,' he promised. 'Later.'

* * *

How late was 'later'?

Flipper had been asleep for hours now. Ten p.m. came and went. Eleven. The minutes ticked past and Kelly tried to stop herself watching the door.

Waiting.

He'd promised he'd come back and he would. The trust was there.

The hope.

As the figures on her watch changed to show midnight, Kelly became aware of an odd sound.

A kind of swishing outside the door.

She got up and peered into the dimly lit corridor. A janitor was mopping the floor.

Disappointment coursed through her so intense she just stood there for a few seconds, watching the mop as it swept in arcs that brought it closer and closer to her door.

And then the janitor in the stained grey coat looked up, and Kelly gasped.

'Oh, my God! *Tony!*'

He grinned.

'What on earth are you doing?'

'Cleaning.'

'Why?'

Tony propped the mop back into the bucket. He stepped towards Kelly and took hold of both her hands.

'Because I love you, Kelly Adams, and I couldn't think of a better way to show you.'

'By mopping the floor? I don't understand.'

'It's about who we are, not what we do,' Tony told

her quietly. 'It's about being real. Cleaning floors seems pretty real.'

'What if someone had seen you?'

'Someone *did* see me.'

'Oh, no! Who?'

'You.'

Kelly gave a soft huff. 'But that's not embarrassing. I don't matter.'

'On the contrary.' Tony's thumbs made circles on the backs of Kelly's hands. 'You matter more than anyone else could ever hope to. Except maybe my other dance partner. The short one. Is she asleep?'

'Yes. With Ribby clutched in her arms, of course.'

'Ah. The frog prince.' Tony smiled, and suddenly Kelly understood.

'You're doing this because of the way we met?' Kelly bit her lip, not quite ready to release the bubble of joy inside her in the form of a smile. 'The Cinderella thing?'

'Yes. I know it's the wrong way round, and I'm not the one who should be doing the cleaning—but, hey, I'm no prince either. I'm nowhere near perfect enough.'

The smile began to escape. He was perfect enough for *her*.

'What I am is a bit older and wiser than I've ever been before,' Tony continued. 'And I have to thank you for teaching me something I might never have learned otherwise. For teaching me about love.'

The look on Tony's face was so tender it made Kelly want to cry. Her smile wobbled.

'I think I fell in love with you the first time I saw you,' Tony said. 'I fell in love with a princess.'

'I'm no princess.'

But Tony didn't seem to be listening. He had let go of her hands and was fishing in the pocket of the horrible grey coat he was wearing. 'I know this is all inside out and upside down, but I really wanted to do this.' He pulled something out of his pocket. 'It's the slipper,' he said sombrely. 'And I'm really hoping it fits.'

Kelly's laugh was a gurgle of pure joy.

'It's a disposable theatre bootee,' she whispered. 'It would fit anyone.'

'But it's you I want it to fit.' Tony dropped to one knee and touched her foot. 'Will you try it on?'

Kelly just smiled down at him. 'I love you, Tony Grimshaw.'

He stayed on his knee. He fished inside the bootee. 'If you won't try the shoe on,' he said, 'could you see if this fits instead?'

'Oh!'

Tony was holding a ring. A simple, solitaire diamond ring that could only mean one thing.

The intensity of what she was feeling made Kelly's knees distinctly wobbly. She sank down. And there she was, kneeling on the floor in front of Tony.

'I love you,' he said softly. 'More than I can ever say, but I'm going to keep trying. Every day for as long as I live. If you'll let me.'

'Oh…' Kelly still couldn't find any words. She

held out her hand, aware of the moisture on her cheeks as Tony slid the ring onto her finger.

'Will you marry me?' he asked. 'And dance with me and clean floors with me? Now and for ever?'

'Yes,' Kelly managed. 'Oh, *Tony!*'

He kissed her. A long, tender kiss that made her tears fall even faster. Tears of joy. He kissed her again, and then brushed her cheeks with his thumbs. 'Don't move,' he smiled. 'I think I'd better get my mop.'

™ MILLS & BOON®

Pure reading pleasure™

JUNE 2009 HARDBACK TITLES

ROMANCE

The Sicilian's Baby Bargain	Penny Jordan
Mistress: Pregnant by the Spanish Billionaire	Kim Lawrence
Bound by the Marcolini Diamonds	Melanie Milburne
Blackmailed into the Greek Tycoon's Bed	Carol Marinelli
The Ruthless Greek's Virgin Princess	Trish Morey
Veretti's Dark Vengeance	Lucy Gordon
Spanish Magnate, Red-Hot Revenge	Lynn Raye Harris
Argentinian Playboy, Unexpected Love-Child	Chantelle Shaw
The Savakis Mistress	Annie West
Captive in the Millionaire's Castle	Lee Wilkinson
Cattle Baron: Nanny Needed	Margaret Way
Greek Boss, Dream Proposal	Barbara McMahon
Boardroom Baby Surprise	Jackie Braun
Bachelor Dad on Her Doorstep	Michelle Douglas
Hired: Cinderella Chef	Myrna Mackenzie
Miss Maple and the Playboy	Cara Colter
A Special Kind of Family	Marion Lennox
Hot Shot Surgeon, Cinderella Bride	Alison Roberts

HISTORICAL

The Rake's Wicked Proposal	Carole Mortimer
The Transformation of Miss Ashworth	Anne Ashley
Mistress Below Deck	Helen Dickson

MEDICAL™

Emergency: Wife Lost and Found	Carol Marinelli
A Summer Wedding at Willowmere	Abigail Gordon
The Playboy Doctor Claims His Bride	Janice Lynn
Miracle: Twin Babies	Fiona Lowe

0509 Gen Std LP

⊚ MILLS & BOON®
Pure reading pleasure™

JUNE 2009 LARGE PRINT TITLES

ROMANCE

The Ruthless Magnate's Virgin Mistress	Lynne Graham
The Greek's Forced Bride	Michelle Reid
The Sheikh's Rebellious Mistress	Sandra Marton
The Prince's Waitress Wife	Sarah Morgan
The Australian's Society Bride	Margaret Way
The Royal Marriage Arrangement	Rebecca Winters
Two Little Miracles	Caroline Anderson
Manhattan Boss, Diamond Proposal	Trish Wylie

HISTORICAL

Marrying the Mistress	Juliet Landon
To Deceive a Duke	Amanda McCabe
Knight of Grace	Sophia James

MEDICAL™

A Mummy for Christmas	Caroline Anderson
A Bride and Child Worth Waiting For	Marion Lennox
One Magical Christmas	Carol Marinelli
The GP's Meant-To-Be Bride	Jennifer Taylor
The Italian Surgeon's Christmas Miracle	Alison Roberts
Children's Doctor, Christmas Bride	Lucy Clark

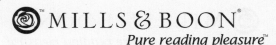

MILLS & BOON®
Pure reading pleasure™

JULY 2009 HARDBACK TITLES

ROMANCE

Marchese's Forgotten Bride	Michelle Reid
The Brazilian Millionaire's Love-Child	Anne Mather
Powerful Greek, Unworldly Wife	Sarah Morgan
The Virgin Secretary's Impossible Boss	Carole Mortimer
Kyriakis's Innocent Mistress	Diana Hamilton
Rich, Ruthless and Secretly Royal	Robyn Donald
Spanish Aristocrat, Forced Bride	India Grey
Kept for Her Baby	Kate Walker
The Costanzo Baby Secret	Catherine Spencer
The Mediterranean's Wife by Contract	Kathryn Ross
Claimed: Secret Royal Son	Marion Lennox
Expecting Miracle Twins	Barbara Hannay
A Trip with the Tycoon	Nicola Marsh
Invitation to the Boss's Ball	Fiona Harper
Keeping Her Baby's Secret	Raye Morgan
Memo: The Billionaire's Proposal	Melissa McClone
Secret Sheikh, Secret Baby	Carol Marinelli
The Playboy Doctor's Surprise Proposal	Anne Fraser

HISTORICAL

The Piratical Miss Ravenhurst	Louise Allen
His Forbidden Liaison	Joanna Maitland
An Innocent Debutante in Hanover Square	Anne Herries

MEDICAL™

Pregnant Midwife: Father Needed	Fiona McArthur
His Baby Bombshell	Jessica Matthews
Found: A Mother for His Son	Dianne Drake
Hired: GP and Wife	Judy Campbell

0609 Gen Std LP

⊚™ MILLS & BOON®

Pure reading pleasure™

JULY 2009 LARGE PRINT TITLES

ROMANCE

Captive At The Sicilian Billionaire's Command	Penny Jordan
The Greek's Million-Dollar Baby Bargain	Julia James
Bedded for the Spaniard's Pleasure	Carole Mortimer
At the Argentinean Billionaire's Bidding	India Grey
Italian Groom, Princess Bride	Rebecca Winters
Falling for her Convenient Husband	Jessica Steele
Cinderella's Wedding Wish	Jessica Hart
The Rebel Heir's Bride	Patricia Thayer

HISTORICAL

The Rake's Defiant Mistress	Mary Brendan
The Viscount Claims His Bride	Bronwyn Scott
The Major and the Country Miss	Dorothy Elbury

MEDICAL™

The Greek Doctor's New-Year Baby	Kate Hardy
The Heart Surgeon's Secret Child	Meredith Webber
The Midwife's Little Miracle	Fiona McArthur
The Single Dad's New-Year Bride	Amy Andrews
The Wife He's Been Waiting For	Dianne Drake
Posh Doc Claims His Bride	Anne Fraser